DEVELOPING THE CAPABLE PRACTITIONER

PROFESSIONAL CAPABILITY THROUGH HIGHER EDUCATION

Edited by

Dave O'Reilly • Lynne Cunningham • Stan Lester

First published in 1999
Reprinted in 1999

Kogan Page Limited
120 Pentonville Road
London N1 9JN
UK

British Library Cataloguing in Publication Data
A CIP record for this book is available from the British Library.
ISBN 0 7494 2876 7

Typeset by Saxon Graphics Ltd, Derby
Printed and bound in Great Britain by Clays Ltd, St Ives plc

Contents

The contributors

Ann-Marie Bathmaker is a Senior Lecturer in the University of Wolverhampton School of Education. She has worked in education in England and Germany in modern languages, English as a Second Language and staff development. Her current professional and research interests are vocational education and lifelong learning.

Professor Geoffrey W. Beeson is Pro vice-chancellor (Development) at Deakin University, Australia. His interests include the design of learning to meet the specific needs of learners, educational administration and policy, and higher education linkages with vocational education and industry. His current work is focused on designing education and training appropriate for capable professionals in a context of rapid change and globalization.

Dr Reva Berman Brown is Research Reader in Management in the Faculty of Management and Business at Nene – University College Northampton. She has published widely in the areas of organizational culture, management education and management practice, and her current research interests include aspects of professionalism, business history and the teaching/learning/knowledge continuum.

Jennifer A. Butler is Principal Lecturer at Oxford Brookes University in the School of Health Care. She is mainly involved with the Occupational Therapy programme and is pro-active in teaching developments. Current research projects include the use of IT in health professions education, particularly in the biological and behavioural sciences. Her other research interests include assessment and rehabilitation of apraxia following brain damage (with Rivermead Rehabilitation Centre, Oxford) and teaching sexuality and disability issues to the health professions.

Maggie Challis is currently Senior Lecturer in Medical Education at Nottingham University Medical School. She was formerly based in the Learning and Teaching Institute at Sheffield Hallam University. Specific research interests are professional competence and expertise and accreditation of prior experiential learning.

Graham Cheetham is a Senior Training Adviser with the UK Department for Education and Employment. He originally qualified as a Chartered Engineer and has been involved in vocational training for around 20 years. He is currently responsible for advising on government policy relating to the training and education of managers and continuing professional development across all professions. Alongside this, he is conducting part-time doctoral research in the area of professional development at the University of Sheffield.

Geoff Chivers is Professor of Continuing Education at the University of Sheffield. A chemist by background, he has been involved in continuing education with a bias towards vocational provision for the past 24 years. He has a particular interest in continuing professional development and is currently supervising a range of research projects in this area, including a number within the health care professions.

Dr Ian Cunningham chairs Strategic Developments International Ltd and the not-for-profit Centre for Self Managed Learning. He is a Visiting Professor at Middlesex University and he is on the Adjunct Faculty of the Fielding Institute, California. He works with organizations at various levels, including assisting with organization-wide change, with teams (on their development) and on individual mentoring and coaching of managers, directors and CEOs.

Geraldine Doherty is the Head of the Central Council for Education and Training in Social Work (CCETSW) in Scotland. In 1994 Geraldine worked as a Social Work Education Adviser for CCETSW and was the lead officer for the UK review of the rules and requirements for the Diploma in Social Work, the professional qualification for social work. Geraldine is a qualified social worker who worked predominantly in the field of mental health, before moving into training and education. Prior to working for CCETSW, Geraldine was the Manager of Training for Social Services and Housing in the London Borough of Bromley.

Alex Dunlop is currently Senior Lecturer in Accounting at Sheffield Hallam University. His primary research interest is in the area of accounting and professional education – an area in which he has published in both professional and academic journals and presented papers at national and international conferences. This research has been funded by several major professional bodies. Specific interests include professional competence and expertise and continuing professional development.

Dave Evans is a Principal Lecturer at the University College Suffolk. His professional background is in social work and schoolteaching. However, in recent years, he has researched and published on a number of aspects of professional learning that are common to a broader range of caring professions. He is currently writing on practice learning and assessing transfer of learning.

Trevor Hassall is currently Principal Lecturer in Accounting at Sheffield Hallam University. His current research interests are in the area of accounting, in which he has published widely and presented papers at both national and international conferences. Specific research interests include professional competence and expertise and its associated assessment. He is currently working on projects in this area with research associates both in the UK and at the University of Seville.

Len Holmes is currently Principal Lecturer in Employment Studies and HRM at the University of North London. He has a practical background as a manager in the hospitality industry, a training specialist working with organizations in the private, public and voluntary sectors, and a teacher and researcher in higher education. From 1991 to 1995 he was the Business School co-ordinator at UNL for the Enterprise in Higher Education initiative. He has written extensively on issues of competence and capability.

Mary Issitt is a Senior Lecturer in the Department of Humanities and Applied Social Studies at Crewe and Alsager Faculty, Manchester Metropolitan University, where she is currently Course Leader of the MA and Post-graduate Diploma in Personal, Social and Health Education. She worked as a practitioner in a wide range of human service contexts prior to becoming a lecturer in Higher Education. She has been conducting research and publishing in the sphere of competence and reflective practice for several years.

Jackie Langley is a Senior Lecturer in Social Work at the University of Brighton. Her professional background is in social work and in training within the Social Services Department. In recent years she has been involved in the development and delivery of professional courses, mainly for social workers, but also for nurses.

Stan Lester is a consultant and researcher in the fields of professional and vocational development and rural economic and enterprise issues. He has previously worked in training management in local government, teaching and inspection in further education, agricultural research in the Gambia, accountancy and landscape design. Stan has also been a visiting lecturer at the University of the West of England, an Inspector for the Further Education Funding Council, and an NVQ external verifier.

Sean McCartney is a Lecturer in Accounting in the Department of Accounting, Finance and Management at the University of Essex. He is a Fellow of the Institute of Chartered Accountants in England and Wales, and worked in practice and industry before becoming an academic. His research interests include accounting and management education, auditing and accounting and business history.

Rachel Pierce is currently an independent social work education consultant. Until her retirement in September 1995 she was Assistant Director (Education and Training) of the Central Council for Education and Training in Social work (CCETSW). She was, in particular, responsible for developing CCETSW's work to achieve a progressive continuum of education, training and awards: Vocational Qualifications in Social Care, the qualifying Diploma in Social Work (DipSW) and Post Qualifying Awards and Advanced Awards in Social Work (PQSW and AASW).

Steve Reeve is a Principal Lecturer at the University of Brighton. As programme leader for regional management post-graduate activity, he is involved and enjoys working with mature managers on part-time courses. His research interest is on the nature of learning, and he draws on his wide experience of open learning and action learning when writing about learning and teaching, innovative methods and technological enhancement. He has conducted joint research into the nature of assessment, and the pursuit of research amongst business school academics.

Lynda M. Stansfield is currently Senior Lecturer and MBA Course Director (part-time route) at Huddersfield University Business School. She has degrees in law and psychology, and an MSc in applied psychology. She researches in management learning, stress and assessment, and has published extensively. Lynda has many years of professional experience in HRM and consulting, is a Fellow of the Institute of Personnel and Development, and a Graduate Member of the British Psychological Society.

David Stoker is a Senior Lecturer in the University of Wolverhampton School of Education. His initial professional education was in nursing. He has many years of experience of programmes that prepare teachers for work in further, adult and higher education, both at home and abroad. His current professional interests include the communication process in teaching and learning situations, and how teachers incorporate theoretical principles into their professional practice.

Professor Diana Tribe is Dean of the Faculty of Law at the University of Hertfordshire, where she has researched and published extensively in the area of medical law. In addition, she has completed research projects in the field of legal education, most notably the *Law Assessment Project* and the *Skills of Magistrates and their Court Clerks*, which she carried out as an Associate Research Fellow of the Institute of Advanced Legal Studies.

Mantz Yorke is Director of the Centre for Higher Education Development at Liverpool John Moores University. Previously he served the then Liverpool Polytechnic as Executive Director responsible for quality and standards before being seconded to the Higher Education Quality Council as Director of Quality Enhancement. He has collaborated with John Stephenson (HEC) in recent years, running conferences and workshops on the assessment of capability and contributing actively to HEC's Assessment Network. He is a member of the Governing Council of the Society for Research into Higher Education and is Editor of the society's journal *Studies in Higher Education*. He has published widely on matters relating to quality assurance and quality enhancement in higher education.

Glossary

AASW	Advanced Award in Social Work
AECC	Accounting Education Change Commission
AGR	Association of Graduate Recruiters
ASSET	Accreditation and Support for Specified Experience and Training
CAT(S)	Credit Accumulation and Transfer (Scheme / System)
CBOK	Common Body of Knowledge for the practice of internal auditing
CCETSW	Central Council for Education and Training in Social Work
CETYCW	Council for Education and Training in Youth and Community Work
CML	Computer-managed / computer-mediated learning
CPD	Continuing professional development
CSC	Care Sector Consortium
CVCP	Committee of Vice-chancellors and Principals
DipSW	Diploma in Social Work
DfE	Department for Education
DfEE	Department for Education and Employment
DMS	Diploma in Management Studies
DTI	Department for Trade and Industry
ED	Employment Department
ESF	European Social Fund
GNVQ	General National Vocational Qualification
HE	Higher Education
HEC	Higher Education for Capability
HEI	Higher Education Institution
HEQC	Higher Education Quality Council
IIA	Institute of Internal Auditors
ILB	Industry Lead Body
IRS	Industrial Relations Services
IT	Information Technology
MBA	Master of Business Administration
MCI	Management Charter Initiative
MIT	Massachusetts Institute of Technology

NAB	National Advisory Board for Public Sector Higher Education
NCVQ	National Council for Vocational Qualifications
NELP	North-East London Polytechnic
NVQ	National Vocational Qualification
OU	Open University
PQSW	Post Qualifying Award in Social Work
PSQ	Personal Skills and Qualities
QCA	Qualifications and Curriculum Authority
RSA	Royal Society for the Encouragement of Arts, Manufactures and Commerce
SME	Small / Medium Enterprise
SQA	Scottish Qualifications Authority
SVQ	Scottish Vocational Qualification
TAFE	Technical and Further Education
UGC	University Grants Council
WEF	World Educational Fellowship

Introduction

The notion of the 'capable practitioner' is not a new one, but it is a very relevant one as we move from an industrially dominated society, with its patterns of taken-for-granted relationships and more or less incremental rates of progress, to what some have called an information society characterized by discontinuous change and challenges to some of our most basic assumptions.

Professional development has moved through various conceptions including the classical notion of the educated person, the mediaeval apprenticeship, the dominant twentieth-century technical-rational approach, and more recently the search for models based on competence and proficiency in the workplace; all of these traditions provide resources on which current debates draw. Higher education has tended to focus on the classical and the technical–rational, at one end concentrating on understanding and development of the intellect, and at the other on the principles, information and facts pertinent to the given field. On the other hand the competence agenda is now beginning to impact on professional higher education, if nothing else prompting institutions to question their curricula, teaching and assessment methods. 'Competence', in the sense of effective practice, has a pragmatic validity and sense of appeal: so moves have taken hold over the last decade or so to be more explicit about what practitioners can do, even if some of the methods used are too fragmented and simplistic to have any real fitness for purpose.

However, there is more to the capable practitioner than command of a body of professional knowledge or the ability to demonstrate competence at work; these may be sufficient in the short term, the period when the wider implications of actions are unknown or can be ignored, but neither is adequate for conditions at the end of the twentieth century. Those involved in professional development and higher education face a challenge to move beyond considerations of knowledge and competence to helping people develop as capable practitioners equal to the challenges of fluid environments and unpredictable change, taking responsibility for their careers and their learning, and able to exercise the kind of practical judgement and systemic wisdom needed for a sustainable future.

While political thinking has traditionally been slow to respond to these kinds of issues, the climate in the UK at the time of publication is perhaps at its most positive in this respect for many years. In his foreword to the Green Paper 'The Learning Age' (DfEE, 1998), David Blunkett, the Secretary of State for Education and Employment, recognizes that 'the fostering of an enquiring mind and the love of learning are essential for our future success' and goes on to call for 'a renewed commitment to self-improvement and... recognition of the enormous contribution learning makes to our society' (p 7). Although in places the paper doesn't live up to this vision, it does demonstrate a will to engage with the issue of learning needing to be endemic within our society.

A similar positive mood, while struggling to move beyond current frames of reference, pervades much of the recent investigation into UK post-compulsory education. Helena Kennedy's report for the Further Education Funding Council (Kennedy, 1997) is primarily concerned with widening participation in further education. Nevertheless, it also has implications for higher education, particularly in terms of continuing to widen the scope and types of provision offered and the markets that are served. The National Committee of Enquiry chaired by Sir Ron Dearing has produced the most thorough public report into higher education since the Robbins report of 1963; it includes recommendations for widening and expanding higher education, increasing flexibility and quality, and a more visible relationship between institutions and the needs and contributions of individuals, employers and society in general (Dearing, 1997). It clearly sets higher education in the context of the 'learning society,' emphasizing the need for institutions to play a central role in supporting continuous learning and ongoing professional development. Finally, Bob Fryer's report *Learning for the twenty-first century* (Fryer, 1997) further develops the goal of a 'learning culture' where learning is endemic, a project in which professional and higher education are fundamental.

Also within the last two years the bodies responsible for school curricula in the UK have merged with those responsible for occupational standards and Scottish and National Vocational Qualifications, resulting in the formation of the Scottish Qualifications Authority and the Qualifications and Curriculum Authority. The effect on the now-familiar UK occupational competence and standards programme is as yet unclear, but there are already signs that some of the rigidity associated with the programme over its first decade is beginning to soften.

The chapters in this book provide an eclectic collection of examples working to address both practical and conceptual issues against these backgrounds. Taken together, they offer a fascinating glimpse into the current state of the debate about professional education in the UK. They cover a wide range of professions, considered from the perspectives of educators and researchers, professional bodies and government agencies. Throughout we find, again and again:

- an explicit awareness of the need to move beyond competence to a more dynamic concept of capability, embracing learning, culture and values;
- a concern with the education of the whole person for professional and social responsibility;
- a commitment to fostering critical, reflective professional practice through critical, reflective learning experiences;
- a willingness to grapple with the intellectual challenges of conceptualizing these new models of professional education for lifelong learning;
- an engagement in constructive dialogue between academia, professional bodies, employers and other interest groups about the purposes and methods of professional formation, assessment and accreditation.

As the Director of Higher Education for Capability wrote in his report on a recent conference entitled *Beyond competence to capability and the learning society*, 'We live in a world of change where individuals and groups are having to take responsibility for managing their own development in work, the community and their personal lives' (Stephenson, 1996). In this sense, the learning society is also the risk society (Beck, 1986), with its attendant dangers of individualism, social fragmentation and exclusion, of complex systems in a delicate global balance. If the professions are to play an effective role in ensuring a saner and more just society, the issues debated in this book are of vital importance.

For ease of reading, we have divided the chapters rather arbitrarily into five roughly equal parts. In fact, several themes (such as the crucial influence of assessment methods) recur often, while all the chapters engage more or less explicitly with concepts and models of professional capability. However, taking account of differences of emphasis, we have tried to group the chapters in clusters that might usefully be read together.

The first part focuses on the reflective practitioner, beginning with an edited summary of a discussion with Donald Schön. As well as illuminating the nature of critical reflection through anecdote and insight, the style of presentation demonstrates critical reflection and critical dialogue in action. The second chapter, 'Multiple mirrors: reflecting the reflections' by Reva Berman Brown and Sean McCartney, explores the application of theories of reflection to learning on an MBA programme and in particular the notion of reciprocal learning between teachers and students. This theme is developed in the final chapter in this part, 'From didactic expert to partner in learning' by Jennifer A. Butler, with reference to the profession of occupational therapy.

The second part is grouped around learner autonomy and action learning. In 'From map-reader to map-maker: approaches to moving beyond knowledge and competence', Stan Lester proposes a metaphor for learning to underpin effective professional practice in environments of uncertainty and change. In 'Towards capability through competence: autonomy or automatism?' Anne-Marie Bathmaker and David Stoker reflect on a teacher training programme that aims to develop capability through autonomous learning encompassing a high degree of student negotiation and individual capability. A comparable programme in management development, incorporating experiential, self-managed learning is discussed by Lynda M. Stansfield in 'Capabilities for successful self-development'. Again in the domain of management education, Steve Reeve considers the development of capability through action learning techniques in 'Action learning and capability: a search for common ground'.

Assessing capability is the theme of part three, introduced by Len Holmes' critique of current models of the capability curriculum in favour of a model which reframes assessment as a social process based on conventions of warrant, 'Competence and capability: from "confidence trick" to the construction of graduate identity'. In his second chapter in this book, 'Assessing the self-managing learner: a contradiction in terms?', Stan Lester argues the case for self-assessment and discusses the issues of ensuring rigour and validity. Finally in this part, Dave Evans and Jackie Langley appraise an approach combining self-assessment and tutor-assessment of experiential learning in 'Practice-based assignments: social work as a case-study'.

The first three chapters in part four also acknowledge the importance of assessment in professional education, though we have grouped them with two further chapters to highlight the role of professional bodies and the needs of employers. In 'Professional capability: requirements and accreditation in the legal profession', Diana Tribe points out the different approaches to education at different stages of legal training and their apparent mismatch in some cases with the expressed needs of employers. In contrast, Geraldine Doherty and Rachel Pierce give an account of a concerted effort to bring together different interest groups in social work in 'Professional capability: a case-study bridging vocational, academic and professional frameworks'. Switching professions, Alex Dunlop, Trevor Hassall and Maggie Challis draw on British and American studies of 'Professional competence development: the internal audit experience' to suggest a case-study model of training. Geoffrey W. Beeson continues with a case-study of a different kind in 'Delivering relevant higher education to the workplace', which describes the development and success of a flexible part-time technology management degree at Deakin University, designed to meet the needs of the Australian manufacturing industry. To complete this part, Mantz Yorke presents the findings of a survey of small enterprises on Merseyside to discover their requirements of graduate employees as compared to the intended outcomes of relevant courses in local higher education institutions, in 'The skills of graduates: a small enterprise perspective'.

The chapters in part five are based on values and models, though, in truth, several of the earlier chapters would sit well here. First, Mary Issitt reminds us that while there are parallels between reflective practitioner and feminist approaches to professional development and practice, functional approaches to competence serve to replicate current power relations and gender inequalities. Her chapter 'Conceptualizing competence and reflective practice: a feminist perspective' is illustrated by reference to human service professions. Second, in 'Beyond competences: lessons from management learning', Ian Cunningham argues passionately for a holistic approach to professional development, which recognizes that denial of the emotions, of moral issues and the social context of learning leads to poor cognitive learning and bad practice. To round off part five, Graham Cheetham and Geoff Chivers offer a model that seeks to pull together the various approaches to conceptualizing competence, in 'Professional competence: harmonizing reflective practitioner and competence-based approaches'.

In part six, the concluding chapter by Stan Lester, 'The challenge of developing the capable practitioner', seeks to pull together some of the key themes and implications emerging from the chapters and points to some possible ways forward.

References

Beck, U. (1986: trans. 1992) *The Risk Society: Towards a new modernity* London, Sage.

Dearing, R. (1997) *Higher education in the learning society* Hayes, NCIHE Publications.

Department for Education and Employment (DfEE) (1998) *The Learning Age: A renaissance for a new Britain* London, The Stationery Office (Cm 3790).

Fryer, R. H. (1997) *Learning for the Twenty-first Century: First report of the National Advisory Group for Continuing Education and Lifelong Learning* London, DfEE.

Kennedy, H. (1997) *Learning Works: Widening participation in further education* Coventry, Further Education Funding Council

Robbins, L. (1963) *Higher Education: Report of the committee* London, HMSO.

Stephenson, J. (1996) 'Conference report: Beyond competence to capability and the learning society', *Capability* 2(1) 60–63.

Part One

The Reflective Practitioner

Chapter 1

In conversation with Donald Schön

Summary

This chapter is based on a series of reflective conversations between Professor Donald Schön and other participants at the Higher Education for Capability seminar, *Professional Capability: Requirements and Accreditation*, held in January 1996. It was collated and edited by Dave O'Reilly, and first appeared in *Capability*, **2**(2), pp 12–16.

The topics touched upon include metaphors for professional practice, the skills of developing reflective practitioners, the nature of reflection-in-action, the relationship between reflective practice and performance outcomes, cultural differences in ways of knowing and the notion of organizational learning. More than that, Professor Schön gave a master class in critical reflection through his use of telling anecdotes from his own experience and his engagement in reflection-in-action on the conversation as it happened.

Among those who contributed to the conversations are Heather Crouch, Michael Eraut, Ray Ison, Stephen McNair, Jenny Naish, John Storan, Imogen Taylor and Edgar Wilson. John Stephenson and James Armstrong chaired the sessions.

The professional as performance artist...

On occasion, when I'm working with groups of people who are managers, or management trainers, or consultants, or teachers, I ask how many people have experience in acting, because I did a lot of amateur theatricals in my youth, in high school and college, and I know that it helped me enormously. How many of you [in the audience] have had theatrical experience of some kind? That's about half.

So we get something from fear, the experience of acting in plays, which we're able to bring to situations that are quite different, on the surface. When I first began to work in industrial consulting, in the late 1950s, I discovered that I was pretty good at going into an organization and trying to figure out what was going on, and 'reading' it, and coming back and writing up my notes about it. You've never done this before, I said to myself, where did you learn how to do it? And then I realized, that in my Freshman year at Yale University, in a course called Directed Studies, we read the 'great books' – Job, Aeschylus, Shakespeare, Lord Byron's *Don Juan* – and we had to write an essay every week about them, and then we had discussions about them. The capability that I was bringing to the reading of organizational phenomena was really a version of what I had been learning to do when reading Lord Byron. These were dramatic situations. I was trying to describe them in a succinct way. I certainly hadn't been trained as an organizational consultant, but that seemed to be what I was drawing on, at least in part, as I went off on my first consulting assignments.

...and the professional as designer

More recently, I've become very interested in designing, in the specific sense of visual, graphic and architectural design, and in the more general sense of designing as making things under conditions of complexity and uncertainty. In this larger sense of 'design', lawyers design cases, business managers design information systems, social workers design treatment strategies. Designing is a critical sort of idea, yet we have no very good theory of design. I've been interested along with a number of other people, in design practice, in what practising designers actually do.

For example, I have a colleague, Crispin Miller, who got me interested in what undergraduate mechanical engineers at MIT were learning. Every year there is a competition where hundreds of students compete to make a device, for example one that picks up an egg and brings it back quickly without breaking it. Crispin's PhD research consisted in working with these students and exploring how they understood what was going on in such mechanisms. He found, for example, that the students, the MIT juniors and seniors who are very good in the sense that they get high marks, couldn't understand in some cases how a lever actually worked in action. So here you have a situation in which students have formal knowledge, in the form of the equations, that describe the behaviour of the lever, and yet do not appear to understand in this immediate situation, face to face with the mechanism, just what it is the lever means in reality. The students had trouble making such connections: only a few did so, and they were not so much the ones who'd done well in the MIT subjects, but those who'd built houses during the summer, or repaired tractors on the family farm.

So we have this issue of different modes of knowledge, different ways of holding knowledge, different strands used in representing things, and the need to link these different strands together, moving back and forth from one to another. This seems to me to be of the essence with respect to the building up of professional engineering capability.

Teaching for capability

One thing that inhibits capability is the conception of what, for example, engineering knowledge is, especially the view that there is always one right answer.

We have a wonderful teacher at MIT who teaches about ocean engineering. He had many ways of describing a wave. First of all, he would write the equation for the wave. Then he would draw a picture of the wave. Then he would mime the wave, and finally he would describe the wave in words. So he was capable of multiple representations of that wave. Most teachers are not so versatile. For most, there's a belief in one appropriate way of describing what a given piece of knowledge is. Now, if I believe there are multiple ways of representing things I'll be very interested in what you understand by what I say, because it may turn out that what you extract from my words is different from what I thought I meant. But if I ask you, I open up the possibility that the dialogue will get away from me.

So, another factor that I think stands in the way of reflective teaching is any theory of action for control, my wish to keep things under control. Unless I give this up, then I can't teach in terms of multiple understandings. I should add that even if I'm willing to give up unilateral control I may lack the skill to discover how you're thinking about the issue, to open up different ways of thinking about it, to inquire into your views, as well as to advocate my own.

Developing teachers as reflective practitioners

An important issue about engaging in reflective teaching is that the teacher may feel slightly unconfident about what she's teaching. Let me just give you an example of that. Two colleagues of mine, Jeanne Bamburgh and Eleran Dodsworth, conducted a project in teacher education some years ago. In one of their sessions there was a videotape of a student working with Montessori bells [they all looked alike but had different pitches]. The student on the videotape was trying to construct 'Twinkle Twinkle Little Star'. He'd go [hums different notes of bells] and search for the first bell, then he'd start at the beginning again, to look for the second, and so on. The teachers looked at that and said 'This kid is a slow learner and he doesn't have his basic music skills.' What was a 'basic music skill'? The teachers said that a student should be able to recognize a pitch, and the name that goes with the pitch – so, for example, to recognize 'C', to recognize 'G' or 'A'. Jeanne then played the first part of 'Twinkle Twinkle', and asked the teachers to sing the first pitch of the second part. And most of the teachers couldn't do it. They were forced to conclude that they too lacked basic music skills. Now, a pitch in isolation is almost unidentifiable. It's only in the context of a relationship of pitches that we can identify a particular pitch. So what the student was doing in that videotape was building up a context of the relationships of pitches. That was why he kept going back to the beginning of the tune.

So the theory of musical knowledge which the teacher held was putting her in the situation of what I would call 'teaching in bad faith'. She was presenting knowledge which didn't correspond to her own real understandings, or how she herself learned. Under these circumstances reflective teaching becomes extremely difficult. I am likely to be put off in a situation by encountering a surprise, since I'm not teaching on the firm foundation of how I myself understand things. So when I work with teachers or teacher educators, it seems to me that the critical issue to begin with is not what the students learn, or their difficulties, but how the teachers have their own understandings of the material at hand.

Reflection in 'hot' and 'cold' action

Is reflection the same in 'hot' and 'cold' action (to borrow McLuhan's metaphor of hot and cold media)? To me, this conversation is an illustration of what I mean by reflection in the actual situation. Is the information here 'hot' or is it 'cold'? I think it's fairly hot, in the sense that quite a lot hinges on what I'm going to do in this moment.

You see, you're asking me questions and I'm trying to respond to them online. Similarly, for example, as [the previous questioner] asks me about teachers, and what it means to help them acquire the 'skills of reflection', I heard her as focusing on how to design a classroom that is full of children all doing different things, I say to myself, 'How am I going to address this?' My problem in doing so is that I think that there's something she's not talking about which is more important than what she is talking about, but I also don't want to downgrade the importance of what she is talking about, especially because I myself am not a teacher, and haven't spent much time in these classrooms. I'm aware of the possibility that I might offend her by being, as a colleague of mine said recently, 'not nice to teachers'.

On the other hand I have a view of what it means to respect teachers, that is to attribute to them an ability to confront challenges to their own understandings, as I myself hope to able to confront challenges to my understandings. So this presents me with a stew of things that I'm thinking about as I respond, and as I listen to myself respond, I may say to myself, 'Wait a minute, you're going overboard – you really haven't dealt enough with this issue of the classroom, it's still there, so you need to make a note and come back to that, deal with it. Do I really understand what she means by what she calls skills of reflection?

Have I asked, have I enquired enough?' I try to work with that material on the spot. I try to design new experiments on the spot in order to respond to what I think may be going on, and try to make sense of the data as it comes back.

In another sense of hot and cold, I know, for example, that there are some situations in which I am disposed to think about what I'm doing much less than in others. These tend to be situations where the very act of reflection is threatening. If I'm involved in an emotional issue, it's much harder for me to reflect on my own behaviour, though sometimes I think I manage to do it. This points to something we really haven't discussed, which is defensiveness on the part of students and teachers, which I think is a greatly underestimated problem of education.

Are reflective practice and measuring performance outcomes compatible?

First of all, let me say something about competence-based education or capability as you may mean it. I'm not sure I have it right in a British context. In the States this phrase suggests the notion that you can establish measures of competent performance without specifying how it's to be delivered, and that you are then able to provide greater freedom to the actors as to how they meet these criteria. But the crucial thing, for a teacher, in terms of how she goes about trying to help someone develop a capability, is that you have criteria measures of performance.

This seems to me to be not incompatible with what I mean by reflective practice. Let me give you an example. The Cog Wheel Experiment was done in the late fifties in the United States. We had something called the SAGE system for targeting and shooting down enemy aircraft. These were complex computer-based systems, and you had teams of about 40 people trying to manage these computer simulations. They never were able to get beyond a 30 per cent hit ratio. They tried lots of different training schemes. A man named John Kennedy, a psychologist, came along and said, 'OK, we're going to give you quantified data about how well you did. We'll give it to you publicly and very fast – public, accurate, quantitative feedback about your performance. And then we'll reiterate, in further episodes of simulation.' This process went on for about three months. The first thing that happened was that performance went down. Then it gradually came back up to 30 per cent. Then, over three months, in step curves, it went up to 70 to 75 per cent.

And if you looked at what was happening, you saw that two different things were going on. One was, people were using less information, so the curve of information usage crossed with the curve of performance improvement. What this says to me is that people weren't getting at theories of what was going on. A theory is a way of getting rid of information. If you build a theory about what enables you to get the target, you're getting rid of everything except what's contained in your theory, so expect people to notice less as they become more skilled within a stable framework.

The other thing that was happening was people were making collective inventions. So, for example, they got rid of the telephones, which were one to one, and substituted hand signals, which were one to many. So they created a collective environment for experimentation, for generating and testing ideas, strategies and assumptions. And that seems to me an important kind of reflection on, and in, action. But it depends on the belief that the measures of performance in question are appropriate. If you can't, or don't get them, then you end up with measures like, for university professors, 'numbers of publications'. Then you create an incentive for 'optimization to the measures'. So the question of the measures that demonstrate performance capability needs to be a subject of inquiry within the organizational setting in which we're trying to establish them. We have to make them problematic, as well.

Tacit knowledge and cultural differences: the indescribable and the undiscussable

Usually what we mean by making things explicit is making them explicit in words, but I think I can give you examples of things which are very difficult to make explicit in words. For example the taste of that *coq au vin* I just ate. That's an important business if you're a chef, or the redness of an inflamed throat if you're a physician. Or the experience of orienting yourself in an unfamiliar environment. All of these things are very hard to make explicit in words, partly because they have to do with behaviour in space or with taste, or with graphic displays, and these are all inherently of their own kind. One can try to convey one's sense of them by painting, or by like representations. I prefer to treat it as an open question, how much you can make explicit, to be tested in each instance in which it arises.

I think it is also important to distinguish between the indescribable and the undiscussable. Some things are very hard to describe, others I don't want to describe. Or I avoid describing them because it would be embarrassing – to say, for example, that our organization conceals negative information about our products.

Across different cultures, there are both differences and similarities as to what's kept tacit. For some of my English friends, I know, there's a very distinct boundary about what it's appropriate to discuss, which is well below my sense of what the boundary is – for instance, the boundary associated with 'gentlemanly' behaviour. If you're in an organizational situation, you would never directly discuss with this individual the fact that you perceive him to be in process of being manipulative and deceptive. To do that, apparently, would be seen by my English friends as ungentlemanly.

There are also connections between the indescribable and the undiscussable. If I treat something as undiscussable, I don't practise trying to make it explicit, so it may also become indescribable for me. If I worked at it, I might be able to do it, but since I never allow myself to do it, it stays under the table.

When I was in Hong Kong not so long ago working with a group of Chinese social workers, I learned something about the idea of 'face'. It was very powerful. I asked them to construct a case scenario drawn from their social work practice. One woman produced her case; she was discussing it, and I was trying to have a dialogue with her about the action strategies she was using. At some point in that dialogue I observed her getting redder and redder and I discovered that what I was trying to do was absolutely impossible for her in that setting. It was a complete failure. But we had a second session whose purpose was to talk about the first session, and that was much more successful. I asked the social worker if she was embarrassed by what I had been doing, and she said, yes, she was. I asked what was it that embarrassed her and she said, 'Because I thought I wasn't getting it right'. So the idea that she would show herself in a group seeming not to be getting it right was extremely threatening for her. And that meant I couldn't teach there the way I would ordinarily do. However, the second session seemed to do better. She was able to think back into the past about the issue in a way that I hadn't been able to deal with in the present.

The connection between individual and organizational learning

What I mean by 'organizational learning' is a process of organizational inquiry through which the organization restructures its theory of action, with respect to the strategies, values or assumptions on which it's operating. By 'organizational inquiry', I mean the business in which individual members of the organization think about problems, talk about them, design experiments, probe situations through interactions with one another and in ways that leave residue that can be embodied in organizational artefacts, such as files, memories, maps and programmes for future organizational life. I think that organizations don't learn, people do. But people can learn on behalf of organizations and individual learning becomes organizational when it results in changes of organizational theory of action, embodied in organizational artefacts.

I think that the quality of organizational learning depends on the ability of the individuals who inhabit the organization to engage in reflective practice and to enquire into issues of ambiguity, especially in the circumstances where embarrassments, risks, and threats come up as a central kind of issue. The environment of the organization, which Chris Argyris and I call the 'learning system of the organization', can be more or less hospitable to reflective inquiry on the part of its members. I think that individuals who live in organizations have a share in shaping their organizational environments, which in turn constrains or enables them. That's the way I'd make the connection.

Chapter 2

Multiple mirrors: reflecting on reflections

Reva Berman Brown and Sean McCartney

Summary

Kolb's (1976) experiential learning model established that one of the four key learning abilities, or processes, is reflective observation, which helps transform experience into knowledge. A common concern of managers is that they have insufficient time to reflect on their organizational actions.

Using the experience of practising managers who are also part-time management students, this chapter combines theoretical insights, philosophical aspects and empirical data to consider the part played by reflection in the cognitive processes that encompass thinking in organizations. The organizational setting, in this case, is extended from the workplace into the classroom.

The authors speculate on the double meaning of 'reflection' – 'to think about' and 'mirroring' – and consider how each of these meanings impacts upon what goes on in the two organizational settings of the reflecting manager's workplace and place of study.

Introduction

... to hold, as 'twere, the mirror up to nature... (Hamlet)

During the last decade, the concept of reflection has grown to become an issue of interest in discussions about teaching and learning. The reason for this is not immediately clear but, as Bengtsson (1995) suggests, it might be a response to the positivist orientation dominant in the social and human sciences. Positivism presents a strongly instrumental view of the relations between science and professional practice. The alternative perspectives provided by other philosophies and methods of investigation, such as phenomenology, existentialism, hermeneutics, critical theory and structuralism, have provided a quite different view on the relationship between science and professional practice.

In 1977, Max van Manen's article, 'Linking ways of knowing with ways of being practical' started a process of considering the importance of reflection in teaching, learning and practice, which has been carried on by Donald Schön's influential books on the topic of reflection – *The Reflective Practitioner* (1983), *Educating the Reflective Practitioner* (1987) and *The Reflective Turn* (1990).

Bengtsson's (1995) list of references provides evidence of the current stream of new contributions on reflection in pedagogical journals, which have devoted special issues to the topic (for example *Theory into Practice*, 1990, no 3, and the *Journal of Teacher Education*, 1989, no 2) as well as edited books on teaching education such as Clift *et al.* (1990), Grimmett and Erikson (1988), Russell and Munby (1992), Valli (1992), Waxman *et al.* (1988) and Zeichner and Tachnick (1991).

There is a problem, however, in the fact that 'reflection' is used by these theorists and writers to mean a number of things. This chapter considers two meanings – reflection as thinking about/meditation on, and reflection as the image returned to the person or object that is being reflected.

The structure of the chapter is as follows: the first section sets the scene, describing the part-time MBA programme of the University of Essex, which is the institutional and pedagogical context that has stimulated the writing of the chapter. In the next two sections, we speculate on the double meaning of 'reflection' – as meditation and as mirroring. We consider these notions to be aids to learning, and 'evidence' is provided by means of a small selection of the relevant Reflections of students on the MBA programme. In the next section, we consider the potential of these Reflections for assessment. In the final section, we reflect on reflection, putting forward tentative conclusions about the significance of the concept of reflection as a pedagogical aid in the two organizational settings concerned – the reflecting manager's workplace and place of study.

The origins and context of the study

An underlying and often unstated assumption about reflection in the learning situation is that it is connected with learning competence. Learning is apparently enhanced if the element of reflection is incorporated into it. Accent is placed on reflection because, it is supposed, self-discovery resulting from reflection will improve and enrich the learning experience. Because those concerned with the design and delivery of the MBA programme at the

University of Essex had accepted this assumption, the element of reflection was explicitly incorporated into the programme design.

The Essex University MBA

There are a number of distinctive features about the Essex MBA:

- The programme lasts two academic years, with students attending one session (afternoon and evening) each week.
- The study sessions are divided into thematic modules, two of which are undertaken in each term.
- The summer term of each year is devoted to a dissertation.

A great deal of discussion has taken place in the 30 years since the introduction of business schools in the UK about where the MBA degree should fit along the generalist/specialist continuum and the topic/technique divide. Many students enrol on an MBA expecting to be taught discrete subjects (marketing, operations management, international business) which will be built up like a jigsaw puzzle into a larger picture. They also expect to receive practical know-how as well as the more theoretical know-about – the tools and techniques of management. As a result, MBA courses are generally composed of core subjects and electives, and knowledge is formally examined. A major innovation at Essex is that we have abolished the core course/elective courses divide; there is no fixed core syllabus that is compulsory and is examined, before students can 'progress' to electives. In a sense, all the modules are core courses or can be viewed as being available as 'electives'.

Programme structure

One thematic area is covered in each of the two class periods in the autumn term and there are a further two modules in the spring term. The modules are thematic, rather than subject or function based. The content of a module is relatively flexible in that students may ask for an area to be included or excluded, and such requests are complied with if they seem educationally sensible. We try to provide them with what they need/want to learn about. At the end of each module, the students must submit a 4,000-word paper demonstrating the application to their own organizations of some of the ideas discussed in the classes. They are required to select the topic they wish to write about. Considerable emphasis is placed on discussion of their ideas for papers by the students with the tutors, and more importantly, with each other.

It should be emphasized that papers are expected to display understanding of theory and familiarity with the literature in the area chosen by the student. The selected area may, however, have formed a small part of the module, and students are not expected to demonstrate any learning beyond what is relevant to their paper. A course text is recommended for each module, which students are required to read. What we expect from students is that they attend classes and participate in discussion, but the subject-based knowledge acquired is probably sketchy, and is not formally assessed. Thus students do not need to know, and are not expected to know, very much about large areas of the notional 'syllabus'. What they do know is therefore self-selected to be relevant to each individual. As Geertz (1973, p 20) puts it:

It is not necessary to know everything in order to understand something.

We go even further: our students do not have to know 'everything' of a (prescribed) syllabus, with the result that they may not know very much (in terms of specific facts or theories) at all, but they understand fully what it is they know. More importantly, they know how to discover and learn that which they do not know, as and when it is relevant to them. As a result, by the end of the programme, they may not know anything in particular, to any depth or in any detail, but they have learned a great deal.

In the summer term, the students continue to attend, although there are no formal classes. They meet together informally and with their tutors if they choose to do so, or use the library facilities and develop their end-of-year dissertation.

At the beginning of the course, the students are encouraged to form learning groups, which meet informally at times and places of their own choice. The place of these groups in the pedagogical process of reflection is more fully discussed in 'Reflection as mirroring' below.

Included in each piece of written work (usually as an appendix) is the 'Reflections' section, where the students discuss and comment on what it is they have learned from undertaking the term paper or the dissertation. These Reflections are the source of our 'evidence' on the value of using reflection as a pedagogical device, supporting our contention that the concept of reflection is more than merely a pedagogical fad suggestive of up-to-date teaching and learning practice. We use the word 'pedagogical' loosely; it would be more exact to say, given the context, 'andragogical' (Knowles, 1984). Whether what we say is as relevant to 'normal' full-time undergraduate students as it is to the part-time adult learners involved here is another matter.

Reflection in general

The word 'reflection' is used in a number of ways, both in everyday life and in educational situations. Reflection is:

- something that occurs in/during action;
- something that is a cognitive activity separated from (physical) action;

- itself an action, in the sense that thinking is an action;
- a kind of self-understanding leading to some kind of enlightenment or learning;
- the image produced in the reflection of light against a smooth surface.

It is the first of these meanings that has concerned Schön, who has now written three books on the subject (1983, 1987, 1990). We discuss his important perspective in more detail in the next section. The second two meanings are interconnected if one accepts that not all actions require physicality, and that thinking and cognitive activity are actions in their own right. The fourth meaning involves the view that reflection (thinking about something after the event) is a necessary part of any action in that it allows for the development of the meaning and understanding that result from that action. And the final meaning, used metaphorically, concerns self-perception and is discussed separately in the section 'Reflection as mirroring'.

Both teaching and learning contain elements of discretion, judgement and forethought. Reflective thinking is important not only as a tool for teaching and learning, but also as an aim of education since

it enables us to know what we are about when we act. It converts action that is merely appetitive, blind and impulsive into intelligent action. (Dewey, 1964, p 211)

Dewey's (1933) views on reflection are as relevant now as when he first put his thoughts forward over 60 years ago. He argued (1973, pp 494–506) that reflection consists of several steps, including perplexity, confusion and doubt, due to the nature of the situation in which one finds oneself; conjectural anticipation and tentative interpretation of given elements or meanings of the situation and their possible consequences; examination, inspection, exploration and analysis of all attainable considerations, which may define and clarify a problem with which one is confronted; elaboration of the tentative hypothesis suggestions; and deciding on a plan of action or doing something about a desired result. For Dewey,

thinking is the accurate and deliberate institution of connections between what is done and its consequences. (p 505)

Reflection on action

What we are concerned with here is not Schön's concept of reflection-in-action, but with reflection on action. The distinction can be made as follows.

Schön was concerned with professional expertise and his books offer an alternative to technical rationality by introducing the process of reflection-in-action, which is intended to be a process of knowledge creation. Schön (1987, pp 28–9) describes three features of reflection-in-action, which represent the past, present and future aspects of the reflective process. First, reflection is at least in some measure conscious, although it need not occur in the medium of words; second, reflection-in-action has a critical function, questioning the assumptional structure of knowing-in-action (the sorts of know-how we reveal when we act):

> I shall use *knowing-in-action* to refer to sorts of know-how we reveal in our intelligent action – publicly observable, physical performances like riding a bicycle and private operations like instant analysis of a balance sheet. In both cases, the knowing is *in* the action. We reveal it by our spontaneous, skilful execution of the performance; and we are characteristically unable to make it verbally explicit. (Schön, 1987, p 25)

Third, reflection gives rise to on-the-spot experiment.

This would imply that, for Schön, reflection suggests a rapid intuitive process with little pause for thought rather than a process of prolonged, deliberative critical questioning. The more that reflection assumes a critical function, the less appropriate it becomes to describe it as being in the action. In *Educating the Reflective Practitioner* (1987), however, Schön provides the image of a ladder of reflection, where people move up a rung to reflect at a metalevel on what they have been doing, then move down again to take consequential action. Here we have reflection-in-action involving thinking (at a metalevel) about the process in which one is engaged. It is this aspect that we consider blurs into what Schön refers to as reflection-on-action, and we call reflection as meditation.

Reflection-on-action refers to the process of making sense of an action after it has occurred, and possibly learning something from the experience, which extends one's knowledge base. It may affect future action, but cannot affect the action being reflected upon because that has already passed.

As Eraut (1995, p 16) suggests, the preposition 'in' refers to the context of reflection while the preposition 'on' refers to the focus of reflection. Schön is primarily concerned with reflection-for-action, reflection whose purpose is to affect action currently in progress. It is here that his use of reflection differs from that of Kolb (1976), whose prime concern is with reflection for learning, which is expected to affect future actions but not usually those still in progress.

When it comes to MBA students, the majority of whom are mature adults, it is obvious that reflective behaviour in a university context is not necessarily the same as such behaviour in a practice/managerial context. The Essex MBA programme has placed emphasis on the process of reflection because we consider that it is relevant to practice and is transferable, despite the obvious differences between reflection in an educational context and in a practice context.

Eraut (1994) provides the factors militating against transfer from the classroom to the workplace: the availability of time to reflect in the busy workday; the erosion of the disposition to reflect, once the obligations of assessed work have been removed; and the post-qualification routinization of professional work. The managers who develop habitual routines are able to cope with the pressures and strains of professional life by limiting the amount of new thinking they have to do. This can increase productivity but can also hinder opportunities for creativity. This makes it even more important to transfer the practice of reflection from the classroom to the workplace despite the difficulties involved in doing so.

Reflection as meditation

Both the practice of management and the studying of it in an academic context share the necessity for many modes of cognition. Decision-making or problem-solving or the absorption of new facts requires the need to superimpose on routinized behaviour hundreds of highly intuitive, but not completely automatic decisions, and to assert a high level of metacognitive control (Eraut, 1995, p 19). It is here that reflection-in-action is helpful – which does not preclude the necessity for reflection-on-action both during and after the event.

Boud *et al.* (1985, p 19) describe reflection in the context of learning as

a generic term for those intellectual and affective activities in which individuals engage to explore their experiences in order to lead to new understandings and appreciations. It may take place in isolation or in association with others.

Reflection on learning – both on content and process – provides many benefits, the chief of which is that it can help students move towards, and then stay within, a deep approach to learning. Reflection is particularly helpful in the context of professional courses as it can help to turn experience into learning. Reflection involves learners in actively processing their learning and provides a learning base that students can apply to new problems and so makes their knowledge more apparent to them.

The models of the learning process developed by Lewin in 1952 and Kolb in 1984 are helpful today. The learning cycle is said to move from new concrete experience, through reflective observation, which examines these experiences from different perspectives, to the formation of abstract concepts and generalizations, which in turn leads to theories that can be used for active experimentation in problem-solving and decision-making, which leads to new concrete experience and so on. Revans' (1983) Action Learning model uses the equation

learning = programmed knowledge + questioning insight

where questioning insight is the result of reflecting on both the programmed knowledge and the process of getting to know.

The term Reflections as used by the Essex MBA encompasses more than reflective observation. It involves the emotions as well as the intellect and contains elements of consideration of, or meditating upon, past knowledge or experience, and is synonymous with contemplation or serious thought or deliberation.

Boud *et al.* (1985) suggest that there are three key elements to the process of reflection. These are:

1. returning to experience: the activity of recalling and 'getting back' to whatever learning event the student is concerned with;
2. attending to feelings: the activity of exploring the positive and beneficial aspects of that experience, as well as exploring and removing feeling that obstructs further consideration of the learning experience;
3. re-evaluating the experience: the activity of examining the experience in the light of the learner's intentions, exploring new knowledge relating this to existing knowledge, and building up the learner's existing conceptual framework.

These three elements tend to overlap in practice and are not intended to be viewed as distinct or independent.

The benefits of writing Reflections

The writing of Reflections is a compulsory part of the MBA programme, taking the form of a non-assessed addition to each term paper and dissertation. We make no formal demands as to the shape or tone of the Reflections. What we get ranges from the stilted through the verbose to the articulate and lucid, from a few (sometimes grudging) paragraphs to pages of insightful comment.

The benefits to the students of writing their Reflections is apparent in what they say. In theoretical terms, we have tapped into Kolb's model (1984) of experiential learning, and the process of reflection helps our students to move round the experiential learning cycle to foster critical reflection at crucial stages.

The benefits to us as designers and deliverers of the programme are also apparent:

- we have a regular and ongoing comment on how the students are reacting to the course;
- we know what we have done well and where they have gained in learning, self-knowledge and confidence;
- we can judge the effectiveness of our educational approach;
- we are made aware of weaknesses in the programme;
- we can draw conclusions about the development of the students.

When we look at the Reflections sections in the term papers and dissertations, it is striking and very gratifying to see how frequently students refer to changes in the way they tackle problems, the way they think about their organization, even the kind of person each one is. Besides their value as teaching and learning aids, these Reflections are also a kind of 'open letter' in which students feel able to express blame, criticism or complaint, as well as praise.

Students' reflections on Reflections

The excerpts we present below concern students' comments about undertaking the Reflections section, rather than reflections on the content or process of their term paper.

By undertaking this section and reflecting on the past month or so, I have found that the research for, and the writing of, this paper has completely changed the way I look at my company, and the way I hope to influence its future. I am beginning to think that before the course is through, I shall have changed the way I look at other parts of my life and even at myself. (first year term paper)

Having just read through the reflections on the early modules of this course, I was surprised how my perspective has changed. I have learnt to be more critical and analytical in my thoughts. (second year term paper)

The way this MBA seems to 'work' (for me anyway) is to force me to increase my knowledge without needing to memorize anything, or to accumulate recipes of procedures and techniques. And having to add this section has forced me to think about what the whole learning process has been about. The project has led me to new ways of making sense of my working environment. You could say that I am beginning to form another way of understanding the reality of my professional world. (second year term paper)

Reflection as meditation is not, however, critical reflection in the sense that the individual is mulling over something in order to question or re-evaluate it. The critical element is a necessary component of reflection, but one can reflect in order to uncover meaning and understanding without adding fault-finding elements. It is reflection as meditation that enables the individual manger to find connections between knowledge, learning and action, and to move forward.

Reflection as mirroring

The word reflection originates from the Latin verb *reflectere* which means to bend or turn (*flectere*) backwards or back (*re*). The term is used in optics to describe the reflection of light against a smooth surface, such as a mirror, and where humans are the object being reflected, this means a physical self-mirroring. In psychology, aspects of consciousness of self have been tested by means of mirrors, not only on animals such as cats or chimpanzees but human infants have been placed in front of mirrors to find out if and when they recognize that the reflected image is of themselves. In literal mirroring, it is assumed that the viewer sees an exact image of that which is being reflected. This is not always the case – the image of themselves that sufferers of anorexia see in the mirror is fatter than the body being reflected. In this instance, the mirror is true, but the perception distorted. On the other hand, mirrors can be deliberately manufactured to distort the image projected on them – the fun derived in a fairground Hall of Mirrors results from the distorted selves that they reflect.

In the main, the term reflection is used metaphorically in human contexts to define aspects of self-exploration. Self-discovery is described in terms of turning towards ourselves and looking inwardly to see ourselves reflected in some intangible inner space. That which is mirrored or reflected is the individual person, our mental activities and the existential aspects of our lives. We gaze upon ourselves reflected in our inner mirror to discover what we are like, although, as in the case of the anorexic, the reflection may be perceived in a distorted form. (A 20th-century metaphor is that we run the film of our lives on a screen in our inner, private cinemas.)

The value of learning groups

Where the manager (as student and practitioner) is concerned, the reflecting surface is other people. In practical terms, for students on the Essex MBA, the mirrors are their colleagues, and mass reflection takes place in their learning groups, possibly more so than in the classroom.

The groups form an important part of the course in that it is there that students are able to support and help each other in an environment that they have chosen. These learning groups are autonomous, self-selected and sometimes very fluid. There is no input from us, the tutors, nor any requirement from us that students should monitor and present to us what they discuss or do when they meet together. The students find these groups very effective in providing meaning and direction for their studies; in many of the term papers, acknowledgements include expressions of thanks, for example:

I wish to thank the four members of my learning group who have provided invaluable advice on organizing [the paper's] contents, when I found I couldn't see the wood for the trees. (first year term paper)

Evidence of the mirror reflecting process is less easy to find in the Reflections section comments. Generally, this aspect of reflection is implied within the remarks made about what has been learned while doing the research for the term paper. We have two explicit comments, however:

I projected my ideas at the others in the group, and what came back revealed the weaknesses in my research design. (first year term paper)

It hasn't been so much a sharing of difficulties about doing our term papers as seeing my difficulties mirrored in the problems of my colleagues. In its own way, this has been a kind of comfort during this time of stress.(second year term paper)

The learning groups provide two types of help to the students – they are able to share information and experience, but they are also a safe environment in which to see reflections of themselves in the mirror of their colleagues. There must be occasions when those mirrors distort the image they reflect, but it would seem from comments made about the usefulness of the learning groups, that in the main, the groups are beneficial to the members.

Even more than experiences or perceptions, it is emotions that are reflected. Learning engages the emotions and students see their emotions reflected in their learning group colleagues, because they meet in one another's homes and the meetings are social as well as studying occasions. The more formal atmosphere of the classroom inhibits this, as does the presence of the tutor.

The potential of reflection if included in assessment

As has already been stated, the MBA programme described above is unusual in dispensing with a set syllabus that all students on the programme must cover. What lies behind this is the rejection of the quasi-scientific/rationalist idea that there is a corpus of management knowledge, which is in the possession of the management educators (us) and which can be easily taught to the manager/students. The scientific paradigm has been the dominant one in theories of management and management education since the Second World War. In this view, management is a science like quantum mechanics, with a known body of knowledge that can be learned.

In this paradigm of education, the problem of assessment appears quite simple: the educators have to examine the students to see whether the appropriate knowledge has been transferred. If, for example, part of the accepted corpus of knowledge is the ability to perform an investment appraisal using a discounted cash flow calculation, then the student must be set a task (a written examination question, an assignment, etc) that requires the demonstration of such knowledge.

If this paradigm is rejected, the problem of assessment is posed afresh. If we cannot measure how much of the prescribed syllabus a manager/student has absorbed, how can we decide whether he/she has 'passed'? Does the word cease to have any meaning?

The solution adopted on our MBA course was to assess the written work produced by the student. Since most of the time and energy that students give to the programme is devoted to preparing these papers, this seems an attractive idea, as we are assessing each student on that which they have done which is specific to themselves. The part of the course that is not assessed is where each student does the same thing (the opposite of assessment by traditional written examination, where the whole point is that the students are all sitting exactly the same paper). This approach also has the advantage that it avoids the distortions created by a mechanical separation of the learning from the assessment of the learning.

We are still assessing the acquisition of knowledge, however. The term papers and dissertations will contain, for example, a literature review, and the tutor will assess this to see whether the student has made a critical appraisal of the literature relevant to the theme of the paper. This may be only a very small fraction of the literature relevant to the module, and the theme will have been chosen by the student to be of relevance to his or her managerial role, but still there is a syllabus, and the expectation of knowledge acquisition.

But this is only indirectly related to the object of the exercise: helping the students to become better managers. The fact that student X has written a number of good papers during the programme does not prove that X is a better manager after experiencing the programme than he or she was before. We want to think so, and we take the quality of the term papers and dissertations as evidence that it is. A student whose written work is not 'good enough' is deemed to have 'failed', ie he or she is not a better manager.

Self-evidently, the students' written work, like any examination, is only an outward manifestation of the process of change in the students. Earlier in the chapter we pointed out that one of the meanings of reflection is 'a kind of self-understanding leading to some kind of enlightenment or learning'. One student, in his Reflections, explicitly compared the self-discovery he had experienced on the programme with the enlightenment central to Eastern mysticism:

One can, perhaps, draw many parallels between the MBA course and the teaching of a Zen master... One of the central themes of Zen Buddhism is the impossibility of teaching enlightenment: the master, instead, having to guide the pupil into self-realization. I hope that by reflecting on the subjects studied I will have learned more than just a collection of facts, and, at least, have achieved some understanding – enlightenment may be too much to hope for! (second year MBA student)

But how can 'enlightenment' be measured and assessed? Like the Gorgon, it can be viewed only indirectly, by studying its reflection, and here, the clearest image we can have is the explicit articulation of the process by the subject of it. The papers to which Reflections are appended are really devices to facilitate the students' self-development, which is most clearly reflected in their Reflections, where they are compelled to articulate the process of enlightenment. It is paradoxical, therefore, that although we require students to submit both papers and Reflections based on the process of writing them, we assess the students on the former, and only use the Reflections to assess ourselves, examining them for evidence of our own educational success or failure.

The logic of our educational approach suggests that we should assess the Reflections, as well as the papers to which they are attached. But this, in turn, would raise new, and possibly insurmountable, problems. Three in particular occur to us.

First, it is difficult to envisage how a tutor can assess Reflections with any pretence of objectivity; teachers know that all marking of written work is a subjective exercise, but marking Reflections would seem to be an extreme case. Second, if the students' Reflections are a reflection of their self-develop-ment, then greater opportunity for progress is open to those who, a priori, have most need of it. In other words, the assessment of Reflections may put a premium on an initial lack of self-development. Finally, and most problemat-ically, if students know that their Reflections are being assessed, they have an incentive to concoct the Reflections which they think the tutor wants to see. Writing Reflections could become just another example of the process of stu-dents 'pleasing the teacher' which has been referred to as an example of 'impression management' (Al-Maskati and Thomas, 1995).

Concluding reflections

Can we take it as read that the explicit practice of reflection has a pedagogical value? If our experience as teachers can be relied on, the answer is 'yes'. With its help, it is possible for students to get self-knowledge of themselves and of their practice, and to take an informed position on knowledge and action.

'Teaching' reflection, like teaching critical thinking, is probably as impossi-ble as 'teaching' the enlightenment (see student Reflection above). Like many other things in life, it is something one needs to learn but which cannot be taught other than by and from oneself. Learning to reflect is like learning to ride a bicycle; we can often remember the moment when balance 'just came' and we became not learners-to-ride but riders, and we cannot say exactly how we know to keep our balance. If we had a person with us who was sup-posed to be teaching us to ride, the 'teacher' turned out to be a helper and a confidence-booster, but in achieving balance, we taught ourselves. Schön's observation about knowledge in action – that we reveal it by our execution of the performance although we are unable to make it verbally explicit – has rel-evance to reflection as meditation.

Reflection methods

There are a number of methods that are held to encourage reflection. These include learning diaries, reflection journals, portfolios of work, discussions of learning strategies, and the use of video, audio and observers in a learning context, which involves the performance of behavioural skills (Gibbs, 1992, p 14).

Reflection on learning reinforces that which has been learned, and if only for that reason, is a valuable pedagogical aid. But it is more than that. Reflection is an essential component of both study and practice. In the work situation, it allows for development and growth, which is why it is unfortunate that there is so little time to reflect during working hours. It is a commonplace that sitting and thinking/reflecting at one's desk is interpreted as not working.

Because the Reflections section is an explicit requirement for the production of term papers and dissertations, our MBA students, over the two years that they are with us, have ten formal occasions when they are required to reflect on the why, what, where, when, and how of their organizational reality. Of all transferable skills, reflection is the easiest to move from the classroom to the workplace.

Gardner's Theory of Multiple Intelligences

Gardner (1993a, 1993b) has produced the Theory of Multiple Intelligences, which rejects the notion of a single intelligence as measured by a standard intelligence test. Drawing on various strands of information, ranging from studies of prodigies to explorations of the brain, Gardner proposed that a more adequate view of cognition can be secured if we think of human beings as having evolved over the millennia to carry out at least seven kinds of information processing and problem-solving. Gardner's seven intelligences encompass:

- type 1 language;
- type 2 logic and mathematics;
- type 3 spatial thinking;
- type 4 musical;
- type 5 bodily-kinaesthetic problem-solving;
- type 6 interpersonal;
- type 7 intrapersonal.

In a lecture at the Royal Society of Arts (1995), Gardner discussed his current work on creativity, from the point of view that each form of intelligence may harbour within it its own form of creativity. Whatever creativity is, it carries with it the capacity to integrate learning and experience so as to be able to channel abilities in new directions. We would suggest that here, too, reflection has a value beyond its pedagogical merit. One might well see 'the new' in a flash of intuition or inspiration, but very often, the new emerges from creative consideration of the old or the current.

Can we relate the discussion on reflections to the intelligences differentiated by Gardner? It seems clear, for example, that Schön's 'reflection-in-action' is closely linked to type 5 (bodily-kinaesthetic problem-solving – riding a bicycle).

Turning back to the question of assessment, traditional methods of assessment (written examinations, for example) obviously focus almost exclusively on types 1 (language) and 2 (logic and mathematics). Our students' Reflections, however, tend to focus on types 6 and 7 (inter- and intrapersonal intelligences). Thus the Reflections are not simply measuring 'intelligence' in a different way; they are measuring different types of intelligence altogether, types of intelligence that are arguably more relevant to the function of a manager.

This brings us back to the beginning of this paper, the suggestion of Bengtsson (1995) that the recent rise in the popularity of reflections (often in the guise of 'critical reflection') is a reaction to a hitherto dominant positivist orientation, which lies behind the scientific paradigm of management. This paradigm, which sees the essence of management as residing in a known, or at any rate knowable, body of facts and techniques is obviously orientated towards types 1 and 2. We have tried in our MBA programme to move the emphasis away from an exclusive concern with knowledge acquisition towards the less definite, less tangible, less measurable attributes associated with types 6 and 7. These intelligences cannot be 'learned' in the way that investment appraisal techniques, for example, can be learned, but they can be developed through a processes of reflection as meditation and reflection as mirroring.

In that sense, everyone 'reflects' with a greater or lesser degree of consciousness that they are doing it. Our requirement that MBA students write Reflections merely guides (or pushes) the students into doing so explicitly and on paper.

I must admit I couldn't see the point in your insistence on producing a reflection on what I have learned by doing this term paper – before I settled down to write it. It would appear that I have gained a kind of confidence in myself by the act of doing it, and I wouldn't have been aware of that, if I hadn't been required to sit down and reflect on what I learned and how I went about learning it. So here is a public acknowledgement that at least one sceptical student has realized that there is an excellent method in your apparent madness. (first year term paper)

In conversation, a couple of students have told us that after attempting, for the first time, to meet the bizarre requirement to write Reflections, they now realize they had always been reflecting, just as Molière's Bourgeois Gentilhomme discovered that he had always been speaking prose.

Reflections can make reflection conscious, and can also make it visible, so that it becomes part of the dialogue between tutor and student. For this reason, we are convinced that the systematic use of Reflections has much pedagogical virtue. Such an approach raises considerable difficulties, not least in the area of assessment, as we have tried to indicate in the chapter, and we do not pretend to have all the answers. On the Essex MBA, we are in an apparently illogical position – on the one hand, we require that students write Reflections (in principle, though we must admit, not in practice so far, a paper fails if Reflections are not included) and on the other hand, we give no prescription to the students as to the content, which is not assessed. In theory, therefore, a student can write anything, however ridiculous, and we must accept it as satisfying our demand. But we think that despite the elements of 'impression management' (tutor management?) that must be present, most students do make an honest effort to enter into the spirit of the exercise and, in consequence, gain something of personal and professional significance from it.

References

Al-Maskati, H. and Thomas, A. B. (1995) 'Contextual influences on thinking in organizations: Tutor versus learner orientations to organizational learning', paper presented at the 12th Egos Colloquium *Contrasts and Contradictions in Organizations*, Istanbul, July.

Bengtsson, Jan (1995) 'What is reflection? On reflection in the teaching profession and teacher education', *Teachers and Teaching: Theory and practice*, 1(1), pp 23–32.

Boud, D., Keogh, R. and Walker, D. (eds) (1985) *Reflection: Turning experience into learning*, London, Kogan Page.

Clift, R. T., Houston, W. R. and Pugach, M. C. (eds) (1990) *Encouraging Reflective Practice in Education: An analysis of issues and programs*, New York, Teachers College Press.

Dewey, John (1933) *How We Think: A restatement of the relation of reflective thinking to the education process*, Boston, Heath.

Dewey, John (1964) *John Dewey: Selected writings*, New York, Modern Library.

Dewey, John (1973) *The Philosophy of John Dewey*, Vols 1 and 2, ed. J. McDermot, New York, G. P. Putnam's.

Eraut, Michael (1994) *Developing Professional Knowledge and Competence*, London, Falmer Press.

Eraut, Michael (1995) 'Schön shock: A case for reframing reflection-in-action?', *Teachers and Teaching: Theory and practice*, 1 (1), pp 9–22.

Gardner, H. (1993a) *Frames of Mind: The theory of multiple intelligences*, London, HarperCollins.

Gardner, H. (1993b) *Multiple Intelligences: The theory in practice*, London, HarperCollins.

Gardner, H. (1995) 'Creativity: New views from psychology and education', *RSA Journal*, **CXLIII** (5459), May, pp 33–42.

Geertz, Clifford (1973) *The Interpretation of Cultures*, New York, Basic Books.

Gibbs, G. (1992) *Improving the Quality of Student Learning*, Bristol, Technical and Educational Services.

Grimmett, P. P. and Erikson, G. L. (eds) (1988) *Reflection in Teacher Education*, New York, Teachers College Press.

Knowles, Malcolm (1984) *The Adult Learner: A neglected species*, Houston, Gulf Publishing Company.

Kolb, D. A. (1984) *Experiential Learning: Experience as the source of learning and development*, Englewood Cliffs, NJ, Prentice-Hall.

Kolb, D. A. (1976) 'Management and the learning process', *California Management Review*, **18** (3), Spring, pp 21–31.

Lewin, Kurt (1952) 'Field theory in social science', in D. Cartwright (ed.) *Selected Theoretical Papers*, London, Tavistock.

Revans, R. (1983) *ABC of Action Learning*, 2nd edn, Southall, Chartwell-Bratt.

Russell, T. and Munby, H. (eds) (1992) *Teachers and Teaching: From classroom to reflection*, London, Falmer Press.

Schön, Donald (1983) *The Reflective Practitioner: How professionals think in action*, New York, Basic Books.

Schön, Donald (1987) *Educating the Reflective Practitioner: Towards a new design for teaching and learning in the professions*, San Francisco, Jossey-Bass.

Schön, Donald (1990) *The Reflective Turn: Case studies in and on educational practice*, New York, Teachers College Press.

Valli, L. (ed.) (1992) *Reflective Teacher Education: Cases and critiques*, Albany, NY, State University of New York Press.

Van Manen, Max (1977) 'Linking ways of knowing with ways of being practical', *Curriculum Inquiry*, **6**, pp 205–28.

Waxman, H. C., Freiberg, J. C., Vaughn, J. and Veil, M. (eds) (1988) *Images of Reflection in Teacher Education*, Reston, VA, Association of Teachers Educators.

Zeichner, K. M. and Tachnick, B. R. (eds) (1991) *Issues and Practices in Inquiry-oriented Teacher Education*, London, Falmer Press.

Further reading

Boud, D. (ed.) (1988) *Developing Student Autonomy in Learning*, London, Kogan Page.

Boud, D. and Felletti, G. (1991) *The Challenge of Problem Based Learning*, London, Croom Helm.

Chapter 3

From didactic expert to partner in learning

Jennifer A. Butler

Summary

This chapter is set in the constantly changing context of professional practice, in which practitioners need to be prepared for professional competence and problem-solving in a multiplicity of settings and to take responsibility for their own lifelong learning and continuing professional development.

Jennifer Butler demonstrates how the Oxford Brookes Occupational Therapy programme recognized the need to develop capability by building upon students' existing skills, prior learning and life experiences, as well as providing opportunities for developing skills in independent learning, problem-solving, reflective practice and team-working. This required a move away from traditional teaching to incorporate self-directed and distance-learning, and more experiential methods.

She describes the processes involved in introducing a radical change in teaching and learning style and philosophy, with associated benefits for students, teachers and future employers.

Introduction

Occupational therapy students need an education that will prepare them for competent professional practice and lifelong learning in a rapidly changing world of health and social care practice. They need the knowledge, skills and professional competence to enable them to respond and adapt to change, to manage their continuing professional education and to prepare them for working in a multiplicity of service environments. Such environments include individuals' own homes, Social Services, the community, hospital settings (both in physical medicine and mental health), working with GPs, with voluntary agencies, in industry and in private practice. Such diverse professional practice requires therapists to solve problems as a member of an interdisciplinary team in situations that are virtually unique in each case (Cohn, 1991). Hilton (1995) suggests that educational opportunities need to be provided to prepare therapists for such work experiences.

Thus, students in occupational therapy arriving at university in their first year need, from the outset, to build upon and have value given to their existing skills, their prior learning and their life experiences. In addition, the opportunities for developing skills in independent learning, problem-solving, reflective practice and team-working should form a critical part of the learning environment.

Increasingly the student cohort has a diverse profile. No longer is the 'traditional' route of 'A' levels the norm. Access courses, first degrees, overseas students and other non-traditional routes of entry, coupled with an increasing number of mature students, indicate the need to examine and modify certain areas of teaching to capitalize on diverse learning styles and experiences.

Many modules within the occupational therapy course at Oxford Brookes University are experiential in nature, are skills based, employ distance-learning strategies, require group work and increasingly as the course progresses, require the students to self-direct their learning. Indeed, the course offers a wide range of different opportunities for student learning over the three years, and encourages all the well-known aspects of good teaching and learning practice.

This chapter illustrates the processes involved in a radical change in teaching and learning style and philosophy to the module in human anatomy and physiology, and the anticipated benefits for the students, staff and future employers.

The motivation to change

Biological science is an area that has a long tradition of didactic teaching (in an increasingly overloaded curriculum) with the 'expert' lecturer sharing knowledge in a master/apprentice manner. The perceived advantages from this traditionalist viewpoint have been well documented by pedagogic research in recent years and include:

- Reassurance that all the topic areas in the curriculum are covered.
- There is a potential to inspire students by oratory and excitement in one's topic area.

- Students hear and become familiar with complex terminology and the language of the subject.
- Complex systems, concepts and ideas can be explained in a more straightforward manner.

There is also the pleasure of 'performance' experienced by the lecturer, which should be recognized as a powerful influence on such teaching practices.
Disadvantages are many, however, including:

- No account is taken of the diverse backgrounds of the students, nor of their differing levels of knowledge or skill, nor of their learning styles.
- The student is a passive recipient of 'wisdom', rather than an active participant in learning (Jackson and Prosser, 1989).
- The students are encouraged to direct all questions to the lecturer as the fount of all knowledge, rather than having the confidence and skills to seek out information for themselves.
- Students may be impeded or inhibited in their learning and exploring by 'boundary setting'. For example, a reliance upon what is needed to be learnt for the hurdle of examination, leading to an evaporation of interest and limited recall following such assessments (Coles, 1987).
- Discussion is deterred, particularly in large lecture theatres.
- Students may not necessarily make the links between theory and professional practice that makes the material relevant for their learning.

Research into active learning incorporates the medical domain where there is a wealth of published evidence indicating that traditional, lecture-based teaching in human anatomy and physiology is not effective in the transfer of knowledge to clinical skills acquisition (Cox, 1987; Mitchell, 1988; Schwartz, 1989; Scott, 1993; Pereira *et al.*, 1993; Association of British Neurologists, 1995).

Compelling reasons for change

Such an accumulation of reasons for change could not be ignored. Indeed, this author's own published work (Butler and Howells, 1993) demonstrates the changes and progress already made in practical biology classes towards active learning, but it seemed that tinkering with elements of the module was no longer sufficient when the major part of the teaching was still based on a didactic lecture and seminar format. A radical rethink and reorganization of the whole approach to biological sciences was necessary.

Retaining best practice

It was intended that the best practice from the current module should be retained, to focus on active student learning to provide opportunities for students to work, co-operate and learn in groups, and to enhance the contextual appreciation of the biological sciences.

By so doing we would:

- reflect changing practice needs;
- help students prepare for continuing professional education;
- suit the needs of a heterogeneous learning group as manifest in the changing student cohort profile;
- promote student-centred education with emphasis on relevance and application to professional practice;
- develop and facilitate problem-solving skills from the very beginning of the course.

Processes of managing change

This change process was managed on several fronts:

- personal and team support;
- philosophically;
- environmentally;
- experimentally.

Personal reflections and team needs

At a personal level each team member had to agree to pursue this new route, to be committed to change. This entailed giving up:

- known and well-used teaching methods;
- territories' of expertise;
- the safety of didactic methods;
- the pleasures of 'performance' in lecturing;
- the 'expert' role.

The pain involved in this process was counterbalanced by the opportunities such change affords. The lecturing team, as a group, needed to recognize the advantages of mutual support in their new roles, including supportive discussion in trying out new methods. The opportunity for open reflection of the teaching and learning process, its successes and difficulties, was also deemed important. Particularly important was the recognition that we would no longer be 'in control'. We would be learning with the students and needed to be comfortable with the new role of partner in learning. These personal adjustments to change have been highlighted by Majoor (1992), including lecturer discontent in losing his/her 'expert' status. Clearly, time spent addressing such issues during the change process is well spent.

Philosophy

The team needed to acknowledge the principle of partnership in learning endeavour. Certain values and beliefs had to be articulated:

- belief in the potential of learners;
- that students had the motivation to learn and the ability to learn in a self-directed manner;
- that students could take on responsibility to learn for themselves;
- that a drastic reduction in didactic teaching would enhance individual student learning;
- to accept and acknowledge that current didactic methods did not achieve the degree of success in learning that one would wish for in the ability to transfer information to practice-relevant clinical skills;
- to acknowledge that what the students need for professional practice were the problem-solving and enquiry skills that would enable them to explore and discover biological bases of any novel dysfunction, disease or disability they may encounter in their working lives to inform professional interventions.

In other words, education should provide these students with the skills to respond to the needs of any client, underpinned by biological and behavioural sciences, but recognizing that for the occupational therapist, 'the key concerns are the functional independence of the individual, the rights of people with disabilities and the provision of opportunities for self-actualisation' (Hollis and Fraser-Holland, 1994).

For this to occur, the learning environment cannot be prescriptive for every unique situation in which the therapist finds him- or herself.

The role of mentors

These changes in thinking and philosophy were facilitated through meetings with a skilled mentor with extensive experience in the area of self-directed learning.

Meetings focused on two main areas – the practicalities of teaching and learning and philosophy.

PRACTICALITIES OF TEACHING AND LEARNING

The lecturing team was able to talk through the logistics of managing such a programme, taking into account limited time, resources and large student numbers. The team looked at where tutor-led sessions could still be appropriate and could complement student-led sessions and explored how the students could be aided in the development of their learning skills, and to consider the framework and support they would need to manage their studies successfully.

PHILOSOPHY

Progress through change was aided by reviewing research literature on problem-focused and self-directed learning in professional education, with the
addition of the practical experiences of the mentor. The current taught curriculum was examined to consider which elements might be 'redundant' in
the climate of modern professional practice. Assessment methods were
explored with a view to devising assignments that would enable students to
demonstrate skills and abilities to access appropriate information and apply
that information to practice-relevant situations, rather than relying on traditional rote memory and factual recall in examinations.

The process of change also involved visiting colleagues running other professional courses that had adopted similar self-learning or problem-focused
approaches. Learning from these colleagues, who were extremely open and
honest, was exceptionally useful in progressing our development.

Environment

The teaching and learning environment had to be considered in the management of change. What may have been appropriate for, and indeed dictating,
certain didactic practices could no longer be considered conducive to enhancing self-directed, student-centred learning. The influence of the environment
upon both teaching practice and upon student behaviour and attitude in
education is well documented. Sitting in rows behind desks predisposes the
student to take a passive, subservient role in learning. Thus, it was critical that
we provided a learning environment and atmosphere in which:

- group discussion was encouraged;
- individual learners were involved equally with others;
- the lecturer was not automatically a central focus of the room.

Both the School and University supported these changes in every way,
including funding provision.

Experimenting with methods

The process of change takes time to work through whilst normal teaching
continues. It is interesting to note that once philosophy and thinking starts to
change, satisfaction with the *status quo* diminishes and justifying current
practice becomes very difficult. An enthusiasm and excitement for all the
opportunities that change offers can be generated and have been shown to
occur in other courses (Schmidt *et al.*, 1987). The way in which this course
team managed this time of transition was to 'experiment' (using the term
loosely) with traditionally taught sessions and topic areas.

One example involved giving students self-directed study time with appropriate guidelines instead of lectures. Following up these with seminar support, it was clear that students had done all, and more, of what was outlined for their study. They had understood what they had studied, and their feedback indicated a positive response to this style of learning, which allowed them to work at their own pace and level, to be actively involved in what they were doing, and yet still feel 'secure' because the seminar could address any outstanding issues that needed clarifying. Such experiences add to the confidence of the students in their abilities to study, learn and understand as autonomous learners. They also enhance the confidence of the lecturing team within the new practice and philosophy.

Benefits of change

The benefits for the students are:

- value and acknowledgement of existing skills in learning;
- active involvement in learning;
- encouragement of attributes desired by the students themselves (analytic thinking, problem-solving and imaginative powers);
- capitalizing on initial enthusiasm at point of entry to the course by emphasizing relevance and applicability of biological science to professional practice;
- fostering team-working and skills;
- promoting academic self-reliance and autonomy.

For future employers the benefit is that therapists will have additional practice in self-directed learning and consequently:

- have the skills and problem-solving abilities to respond to client need;
- are independent, autonomous workers with self-management skills;
- are able to adapt and change to suit the various service environments in which they work;
- are adept at assessing and dealing with problems;
- are experienced in teamwork for interdisciplinary co-operation;
- have independent learning skills for continued professional development.

Much additional work is required in preparation of such major change – both in developing and planning the module and in personal reflection and adaptation. Nevertheless, the educational and professional opportunities and benefits for lecturers are clear, for example:

- professional development of skills and knowledge in a new aspect of education;
- increased personal interactions with students;

- new learning insights and knowledge acquisition;
- professional challenge and opportunities;
- potential for pedagogic research to monitor and evaluate change.

The experience of our Occupational Therapy School in progressing from a safe platform of didactic 'expert' to the insecurities of partnership in learning endeavour involved time, effort, financial resources and risk-taking. This investment was vindicated by the subsequent benefits for the student learning experience. It may well be an essential rather than optional journey on the road to capability, one that is necessary for both present and future employment needs, and ultimately, one well worth making in the interests of lifelong learning.

References

Association of British Neurologists (1995) 'Teaching neurology in the 21st century: Suggestions from the Association of British Neurologists for UK medical schools planning their core curriculum', *Medical Teacher*, **17**(1), 5–12.

Butler, J. A. and Howells, K. F. (1993) 'Health profiles in physiology teaching: An active learning experience', *British Journal of Occupational Therapy*, **56**(2), 55–8.

Cohn, E. (1991) 'Clinical reasoning: Explicating complexity', *American Journal of Occupational Therapy*, **45**(11), 969–71.

Coles, C. (1987) 'The actual effects of examinations on medical students' learning', *Assessment and Evaluation in Higher Education*, **12**(3), 209–19.

Cox, K. (1987) 'Knowledge which cannot be learned is useless', *Medical Teacher*, **9**(2), 57–67.

Hilton, R. W. (1995) 'Fragmentation within interprofessional work: A result of isolationism in health care professional education programmes and the preparation of students to function only in the confines of their own disciplines', *Journal of Interprofessional Care*, **9**(1), 33–40.

Hollis, V. and Fraser-Holland, E. N. (1994) Course document for the Post graduate Diploma in Occupational Therapy, University of Brighton.

Jackson, M. and Prosser, M. (1989) 'Less lecturing, more learning', *Studies in Higher Education*, **14**(1), 55–68.

Majoor, G. (1992) 'Introspection at the Faculty of Medicine of the University of Limberg', *Annals Community-oriented Education* **5**, 199–200.

Mitchell, G. (1988) 'Problem-based learning in medical schools: A new approach', *Medical Teacher*, **10**(1), 57–67.

Pereira, L., Telang, B., Butler, K. and Joseph, S. (1993) 'Preliminary evaluation of a new curriculum: Incorporation of problem-based learning into the traditional format', *Medical Teacher*, **15**(4), 351–64.

Schmidt, H. G., Dauphinee, W. D. and Patel, V. L. (1987) 'Comparing the effects of problem-based and conventional curricula in an international sample', *Journal of Medical Education* **62**(4), 305–15.

Schwartz, P. L. (1989) 'Active small group learning with a large group: A practical example', *Medical Teacher*, **11**(1), 81–6.

Scott, T. M. (1993) 'How we teach anatomy efficiently and effectively', *Medical Teacher*, 15(1), 67–75.

Further reading

Collins, R. and Hammond, M. (1987) 'Self-directed learning to educate medical educators: How do we use self-directed learning?', *Medical Teacher*, 9(3).
Sadlow, G., Piper, D. and Agnew, P. (1994) 'Problem-based learning in the development of an occupational therapy curriculum, part 1: The process of problem-based learning', *British Journal of Occupational Therapy*, 57(2), 49–54.

Part Two

Learner Autonomy and Action Learning

Chapter 4

From map-reader to map-maker: approaches to moving beyond knowledge and competence

Stan Lester

Summary

Through the metaphor of mapping, this chapter proposes a model of professional development that moves beyond the dominant ideology of acquisition of technical–rational expertise and that offers a reframing of the relationship between vocational and academic awards.

Stan Lester argues that the majority of formative professional development programmes are based on a conceptual 'map' such as a syllabus or standards framework. However, encouraging people to develop through 'map-reading' does not necessarily help them to become good map-makers – that is, self-managed, intelligent practitioners capable of advancing their practice and operating effectively in environments of uncertainty and change. To support development towards this latter kind of professionalism, it is necessary to encourage an enquiring, critical and creative approach at the same time as meeting the demands of the knowledge or competence curriculum.

This chapter may usefully be read alongside Chapter 9, 'Assessing the self-managing learner: a contradiction in terms?'

Introduction

Initial professional development programmes are commonly based on models containing notions of what practitioners ought to know and be able to do in order to practise effectively. In the technical–rational tradition, these take the form of a body of knowledge and technique to be learned and applied, or more recently in some occupations, a theory of practice articulated in the form of a set of competence standards. Both kinds of framework can be thought of as conceptual 'maps' designed to help student and developing practitioners find their way in their professional 'territories'.

Although technical–rational models have been dominant throughout 19th- and 20th-century professionalization, they are nevertheless limited, particularly as the nature and context of professional work becomes (and is re-interpreted as) more than technical and administrative problem-solving. Perspectives provided by for instance Ackoff's (1974) systems approach, Toffler's (1980) *The Third Wave*, Reich's (1991) notion of the symbolic analyst, Handy's (1989) *The Age of Unreason*, as well as recent thought on modernism and postmodernism such as that of Habermas (1977), Harvey (1990) and Law (1994), point to professional work as an interpretative and creative activity as much as a technical one. Practice is involved with dilemmas of value, with creating congruent outcomes in complex social, ethical and economic contexts, with 'managing messes' (Ackoff, 1974) and 'setting' as well as solving problems (Schön, 1983), and with situations where not only is the nature of the territory constantly changing, but territorial boundaries are beginning to blur and dissolve.

Within this context there is still room – and need – for the kind of map-reading or Model A practice characterized by technical knowledge, standards and professional boundaries (Lester, 1995a), but by itself it is an inadequate conceptualization of professional work at the close of the 20th century. Increasingly, practitioners need to move beyond map-reading and become active experimenters and constructors of their own practice and the theory on which it is based. This map-making or Model B practice (Lester, 1995a) in effect involves moving up a level from the frameworks offered by professional bodies and curriculum designers, and seeing them as perspectives or frames of reference from which to approach the territory, rather than as the territory itself. It then becomes possible to move between frames of reference, create new ones, and work in the spaces where practice creates rather than follows the map.

In some fields this kind of practice is recognized through the idea of extended professionalism, and through approaches such as reflective practice, action learning, action research and other forms of generally self-managed learning, which are increasingly being used at the level of continuing professional development (CPD). However, to make a division between 'map-reading' initial training and 'map-making' extended development is not entirely helpful, because proficiency at map-reading, at following other people's structures, does not necessarily transfer to the confidence, exploration and experimentation required to map uncharted territories and redraw the maps of known ones. More than this, an education in map-reading does not guarantee development of the abilities required for map-making, and may encourage limiting beliefs that blunt them.

The challenge is therefore how to develop map-making abilities while working within the constraints of the curricula that characterize initial professional frameworks. The remainder of this chapter briefly considers the nature of maps and guidance structures, then goes on to explore ways of developing beyond them from within competence-led and syllabus-led programmes.

Maps and safety nets

Given the predominance of content frameworks, by which term I include defined knowledge, skills, ethics and competence outcomes, it is worth briefly exploring what they achieve. The framework can be thought of as a guidance structure or map to enable the developing or would-be practitioner to gain familiarity with the professional territory quickly, to begin to operate coherently within it, and to give meaning to the jargon and cultural artefacts of the profession, as well as a safety net designed to prevent damaging mistakes. It can be argued that many content frameworks are influenced by factors of professionalization and power (eg Larson, 1977), but for practical purposes there is perhaps little argument that they have pragmatic value, both to assist practitioners to develop to a stage where they can operate competently, and to give recipients of professional services some degree of confidence that minimum standards will be reached.

Despite this utility, content frameworks have limitations that often remain hidden and are sometimes actively covered up within development programmes. Creating the map is a subjective exercise which involves value judgements about how to interpret, what to put in and what to leave out, and what is appropriate professional behaviour. It also necessarily involves at least tacit assumptions about the future, for the environments and contexts of practice change while the temporal contexts of development frameworks are rarely made clear; yet many are heavily influenced by practice that is being questioned and overtaken even as it is introduced into the framework.

Whatever map is chosen, in the end it will always be an interpretation from a perspective, whether given legitimacy through discourse in professional communities or through technical–rational logic. The developing practitioner will therefore be presented with a necessarily subjective model that may well be held up as a 'correct' one for the particular profession and, except within defined limits, as beyond his or her critique. The more codified and ostensibly objective the model, the less it is amenable to developing anything other than map-reading professionalism.

Encouraging map-making professionalism suggests starting from a different point – that of enquiry, critique, reflection and reconstruction. This is not to suggest that the map is abandoned, but that it is offered explicitly as a map that can be seen as useful, but also as one of many possible interpretations of a professional territory. While the map may form the basis of the development programme or assessment framework, practitioner-learners are nevertheless encouraged from the outset to see it as a set of theories with which to engage in a practical dialectic, becoming aware of the assumptions it implies and reconceptualizing and recreating it to develop their own frameworks for use and testing. In this model therefore development operates simultaneously at two levels; one being concerned with understanding and using maps, and the other with critique, exploration and map-making.

The distinction between guidance structures and safety nets gains added importance here, for the most essential aspects of professional competence and ethics can initially be introduced as rules, providing a safety net for the novice and a basic structure for assessment; while much of what tends to pass as essential knowledge and skills to be learned might better be treated as a guidance structure, and opened up to critique and enquiry from the outset. However, as the practitioner develops to a stage associated with fitness to practice unaided, the safety net will also have become subject to enquiry, even if reconstruction is in places limited to long-term options for change.

Beyond competence: map-making within NVQ frameworks

The competence frameworks provided by UK National and Scottish Vocational Qualifications (here abbreviated to NVQs) essentially lend themselves to use in two ways. One method is to approach them as the end point of development, where the programme is essentially concerned with gathering evidence and 'proving' competence. While this can be managed by the learner, it is still an exercise in map-reading, and if pursued in a purely instrumental way it may improve practice in line with the standards, but it does little to enhance the practitioner's capability beyond them. The other is to use the framework as the starting point for development, seeing it explicitly as a guidance structure, an initial model to be challenged and reconceptualized as the practitioner builds a personal and developing map of the field. Used in this way, standards frameworks need not be antagonistic to a map-making approach to development; although their predefined nature looks rigid, the explicit and purposive nature of the standards makes them relatively straightforward to use as a starting point for more critical and creative development.

While there are now an increasing number of NVQs that are on a level with full professional qualifications, by far the greatest experience at the 'higher' levels is with the Management Charter Initiative (MCI) standards. MCI initially produced standards at four levels, described as supervisory, first-line, middle and senior management, the first three of these being used as the basis for NVQs at Levels 3, 4 and 5 respectively (NCVQ, 1995, p11); subsequent review has maintained the three levels of qualification but incorporated a strategic management stream into Level 5.

The management standards are based on three components: a competence framework derived through a form of functional analysis (Mansfield, 1991), describing activities such as managing operations and resources, recruiting and selecting staff, planning and evaluating work and managing information; a Personal Competence Model, which describes behaviours relating to, for instance, managing oneself, managing others, communicating and thinking and taking decisions; and an outline of knowledge that is assumed to guide action in the functional areas. Rather than demanding familiarity with prescribed theories of management, the knowledge component is open to recognizing practitioners' practical theories of action provided they are sufficient to enable practise at the level and breadth of competence defined in the functional standards. The standards are not without criticism (Lester, 1994) and even in revised form they still favour large-organization, bureaucratic environments, but they nevertheless represent an attempt to describe the work of managing in a reasonably generic way.

Several different approaches to using the MCI standards can be distinguished, whether or not they are being used for NVQ accreditation. These can be categorized as:

- using the standards to develop a syllabus, which is then provided through a taught course;
- concentrating on assessment for an NVQ, often (but not exclusively, see MCI, 1996) through presenting a portfolio of evidence, which attests to existing competence;
- using a developmental approach (such as a form of action learning) within an evidence-based NVQ model.

The first approach is one which was initially popular in higher education, but it suffers from defining both the inputs and objectives of learning, in some respects detracting from the flexibility offered by the NVQ model; of the three, it can provide the least scope for developing beyond a map-reading level of learning. The second is perhaps the most common variant for commercial provision and in-house assessment centres, although as mentioned above it can encourage instrumentalism, which acts as a barrier to more than a superficial level of development. The third model is perhaps the most successful at encouraging development within an NVQ-type framework, as it encourages practitioners to engage with the standards and integrate them into their work. However, although it is more supportive of alternative ideas, it is still ultimately restricted by the frame of reference provided by the MCI map.

An alternative that builds on this third approach is for the practitioner to develop and use a personal model of practice, for which the competence framework forms a starting point. Taking the statements of competence from the MCI standards, the practitioner engages with these in a dialectic with his or her work and develops through action and reflection, in the process creating a personal map, which reflects developing theory-in-use. The result is likely to be not only a manager who is competent in his/her current context, but who is also capable and contextually aware, and able to extend his/her map proactively into new areas and redraw it in explored ones as needs and opportunities arise.

A significant obstacle to this approach is that assessment for the NVQ leaves little room for negotiation, and aware practitioners may find they have developed a perfectly valid model that is significantly at odds with the expectations of the assessment system. However, the MCI standards are explicit enough to make it practicable to develop critical awareness of the process of assessment as expecting conformance to a particular theory of action, such that participants will separate what they need to do as competent and capable practitioners from the precise requirements of the assessment process. This is not an entirely satisfactory situation, but it does enable participants to recognize the artificiality of external assessment, and contrast it with practical tests of validity they can apply to their theory and practice from considering its fitness for purpose and wisdom for wider contexts (see Lester, 1995b).

A second assessment option with great potential for exploration and use is to locate an MCI-based development programme within a higher education assessment framework such as one based on Credit Accumulation and Transfer (CATS). In this case, the aim is to base the higher education accreditation structure in a horizontal or map-making dimension, so that it explicitly supports critique, reflection, enquiry and constructive action, without linking it to achievement of the NVQ standards. This type of framework makes no attempt to assess the practitioner's map directly, but considers the extent to which it has been internally evaluated for fitness for purpose and contextual congruence (Lester, 1995b).

This approach also overcomes the problematic question of equating NVQ levels within higher education, for it removes any attempt to make a direct link between the complexity (and to some extent responsibility) of function on which the NVQ system is based, and the level of rigour, critique, reconstruction and creativity demonstrated (cf Lester, 1995c). As an example, a recent programme proposal developed for use with teachers with varying management roles uses all levels of management standards as a starting point, and offers accreditation through CATS at degree or master's level as well as via NVQs. Participants will be able to select whatever standards are most suitable for them – including, if NVQ accreditation is not a priority, combinations of competence standards from different levels – and develop from them a dynamic personal model of management practice appropriate to their current situations and future plans. The CATS accreditation is based on a set of negotiable criteria relating to enquiry, reflection, learning through action and developing concepts, with work at M-level broadly demanding greater contextual awareness, exposure and questioning of basic assumptions, and critical and creative (as opposed to purely problem-solving) theory and action.

Beyond knowledge: map-making in syllabus-based programmes

Opportunities for applying similar principles in syllabus-based programmes vary with the nature of the assessment system and degree of latitude available within the professional curriculum. At one end of the spectrum are schemes where assessment is wholly external, typically through unseen examinations, and the syllabus closely defined; in some instances the programme is dominated by assessment to such an extent that it becomes a low-level cramming exercise that relates only marginally to practice even at a map-reading level. However, the spectrum also extends to programmes where the provider effectively controls the curriculum and assessment within the overall requirements of the external body, and there is considerable scope for building in creative approaches.

While the more restrictive end of the spectrum limits opportunities to build in map-making activity, it does not circumscribe them completely. Presenting the curriculum or syllabus so that it is understood holistically as a map, rather than in piecemeal or sequential form, provides a first step in this direction, enabling the assessment strategy to be explained in context and contrasted with practice-based evaluation. The learner can then move up and down through levels of detail to gain an understanding of the curriculum in a way that is consistent with assessment requirements, as well as aiding location against practice and facilitating critical comparison. Further developing students' use of conceptual mapping as a thinking and learning tool – for instance through Buzan's mind-mapping approach (Buzan, 1974) – is capable of enhancing learning more generally, with potentially significant benefits in terms of assessment outcomes. Even in the case of full-time students with limited access to practice experience, encouraging systemic rather than linear approaches to thinking about professional territories has greater potential to develop a more critical and creative approach later on.

At the other end of the spectrum, providers have latitude to design their own programmes and assessment systems within a set of written or tacit guidelines provided by the professional body or registration authority acting as an accrediting agency. While the guidelines may imply an outline curriculum in the content dimension, this should not detract from the provider's ability to build critique, reflection, enquiry and creative synthesis into the programme's methodology. For instance, in initial teacher education an interesting dynamic has arisen through external concerns that are tending to focus on subject knowledge and measurable competence, while many pro-grammes are rooted in a reflective practitioner philosophy (Fish, 1995). In meeting the external requirements, these programmes also aim explicitly to develop practitioners beyond them as map-making professionals; critical enquiry and the development of 'practical discourse' (Fish, 1995) are typically encouraged, and approaches incorporated such as negotiated learning con-tracts, self-identification of areas for development, self-development diaries and collaborative enquiry (Weil and Bridges, 1992).

In both cases it is clear that the approach taken within the constraints of the curriculum framework and assessment process has potential to influence whether the programme is primarily concerned with training in map-read-ing, or becomes an introduction to map-making. In the latter, students will be achieving the outcomes required by the framework, but will also be relating them critically to their own practice – or to real-life case-studies – and con-sciously developing their own theories of practice and constructing and test-ing personal models of professionalism.

Conclusions

Moving from a map-reading, Model A approach to professional development to one which encourages self-managed Model B practice requires action at several levels. Organizations that develop curricula, standards and assess-ment frameworks can begin to move towards a process-based dimension in which practitioners are recognized as map-makers and creators of their prac-tice rather than purely map-followers, while at the level of institutions and providers, local programme design and assessment strategies can become more visible, open and negotiable. However, action can also be taken within existing frameworks by individual tutors and programme leaders to assist students to become active explorers and constructors of their practice.

At the level of learning about learning, and about conceptual structures used to support and guide learning, an understanding of the map/territory distinc-tion is fundamental, together with an appreciation of the subjective nature of any map and the validity (and inescapability) of personal models, theories and knowledge. Along with this goes awareness of the difference between assess-ment standards, in most cases set from the conceptual maps of others, and fit-ness for the purposes and wider contexts of personal practice, which in a Model B world it is the practitioner's responsibility to develop and evaluate.

In terms of process, methods of supporting learning are needed which support the development of personal models through enquiry, critique, ques-tioning, reflection, dialectic and systemic and creative thinking. One step in this direction follows on from awareness at the level of conceptual structures, and involves making explicit any map or framework being used as the basis for development and assessment. Another involves using and developing approaches, both at a general and a 'micro' level within the programme, which encourage appropriate thinking and action and, where necessary, explicitly support appropriate learning and concept-organizing methodologies within them.

Finally, there is a vital need for consistency. Assessment frameworks can be extremely effective at undermining self-managed, map-making approaches to learning (Lester, 1995b), and while in the context of initial professional programmes it is rarely possible to tackle them at the root, it is possible to make them consistently explicit and help learners look beyond them.

References

Ackoff, R. L. (1974) *Redesigning the Future: A systems approach to societal problems*, New York, John Wiley.

Buzan, T. (1974) *Use your Head*, London, BBC Books.

Fish, D. (1995) *Quality Learning for Student Teachers: University tutors' educational practices*, London, David Fulton.

Habermas, J. (1977) *Knowledge and Human Interests*, Boston, MA, Beacon Press.

Handy, C. (1989) *The Age of Unreason*, London, Century Business.

Harvey, D. (1990) *The Condition of Postmodernity: An enquiry into the origins of cultural change*, Oxford, Blackwell.

Larson, M. S. (1977) *The Rise of Professionalism: A sociological analysis*, Berkeley, University of California Press.

Law, J. (1994) *Organizing Modernity*, Oxford, Blackwell.

Lester, S. (1994) 'Management standards: A critical approach', *Competency*, 2(1), 28-31.

Lester, S. (1995a) 'Beyond knowledge and competence: Towards a framework for professional education', *Capability*, 1(3), 44-52.

Lester, S. (1995b) 'Assessing the self-managing learner: A contradiction in terms?', paper for *Beyond Competence to Capability and the Learning Society*, Higher Education for Capability Conference, Manchester (reproduced in Part Three of this book).

Lester, S. (1995c) 'Professional pathways: A case for measurements in more than one dimension', *Assessment and Evaluation in Higher Education*, 20(3), 237-49.

Management Charter Initiative (1996) *New Methods of Assessing Management Vocational Qualifications*, London, MCI.

Mansfield, B. (1991) 'Deriving standards of competence', in E. Fennell (ed.) *Development of Assessable Standards for National Certification*, Sheffield, Employment Department.

National Council for Vocational Qualifications (1995) *NVQ Criteria and Guidance*, London, NCVQ.

Reich, R. B. (1991) *The Work of Nations*, London, Simon & Schuster.

Schön, D. A. (1983) *The Reflective Practitioner: How professionals think in action*, New York, Basic Books.

Toffler, A. (1980) *The Third Wave*, London, Collins.

Weil, S. and Bridges, D. (1992) 'Capability through teacher education', in J. Stephenson and S. Weil (eds) *Quality in Learning: A capability approach in higher education*, London, Kogan Page.

Chapter 5

Towards capability through competence: autonomy or automatism?

Ann-Marie Bathmaker and David Stoker

Summary

This chapter illuminates the potential for broadening the competence approach in an imaginative way, in order to achieve capability through such processes as autonomous learning, encompassing a high degree of student negotiation and individual creativity.

It is based on the experience of operating a competence-based teacher training programme at the University of Wolverhampton with a particular focus on teachers in the post-16 education sector. In designing the programme two questions were posed: what are the roles of the teacher in further education, and what does the successful teacher do when fulfilling these roles?

The activities of the programme embody a capability approach and are intended 'to develop thinking practitioners who are concerned to question their teaching, and to relate theory to practice' giving rise to the notion of 'restricted' and 'extended' professionals.

Introduction

The University of Wolverhampton runs teacher training programmes for primary, secondary and post-compulsory education. In 1990, the Further, Adult and Higher Education programme was validated as a competence-based course of preparation for teachers in the post-16 education sector. The elements of competence were derived as the result of discussions between staff of the University (the Polytechnic at that time) and teachers in local colleges of further education. They arose in answer to two questions:

- what are the roles of the teacher in further education?
- what does the successful teacher do when fulfilling these roles?

There are presently 50 competence elements, arranged into eight units of competence, seven of which are concerned with the art or craft of teaching. The eighth addresses wider contextual issues surrounding the teacher's work.

Our beliefs

Following five years' experience of the programme, it is our view that a competence-based programme of teacher education can lead towards capability, where capability is understood to relate to notions of an extended professional. We qualify our claim in the light of this. The competences must reflect what a capable teacher should be doing and the performance criteria need to reflect a wider, rather than narrower focus of attention, knowledge and understanding. The assessment process is then concerned with probing these wider issues, and the teaching and learning processes in the programme allow the students to take some responsibility for their education. The collection and presentation of evidence need to allow flexibility of choice in the form the evidence will take and the time at which it is presented. The goal of the programme, then, is to develop in students the qualities of a capable practitioner. Given these circumstances, the concept of competence becomes wider, rather than narrower.

Competence

Competence is often conceived as 'the ability to perform tasks' and competence-based programmes may be characterized by the pejorative epithet of 'the 3 Rs' – Reductionist, Restrictive and Ritualistic. If this is the conception of competence, then it is in danger of becoming a vehicle for training, described by one writer as causing people to behave in certain ways (Barrow, 1976).

In many cases there seems to be a preoccupation with the completion of detailed competence pro formas, leaving no stone unturned, with everyone presenting and assessing similar evidence for competence, in the quest for standardization. If pressed, this might be justified by invoking the educationally respectable terms of validity and reliability. However, this ignores the effect of this approach on feasibility (heavy workload on student and assessor) and discriminating power (students' individuality or creativity being allowed to be demonstrated). The procedure for presentation and assessment of evidence becomes a box-filling and ticking, ritualistic, even automatous, activity.

If, however, competence includes the aspect of 'having command of pertinent skills and knowledge' (Short, 1984), a different vision of a competence-based programme becomes possible, with an educational rather than training orientation. An educational focus opens up the opportunity for critical interaction with skills and knowledge. 'Having command of' subsumes the ability to 'choose and use' the pertinent skills and knowledge. This, in turn, implies rationality, intent, decision-making, foresight and the ability to reflect on (and even in) action. Taken together, these seem to suggest an autonomous, rather than automatous approach.

The purpose of education has been described as an 'understanding of the complexity of the nature of "X" ' (Barrow, 1976), indicating a wider, rather than narrower perspective, but also probing principles (Peters, cited in Barrow, 1976) and doing something with the pertinent knowledge and skills. Whitehead's notion of education, written as early as 1912, is 'the acquisition of the art of the utilisation of knowledge' while Eraut (1995) defines capability as 'knowledge in use'. Capability and education would appear to have similar attributes. A competence-based educational programme, therefore, within this wider view of competence, can lead towards capability, if autonomy (a significant factor in capability) is a feature of the processes involved in the course. Another necessary attribute of such a course would be learner-managed learning – another well-cited feature of capability.

The goal of the Wolverhampton programme: the PRIT model and autonomy

At an early stage in their programme, students are introduced to the kind of teacher it is hoped that they will become. It is not envisaged that they all become identical clones, but that they will each bring their own individuality to their teaching roles and activities. However, it is felt desirable for them to become pro-active, reactive, and interactive teachers.

The pro-active teacher is one who consciously, deliberately and sensitively seeks to create situations in which learning occurs (shades here of Curzon's definition of teaching (1990)). This conscious deliberation, and selection of appropriate methods and milieu, has, at its heart, sensitive decision-making. This requires a base of developed or developing theory, which underpins and guides the teacher's actions in choosing and using pertinent skills and knowledge.

Handy's (1993) assertion about the value to the manager of organization theory – leading to more influence on future events – is felt to apply to the role of theory for the teacher. The theory may have its origins in 'private' theory, generated through reflection on their own experiences of teaching, either as teachers or taught (Eraut, 1994), in 'espoused' public theory, and in negotiation between private and public theory, in which students regard public theory not as a prescription having some universal relevance, to be applied automatically, but rather as principles to be tested out in practice (Stones, 1994). These principles can be modified to make them compatible with particular contexts and personal beliefs. Sensitive decision-making and adaptation of principles seem to reflect an autonomous approach.

The reactive teacher consciously, deliberately and sensitively responds to the changing teaching and learning situation. Sensitivity implies that the teacher can judiciously choose what to do, and the actions will vary from situation to situation. Again, the choice will be influenced by the theories developed and outlined above. The interactive teacher regards teaching and learning as a system in which effective two-way (reciprocally contingent) communication is important – each takes account of the other in their dealings in a teaching and learning transaction.

The sensitivity to, and the reciprocal nature of, the learning situation enables the pro-active, reactive and interactive – the PRI – teacher to make appropriate interventions or non-interventions. This requires an element of 'with it ness', an attribute of effective teachers coined by Kounin in 1970, and more recently promulgated by Kyriacou (1991) and Child (1993). Withitness is the 'demonstration by the teacher that she [sic] is aware of what is happening in the classroom' (Kounin, 1970). It encompasses the teacher's provision of what is needed, the necessary stimuli, resources and activities.

PRI teachers are in control of self, others and the teaching/learning situation. They have command of the pertinent knowledge and skills appropriate to the circumstances in which they find themselves. The above seem to imply autonomy – a feature of capability, and also the ultimate goal of the competence-based teacher education programme.

Learner-managed learning and autonomy

In learner-managed learning, students are involved in deciding what to learn, how to learn and how that learning is to be assessed. We will concentrate on the area of assessment of competences. Whilst it is true that the competence elements in the Wolverhampton programme are pre-specified, students can exercise choice in the assessment process. After reflecting on the competence elements, and their stage of development, students can decide the order in which the competences are to be achieved. Often the assessment involves the recognition of prior certificated or experiential learning. Students then decide the nature of the evidence to be submitted for assessment. In the course documentation some suggestions are made for the type of evidence – these are meant as a guide only, and are not prescriptive. The ultimate choice rests with the student. The performance criteria contain a general indication of the relevant theoretical principles that contribute to the underpinning knowledge and understanding for the competence elements. In the explanation and justification involved in many of the competence elements, students are required to draw on and use those aspects of theory which they consider to be most apposite, and to support the choices that are made.

Students have the opportunity to give an account of the application or testing of theories in practice, and through reflection on the situations encountered, can show how it was decided which principles were suitable as explanations or predictions of phenomena, as prescriptions for action, or which may have needed modification. This decision-making involves 'having command' – and also exercising autonomy.

The features of the PRI teacher and the learner involvement in the assessment process seem to indicate that the approach adopted in the Wolverhampton programme is leading students towards a choice of purposeful, purposive interventions. Purposeful and purposive each have connotations (and also denotations) of intentionality and effectiveness – features of autonomy and capability.

The disposition to theorize and to metacompetence

Many of the activities discussed above indicate that students are moving beyond the skills and outcomes directly related to the work situation, and towards Brown's (1994) notion of metacompetence – which includes the ability to ask the right questions, and Klemp's (1977) suggestion of the ability to learn from experience by reflection, theory and the synthesis of alternatives (cited in Lester, 1995). Evidence for competence is the result of students' reflection on their classroom experiences, and asking themselves questions about the practice and the effectiveness of their actions. Many of the answers may lie in their developing theory.

Much of what has been discussed so far depends on the students' use of theory, and their ability and willingness to use it – what Eraut (1994) calls the disposition to theorize (simply, the reflection on, and selection, use or modification of theory). This 'disposition' is contextually influenced. We feel that there are certain things in the University of Wolverhampton course that contribute to a context conducive to theorizing, linked to factors referred to by Eraut, which can enhance or hinder the students' theorizing. These factors are as follows:

● Theorizing is not likely to be taken seriously unless it engages with students' current concerns. The competence units are one of the major current concerns of student teachers.

- Students need to encounter theorizing in educational settings – in many, minimal attention is given to the importance of theory – it is something to be grown out of, rather than grown into. The assessment of competence is by work-based assessors – practising teachers trained in the assessment procedures and in the links between theory and practice. In this way, theorizing is not seen as something only done by university staff.
- Students need to have some knowledge of alternative courses of action, without which planning becomes a routine, from which practical theorizing becomes excluded. This is covered in the justification of decisions made in lesson proposals, in the evaluation of lessons, and in particular competences that require students to suggest alternative courses of action.
- Students need to have some success in theorizing. The attainment of a competence element should reflect evidence of success in the use of theory.

The restricted or extended professional

The activities of the Wolverhampton programme are intended to develop thinking practitioners, who are encouraged to question their teaching, and to relate theory to practice. These are features of the extended (rather than restricted) professional outlined by Stenhouse (1975) based on Hoyle. Briefly summarized, the features on the continuum of restricted to extended professional are as follows:

- *Restricted professionals* attend short courses of a practical nature, are subject or student centred in their teaching, have a high degree of skill in handling and understanding students, demonstrate a high degree of classroom competence, obtain great satisfaction from personal relationships with students and evaluate their performance in relation to their perceptions of changes in students' behaviour or achievement.
- *Extended professionals* seek to link theory to practice, have a commitment to some form of curriculum theory and mode of evaluation, have a view of their work in the college, community or society context, and participate in a range of professional activities, such as exam boards and subject co-ordination.
- *Extended professionals plus* have a systematic commitment to questioning their own teaching as the basis for development, the commitment and skills to study their own teaching, and the concern to question and test theory in practice. It is these last three which are areas of central interest and concern to those participating in the Wolverhampton programme. The goal can be seen as the 'extended professional plus'.

Conclusion

Competence-based courses can lead to more than competence if certain issues receive attention in the development and implementation of the programme. The notion of competence must not be restricted to 'the ability to perform a task', but broadened to contain constructs such as control and empowerment. The evidence considered legitimate should be amenable to negotiation or creativity on the part of the student. The fulfilment of the performance criteria should encourage or require students to draw on a range of relevant theoretical perspectives, selected on the basis of informed and rational choices from alternative or competing explanations of practice. The process of assessment and verification must go beyond a mechanical box-filling and ticking activity, but require thought, insight and intelligent decision-making by both students and assessors.

We believe that the Wolverhampton competence-based programme for teachers in further, adult and higher education, in its conception and implementation, has the capacity to develop in students an autonomous, rather than automatous approach to their work. The programme can develop students' capability as well as their competence, both during the course and in their subsequent professional careers.

References

Barrow, R. (1976) *Common Sense and the Curriculum*, London, Allen & Unwin.

Brown, R. B. (1994) 'Reframing the competency debate', cited in S. Lester (1995) 'Beyond knowledge and competence: Towards a framework for professional education,' *Capability*, 1(3).

Child, D. (1993) *Psychology and the Teacher*, London, Cassell.

Curzon, L. B. (1990) *Teaching in Further Education*, London, Cassell.

Eraut, M. (1994) *Developing Professional Knowledge and Competence*, London, Falmer.

Eraut, M. (1995) 'Professional knowledge and competence: Analysis, intuition or reflection?', Address, Universities' Professional Development Consortium (UPDC) Conference, 26 October.

Handy, C. (1993) *Understanding Organizations*, Harmondsworth, Penguin.

Hoyle, E. (1972) 'Creativity in the school', unpub. paper, OECD Workshop, Estoril, Portugal.

Klemp, G. O. (1977) 'Three factors in success', cited in S. Lester (1995) 'Beyond knowledge and competence: Towards a framework for professional education', *Capability*.

Kounin, J. S. (1970) *Discipline and Group Management in Classrooms*, New York/London, Holt, Rinehart Winston.

Kyriacou, C. (1991) *Essential Teaching Skills*, Hemel Hempstead, Simon & Schuster.

Lester, S. (1995) 'Beyond knowledge and competence: Towards a framework for professional education', *Capability*, 1(3).

Peters, R. S. (1966) *Ethics and Education*, London, Allen & Unwin.

Short, E. C. (1984) 'Competence re-examined', *Educational Theory*.

Stenhouse, L. (1975) *An Introduction to Curriculum Research and Development*, London, Heinemann.

Stones, E. (1994) *Quality Teaching*, London, Routledge.

Whitehead, A. N. (1962) *The Aims of Education*, London, Ernest Benn.

Chapter 6

Capabilities for successful self-development

Lynda M. Stansfield

Summary

This chapter presents a conceptual model derived from an empirical study of self-managed learners. It proposes that key capabilities can be identified in the personal and social domains that may be able to predict a positive or negative orientation to learning which relies on self-development as a key strategy.

The model is based on evidence drawn from a detailed two-year evaluation study of a post graduate, post-experience management development programme based on the concept of management self-development.

Lynda Stansfield explores the implications of a model of capabilities needed by the responsive self-developer, in particular the apparent desirability of pro-active and creative learning approaches, and the difficulties these can present to less adventurous learners. She concludes by suggesting how this conceptual model of the responsive self-developer may be used by others wishing to encourage greater independent and interdependent learning.

Introduction

The Government's White Paper 'Higher Education: Meeting the Challenge' and employers' continuing moves towards expectations of a motivated and self-directed workforce are but two major influences upon the rise in popularity of the use of self-development techniques in higher education management programmes.

This chapter starts with a model of key attributes and capabilities that learners need to develop, based on evidence generated by a study which has been conducted in the Division of Management of the University of Huddersfield, comprising an evaluation of a new Manager Development module. This programme has been designed to promote personal and professional skill development at the post graduate, post-experience level. It relies heavily on management self-development learning methods.

Self-development is a way of learning that appeals initially to some and not to others. Stansfield and Carmichael (1994) described some of the psychological difficulties some students appear to have when exposed to these non-traditional learning methods, particularly the strength of their resistance. This resistance can be temporary or, in a small number, much longer lasting.

The focus of this chapter is the Diploma in Management Studies (DMS), a well-established post graduate management qualification. Until two years ago, Huddersfield was not unusual in offering a traditional, teacher-centred and syllabus-based programme. As a tutor on the programme and a recent recruit from industry, I formed the view that the development of management skills and capabilities was not approached in a way that was compatible with the changing demands of employers and students in the contemporary employment climate. Management skill development was regarded by students (and some staff) as optional, second-class and very much an adjunct to other management disciplines. Evaluation questionnaires revealed a low level of student satisfaction with this part of the course. In particular, there was a perceived lack of personal relevance.

I designed a new, compulsory stand-alone Manager Development module which was credit rated and scheduled to run at the beginning of the pathway, so that it would attempt to shape the learner's approach to his/her management education from the outset. This was based on a recognized model of management skill development (Pedler, *et al.* 1994) to provide a theoretical framework to underpin the module.

The DMS caters for a variety of participants, which represents a major design challenge in terms of the incorporation of relevant and stretching content. The programme purports to prepare students with a multitude of different backgrounds and needs for middle management. The new Manager Development module covers a diet of key skill and competence areas based on the self-development model. To cater for learners' many differences in development stages, needs, expectations and motivations, the module also requires students to identify, develop and evaluate the outcomes from a range of skills that they choose for themselves to pursue outside the formal business of the module, but that are included in the assessment. This allows the students to tailor their skill development to their own identified needs.

The development of reflection skills and the ability to evaluate learning 'experiences' using Kolb's concept of the learning cycle (1984) is a key feature.

Vital to this process is goal-setting. After completion of the module, when management skills are no longer formally addressed, participants are encouraged to develop habits that will lead to lifelong self-development.

Support structures include relevant texts: recommended readings are Guirdham (1995) and Pedler, *et al.* (1994). Suggestions of additional reading and other materials into which the students could delve according to their needs, interests and motivation were provided via a series of tutor-prepared 'resource guides'. This adds to the 'self-development' nature of the module.

Two weekend workshops form the focus for development, supported by brief weekly discussion sessions to provide guidelines on how and where to obtain learning resources. The theme of the first half of the semester (up to and including the first weekend workshop) is the development of personal skills, such as self-awareness, reflective and experiential learning techniques, career development strategies, presentational skills and creative thinking. The main theme for the remainder of the semester (including the workshop) is the development of interpersonal skills, such as communication, influence and persuasion, interviewing in a variety of contexts, and counselling, coaching and mentoring.

The module is ungraded, but it provides a great deal of self, peer and tutor feedback. Assessment is by way of 'evidence' of the student's work submitted in a development log.

The evaluation study

The details of the evaluation study are provided elsewhere (Stansfield, 1995a, 1995b). The purpose of this chapter is to take the main outcome from the study, a proposed model of the required attributes and capabilities for a learner to derive most benefit from a self-development approach, as its starting point, and discuss the implications of these findings for both learner and tutor.

From the data collected, it would appear that the responsive self-developer possesses many attributes, which can be grouped into personal attributes (internally focused), and social attributes (externally focused).

Personal attributes:

- open-mindedness and a capacity to try new ways of doing things;
- taking responsibility for one's own learning;
- interested in one's own learning processes;
- a recognition of the benefits and limitations of traditional concepts of knowledge and understanding, and of their links with experience;
- an active learning style;
- a thirst for knowledge, understanding and experience;
- being pro-active and enthusiastic about learning.

Social attributes:

- an ability to see the relevance of their development in the wider context beyond themselves (perceptions of value for others);
- an ability to engage with his/her wider environment, to be able to think 'outside the box';
- a desire to develop others;
- a willingness to share;
- an ability to recognize the intrinsic value of his/her peers' contribution;
- a preparedness to put in extra effort beyond following tutors' instructions;
- the ability to exercise independence of thought and restrict reliance on 'experts'.

Implications

The majority of learners embarking upon a programme will possess some but not all of these attributes. In most cases, some element of personal change will be required if these attributes are to be developed when moving from a tutor-led model to a self-led model.

In terms of effecting change, there are distinct differences in the degree of difficulty according to the nature of the change desired. One convenient way of categorizing these differences is as follows:

Knowledge: This is probably the easiest to change. Methods recommended include guided reading, attendance at lectures, watching videos, etc. It is relatively easy to change an individual's knowledge base. From a tutor's point of view also, this is probably the easiest area, as the methods fit most students' 'internal models' of what education is about.

Skills: This is also relatively easy to change. This area is a little more difficult than changing one's knowledge base, as it involves not only knowing how to do things but actually doing them as well. Some students put up resistance to the 'doing' part of skill development.

Attitudes: These are notoriously difficult to change. Dependent upon the strength of feeling attached to the attitude in question, effecting any kind of change can be a long and painful process. In terms of attempts to change attitudes towards, say, the need for more pro-activity on the part of the student in his/her learning activities, these can be met with much resistance. For example, if such change involves attitudes towards the role of the tutor (facilitator rather than teacher) then again there are some powerful internal models to overcome.

Personality traits: These are by far the most difficult to change, and indeed it is not even certain that such changes are possible, dependent on the nature of the change required. For example, it would seem that a positive orientation towards many aspects of learning is required for successful self-development to occur. A change from negative orientation to positive orientation is not easy to achieve. Some writers (eg Seligman, 1975) believe that positive orientations such as optimism can be learned, but acknowledge that it takes a great deal of willingness, effort and time.

Validation of the self-led model

The original observations have been witnessed again in an extension of the evaluation study, which focuses upon the experiences and views of the third cohort.

We still observe that a number of higher education management students are reluctant to take responsibility for their own learning. This can be demonstrated by the discourse used by some learners. They seem to be much more comfortable with a tutor focus rather than a learner focus. Consistently, and despite many briefings to emphasize the different nature of the self-development process, comments include 'what do we have to do?' and 'what do you (tutor) want?' Some students are ill at ease with the idea that they may do things that suit their development needs and styles best, rather than to suit the tutor. These barriers to learning have to be broken down before self-development can take place.

Learning styles (Honey and Mumford, 1992) still seem to have a bearing on positive orientation to self-development. Evidence seems to suggest that those with active learning styles (activist/pragmatist) as natural preferences seem to have an advantage over those with predominantly passive learning styles (reflectors/theorists). It would appear that it is easier to develop reflective and theorizing capabilities starting from an active learning style, rather than vice versa.

Barriers to change include the lack of a perceived need to change. According to Lewin (1951), in order to encourage change, one must first 'unfreeze' the person. In the case of the Manager Development module, the main vehicle for raising awareness of the need for change, or 'unfreezing' is the challenging of traditional assumptions. The external changes taking place in the world of work are introduced, where the models used for discussion are those of the flexible workforce and the fruits of several research projects concerning the changing nature of careers. The drawback to the use of such examples as a way of raising awareness is that the adult learner must see some personal relevance of the arguments to him/herself for the need to change (Knowles, 1980). If the learners are not personally in situations where they can relate these ideas to their own real world, then it is unlikely that they will perceive a need for change.

The expectations of the mature higher education learner cannot be underestimated. Based on previous experience (which may well have been the product of a formal education experienced some time ago) the expectation generally exists that the educational experience will consist of a tutor–pupil model rather than a learner-centred model. It is very easy for the tutor designing and running these courses to fail to take full account of the power of these expectations and the amount of hard work and persuasion required to break them down.

The time and pressures elements are also easily underestimated. In many cases, learners are facing inordinate increases in the pressures at work to perform better. In the educational sense, these pressures manifest themselves in the learner's increasing orientation to immediacy and preference for highly structured tasks. This behaviour has been even more visible in the most recent cohort. Informal conversations with learners reveal instrumental coping strategies based around sequences of deadlines, priorities and simplicity of tasks. To that extent, one is tempted to think that learning is occurring at surface rather than deep levels, and the ability of learners to plan, act and evaluate for themselves is impaired. Motivation to learn appears to be based on a means–end internal model rather than a personal development and growth internal model.

Support structures

A major outcome of the two-year study was to change certain elements of the programme based on the comments from the original cohorts. One of the strongest messages to emerge was that the learners wanted clearer briefings on the nature of the workshops and how to approach them.

An experiment was conducted to see whether or not those clearer briefings would help learners to break down barriers more easily. In previous years, I had designed the first weekend so that learners found out by discovery that it was up to them to take the initiative and shape the event around their, and the group's, development needs. Starting with the 1995 cohort's first workshop session, an additional section was included in the introductory briefing. This was designed to be much more directive about how to approach the workshop. In an attempt to manage expectations right from the start, the new briefing contained the following elements:

- the importance of setting personal objectives for the workshop, not relying on the 'official' objectives;
- the role of the tutors (ie as facilitators, not teachers, to be used as a resource);
- the importance of self and group time management: there were tasks to do and an outline timetable – how these were to be used in detail was up to them;
- how to handle self-disclosure and confidentiality;
- how to give and receive feedback;
- the importance of keeping learning fun and light.

From an initial analysis of the post-workshop feedback questionnaires, it would seem that there is no observable difference between the reactions of 1995's cohort and those of previous years. A number of learners still complained about lack of time, leadership (from the tutors) and tutor input. They still waited to be told, cajoled and directed. Most complained that they did not have time to consider the issues that were important to them, but failed to use the 'slack' time in the programme to organize this task.

Feedback sessions with the students after the workshop were as fraught with confusions and frustrations as the ones held in previous years. They complained about the lack of time in the workshops, despite having been briefed several times about the continuous nature of development, and the need for them to use personal time later to consider their workshop performances. They appeared to be looking for 'one-shot' learning, so that they could move on and concentrate on other parts of the course. A key feature of the workshop was to video each learner's presentation in their development groups and each group could keep their video to use it to continue learning after the event. Some students asked why they needed to be videoed. Others complained that there was not enough time after their presentation to explore all the issues in their personal feedback session. Even though these comments were made by the same groups, they did not make the link that the use of video was precisely to allow them the opportunity (admittedly in their own time) to develop their feedback and learning to suit their own needs and pace.

There again were signs of discomfort at being asked to determine and write their own agendas. It was challenging personal comfort zones and required the acknowledgement of the need to change. There was also some evidence of macho attitudes to the concept of self-development, especially to introspection, from some of the male students, manifesting itself in the poking of fun at the titles of some of the reading recommended for further study. Students quite rightly wanted some feedback from me on their performances in some of the sessions I had led. When I started that feedback by asking for their views, the comment was 'Typical psychologist!'

Not all the feedback was as negative as the examples cited above. Many students displayed behaviour that supported the conceptual model of the essential capabilities. Some other comments were 'inspirational' and 'never learned so much in such a short time'. Many were only too happy to recognize the value of their peers' ideas and contributions.

Conclusions

In the light of such findings, we are left with a number of choices. One is to accept that there will always be a proportion of students who will not respond to the philosophy of self-development, leave it at that and concentrate on those who respond positively. On the other hand, there is a proportion of people who will put up resistance initially, and over a period of time will gradually learn to adopt a more pro-active ownership approach to their learning. As is the case with dispositional optimism and helplessness, it is possible to learn to change one's outlook (Seligman, 1975). My studies have shown, for example, that perceptions do change over the course of the module. Satisfaction ratings show a marked improvement between Time 1 (seven weeks into the programme) and Time 2 (15 weeks into the programme). Comments taken at the end of the second workshop begin to focus on the developmental issues rather than on the more tangible, operational matters at the end of the first workshop. Consistent observations from three consecutive cohorts support this view. Benefit has also been observed in other parts of the course, especially in respect of the capstone action-learning project in Year 2, where the quality of work and the confidence of learners have noticeably increased. An extrapolation of that observation may be that similar changes are happening in the learners' work domains, although I have yet to conduct direct research in that area.

Whilst it is acknowledged that working with learners on self-development programmes is not easy, it is most rewarding in terms of the progress students make. Examples of this include the case where one learner, having made her last presentation in the work context and had her confidence destroyed in the process, was able to make a professional presentation in a safe and supportive environment, and as a result is no longer frightened by the task. Other students have had vague feelings of career dissatisfaction, and have made clearer decisions as a result of self-discovery and action planning in the workshops. Such benefits go beyond the limits of formal course evaluation techniques, and show that, whilst uncomfortable and frustrating at the time for tutor and learners alike, the learning is much deeper and longer lasting than would be the case if knowledge only were to be imparted.

It is proposed that the model of capabilities can be used as a guiding framework for tutors and learners, in order to provide some goals for future development. One thing is certain: the need for effective self-developers in many areas of work life is likely to increase in the future. If we can help our learners develop the capabilities that matter, we shall have met one of our most challenging and difficult objectives in higher education today.

References

Guirdham, M. (1995) *Interpersonal Skills at Work*, London, Prentice-Hall.
Honey, P. and Mumford, A. (1992) *Manual of Learning Styles*, Maidenhead, Peter Honey.
Knowles, M. S. (1980) *The Modern Practice of Adult Education: From pedagogy to andragogy*, Chicago, Follett.
Kolb, D. A. (1984) *Experiential Learning*, Englewood Cliffs, NJ, Prentice-Hall.

Lewin, K. (1951) *Field Theory in Social Sciences*, New York, Harper & Row.

Pedler, M., Burgoyne, J. and Boydell, T. (1994) *Management Self-development*, London, McGraw-Hill.

Seligman, M. E. P. (1975) *Helplessness: On depression, development and death*, San Francisco, W H. Freeman.

Stansfield, L. M. (1995a) 'The independent learner: A study of self-managed learning in post graduate management education'. Paper presented at the SHRE Conference *Changing the Student Experience*, University of Central England, Birmingham, 4–5 July.

Stansfield, L. M. (1995b) 'Is self-development the key to the future? An evaluative study of participant views about self-directed and experiential learning methods in post graduate management education'. Paper presented at the British Academy of Management Conference *Revitalising Organizations: The Academic Contribution*, 11–13 September.

Stansfield, L. M. and Carmichael, J. L. (1994) 'Differences in perceptions of self-directed and experiential learning methods in higher and management education'. Paper presented at the Bolton Business School third Annual Conference, *Challenging Learning: The Experience of Management*, 20–22 November (*published under former name of Smith).

Chapter 7

Action learning and capability: a search for common ground

Steve Reeve

Summary

This chapter attempts to elicit some resonance or overlap between the use of action learning techniques and the nature of capability. It makes critical reference to the use of action learning within the context of award-bearing postgraduate management programmes at the University of Brighton.

This approach is designed to elucidate an appropriate academic definition of competence and how far beyond competence or not the Brighton programme has moved. In discussing the nature of learning, Steve Reeve distinguishes between a learning culture and a competence culture and discusses their relativity and meaning. He contrasts the nature of independent learning with the process of action learning in sets, and suggests that perhaps the terms *by*, *with* or *through* competence more accurately define action learning and similar techniques.

The nature of action learning

The nature of 'action learning' (McGill and Beatty, 1992) has gone through and continues to go through continuous reinterpretation as different and new groups of staff begin working with it. Those working with this model have consciously and experimentally moved the original process from a problem-solving standpoint (somewhat antithetical toward 'programmed knowledge') toward mainstream academia (ie into the heart of 'enemy' territory). There is no doubt that an industrial model purist would consider that the meddling may have gone too far already, and may not even acknowledge some of what we do as action learning. Certainly debate amongst practitioners remains lively, and debate within academic circles where this is being tried can be heated.

Set out below are some principles, guiding structures and processes that we tend to adhere to, and an explanation of some of the environmental context. An attempt is then made to see if these fit (and if so how well) with the concept of capability.

Descriptors

Amongst the collection of descriptors for what we consider successful action learning, one finds the following:

- andragogical approach (a predominant emphasis by staff on adult/adult relationships);
- respect (the notion that mature participants possess an enormous amount of 'lifetime' experience, whether as managers or as adults);
- control shift (staff involved will be attempting to pass over control of the learning experience from themselves – the traditional academic 'owners' of knowledge – to the participants);
- encouragement of co-operative and cohesive attitudes within the set;
- trust (clearly essential if the above is to have any meaning);
- confidentiality (essential to building interpersonal trust within the set);
- time (the allowance of time to every set member such that they feel their problems/contributions are important to and valued by the others);
- engagement at both an intellectual and emotional level;
- the cycles of learning and reflection.

The work of action learning sets

Here is perhaps the furthest lurch away from an original industrial model approach. The sets may be involved with seemingly 'artificial' outcomes. Working together, set members may be generating assessment projects, statements of academic relevance or pure or applied business/management research – but often not classic in-house solutions to immediately pressing real problems. The question then arises as to the efficacy or usefulness of an action learning, set-based, approach to issues that by nature are 'academic' rather than real operational problems (I readily acknowledge that set members do work on real operational problems, but my point is that the academic rationale is primary). Are we merely producing super learning support groups, or is there something else beyond this actually occurring? The answer may well lie with the perceived and acknowledged 'value added' generated for participants over and above merely successful academic outcomes. The nature of this 'value added' may share a great deal with the aspirations for capability.

Contrast with the standard post graduate experience

Experience of working with this model has convinced those involved of the ensuing benefits. This begs the question of what is actually happening that makes this approach different from a standard post graduate experience? Participants moving through the process report the following issues:

- Initial confusion and 'extra' work – with many experienced adults' recollections of university or school relatively far in the past, their expectations are often about being 'told what to do', not being asked what they should do.
- Even highly autonomous decision-making senior managers seem to fall rapidly into a standard default mode of 'dependent student' when entering academic premises. It takes time and effort to fight against this default mode and hand back to such adults their autonomy within this new environment.
- They then have to expend more effort getting to know others in a much more intensive way than required during standard part-time or evening attendance. They may endure some discomfort whilst forming sets if control has been handed to them for this.
- They will be asked to come to terms very specifically with why they are there at all and what they hope to get out of the experience. All of this requires investment of their time and effort.
- In the early stages they may well be asking questions about the necessity for this and gazing ruefully at a standard model of 'night school', with its attendant safety features of familiarity and dependence.

The benefits of working in sets

As sets find their feet, participants begin to value the experience of being listened to by the others in their set. They feel the benefit of reciprocal advice. Suggestions are made about process, methodologies and sources, and advice is informed by case histories, personal experience and managerial events from the set participants. This is a much deeper experience than collective or 'group work' activities during a conventional part-time session.

There will be time in the set sessions where no academic work is discussed at all; instead issues of personal or managerial importance are expressed and discussed within a safe environment. Very often, this is where 'learning blockages' are finally acknowledged and grappled with, freeing up the participant for much more meaningful engagement later. The small and enclosed or exclusive nature of the set really helps to engender this situation.

The strength, safety and security of the set is being constructed, and members are 'buying in' more and more deeply. There is a feeling of support and mutual understanding, which is much greater than that achieved by a cohort feel on a standard type of programme. Co-operation and mutual support often move toward and into realms of emotional commitment, further deepening the experience beyond that attainable on a more standard academic programme. Even on a programme where individual achievement might cynically be said to be the only game in town, set members genuinely care about each others' progress and success.

Furthermore, as the research/academic work is progressing, it is under far greater scrutiny than would normally be the case. There will be several pairs of caring eyes critically examining methodology, work in progress and finished writing. This has often been referred to as invaluable by participants, in their view substantially raising the standard of their academic performance.

There is a degree of similarity in terms of aims to many aspects commonly associated with the independent learning school (albeit that curricula involved range from the given toward the truly negotiated, ie from weak to strong); however, as might be obvious, the use of action learning sets implies a huge amount of inter-dependence.

Where might capability fit into all this?

A significant feature of capability concerns a learner's ability to cope with changing future circumstances. This is not dissimilar to much of the work on 'learning to learn' within the learner managed learning/independent study framework. By implication, action learning as a set of techniques is very much concerned with future states and the ability of individual set members to adapt to changing circumstances based on developed intellectual abilities and the benefit of a great deal of case experience shared within the set. It is to be hoped that the safe environment provided will have enabled individuals to open up to a conscious awareness of 'metalearning', or their operation of the learning to learn process. In fact a good deal of set time is taken up specifically with this issue. Such cognizance is usually never specifically required (although desirable) within conventional programmes, but is fundamentally and clearly addressed within action learning as practised at the University of Brighton.

There is an equal emphasis on the nature of independence in terms of self-esteem, self-confidence, ability to make judgements and power to respond flexibly, which certainly sit well with 'independent capability' (Stephenson, cited in Graves, 1993). To some extent, the influence of the set environment here may be said to lead to a more powerful result than that experienced in a more 'lonely' form by classic independent learners. There is a definite attempt by staff to allow action learners the space to make mistakes, become more confident as self-referencing individuals, and develop (with guidance) an intrinsic (Gibbs, 1981), and deep (Marton and Saljo, 1976) approach to academic study and managerial life. This orientation is particularly suited to mature students, who develop this deeper, achieving approach naturally (Richardson, 1994).

In this sense, it seems that our variants of action learning are much closer in approach to notions of capability than to competence.

So what of competence?

It should also be becoming clear that sets *qua* learning sets within post graduate management programmes require competent individuals in the sense of participants who comprehend how to and in fact do manage (often to very senior levels) in their 'work lives'. If we loosely assume competence here to be to do with proven abilities to operate within certain environments, then an action learning set within such a suite of programmes must assume (whether explicitly or implicitly) a competence base in individual terms before it can begin to function usefully. Of course such individual competence will vary widely depending on past experience, level of responsibility and so on, but this would not seem to obviate the need to start off (on a post graduate management programme) with groups of people who have demonstrated competence in a managerial sense prior to the commencement of a programme – otherwise the programme itself would have the nature of a foundation or introductory model.

However, once assembled, the academic or research aims of a set will not be concerned with increased competence *per se* (although this may come about), but rather with the approach to learning and the achievement of successful academic ends – aims that seem to sit much more easily within a paradigm of capability than competence. There is no doubt that 'action learners' on a programme that is externally referenced (ie qualification based) would expect nothing less than to reach an equivalent standard to that applying to a more traditional model, which mirrors closely the view found in much of the literature on independent learning. In this sense, any personal or managerial development aims are particularly strongly tied to the nature of capability, ie:

- the pursuit of excellence;
- generic active/reactive strategies to cope with changing environments;
- the 'intellectual apparatus' to make sense of the new;
- the facility to recognize patterns and conditions that may lead to pragmatic theory-building and testing.

This is not to suggest that sets are not suitable as competence-building vehicles. If the overall aims were to increase the functional skills of individual set members then that is perfectly possible. It would, however, be seen as a lost opportunity to develop the attributes lauded by proponents of capability, which also sit comfortably with the (andragogical, self-managed) educational ethos and aspirations of staff involved with action learning.

Linking action learning and capability

The kind of issues that might bind action learning and capability would be to do with:

- the nature of learning itself (conscious exploration thereof);
- 'metalearning' or learning to learn;
- a 'futures orientation';
- abilities to cope with new, unknown or unexpected circumstances;
- desire to engage with 'work' in both an intellectual and pragmatic fashion.

The focus must be on helping students in the journey toward intrinsic approaches, deep learning and holistic perspectives, ie the academic approach.

Possibly the most critical conceptual similarity is to do with the 'learning culture' emphasis. Is this distinct from a 'competence culture'? As far as I can ascertain, the emphasis of such a culture is much more on a functionally specific, externally referenced set of received and demonstrated activities, which may or may not have led to a range of abilities to cope with the new. Although this allows the rest of society to feel safer in that practitioners have demonstrated their ability to perform to certain benchmark levels, it is not clear whether this emphasis can deliver anything further.

Much competence-based education seems intrinsically closer to the surface, by its externally referenced, serial, safe and proven approach (as identified by Pask, 1976; Gibbs, 1981; Entwistle and Waterson, 1988), and to dissemination-based learning (Hodgson, *et al.* 1987) than to the meaningful learning identified by supporters of independent, and 'learner managed' learning strategies (Cairns, cited in Graves, 1993).

Thus, essentially classical academic expectations surrounding the pursuit of excellence, the development of the generalist and informed specialist, combined with an emphasis on the nature of specifically adult learning, lead one toward the notion of capability. However, I feel pressed to ask the question, is this really being fair to competence?

Capability and competence: commonalities?

The Brighton experience suggests that capability and competence might lie closer together than the rhetoric of debate might indicate. This may be a specific result of working within the area of management development. If one takes the National Vocational Qualification process for example, there is no doubt that we have managed to combine two ways of doing things, namely – academic route action learners have also demonstrated certain of the MCI (Management Charter Initiative) competences via the operational/managerial projects and research they have tackled. This raises some questions:

- Does the strength of the action/academically based set help toward the demonstration of competence, in a way that would not work in reverse?
- Has the holism and 'metalearning' encountered within action learning enabled them to make much greater sense of a system often pilloried as serialistic, 'bitty', closed and boring?
- Is the very nature of the assessed 'academic' work (in this field) entirely similar to proving a competence that just happens to be very high level, complex and difficult to define?

An academic form of action learning might be analysed as follows:

- A cutting edge to the experience is achieved by the explicit recognition and encouragement of the learning to learn issue. This shares many of the values of independent learning or capability.
- There is protection for the individual learner within the set, which is usually unavailable to a learner on a more conventional programme. Such protection, or safety, is built from the creation of confidentiality, trust and mutual support within the bounded set environment. Thus, many of the shocks and collisions commonly encountered by adult learners within part-time higher education are absorbed. This allows set members to continue under circumstances that often lead to withdrawal on other programmes.
- Intrinsic motivation becomes deeper and more propulsive for sets as intellectual and emotional energy is pooled. The sense of vision and shared purpose is enhanced as individuals mutually value past experience and future expectations. Confidence is generated from the recognition of differing previously acquired skills and managerial competence, again leading to a release of energy for the action learning programme.
- The above three areas overlap and combine, creating an extremely powerful and effective learning vehicle.

This learning vehicle, when engaged with the traditional nature of higher education (ie the stock of knowledge, research and methodologies, creativity, conceptual presentation, etc) allows for a potentially much more fulfilling and successful experience for the learner – particularly stepping back in from the 'real world' to the relatively unknown territory of academia. Whatever the drawbacks may be from this kind of model/approach, what is clear is that it can be a successful way to engage with mainstream academic study (particularly for people with a mix of great experience, high levels of responsibility but long absence from higher education) especially within the management field, or group of related disciplines.

Nevertheless, the thorny issue of surrounding culture must also be addressed. Could this seed be planted in unprepared ground? It is clear to those of us working in this field that there can be major dysfunctional clashes between a capability-based approach (as evident in our interpretation of action learning), and the prevailing university environment. If the environmental culture is based more upon an extrinsic, serialist/surface, 'stock of knowledge' set of approaches, then the introduction of the model explained above will cause friction. Furthermore, the more 'traditional' and previously unchallenged the prevailing structure is, the more friction there will be. Thus, either the new model must occupy 'empty' space (and then develop a whole new ethos and reputation), or it must be moved gradually into traditional space.

There is still debate as to whether action learning (particularly) can sit comfortably within a paradigm based on 'stocks of knowledge, traditional compartmentalism, content driven assessment' (Bourner, 1995). There is a case for widening this to question whether capability-based (or independent learner) approaches can coexist with such paradigms. A large body of evidence proves that it can (see research on former North East London Polytechnic (NELP) plus the Australian experience of 'problem-based learning' in medicine and agricultural higher education institutions, eg Anderson, and Boud and Higgs, cited in Graves (1993). Questions remain over whether this occupies a separate cultural space or whether a new model is being grafted on to an older culture.

There is a continuing debate as to whether a programme of this kind provides sufficiently wide syllabus coverage, given the natural tendency of participants to pursue depth. Such debate has clearly been held within the independent study movement in the past. Within the management field where interdisciplinary study is predominant, this kind of debate is sharpened as those responsible for a unit or module from a specific discipline become even more anxious that their area is covered.

There is a danger of cultural dissonance where an action learning educational orientation is placed within a traditional environment. The messages from the environment could emphasize taught sessions as opposed to research, syllabus coverage as opposed to depth, and the importance of the assessment structure over all else. Such messages might beckon participants towards classic surface strategies and techniques, and away from the reflection and depth deemed important for successful action learning. Furthermore, unless specifically acknowledged and dealt with, there is a danger that disagreement between staff, unclear educational values and divergent views on learning strategies will cause confusion to participants leading to much less favourable outcomes than might be expected.

Depending on the nature and power of the surrounding academic environment, it might be far easier for capability-based approaches (in this case action learning) to inform competence structures rather than traditional academic environments. A competence environment might be a much more amenable host than an academic culture where content-driven, extrinsically orientated, mass educational practices predominate.

(For more information on action learning at the University of Brighton, contact Steve Reeve at the Centre for Management Development, e-mail S.D.Reeve@bton.ac.uk).

References

Anderson, B. (1993) 'The case for learner managed learning in health professionals' education', in Graves, N. (ed.) *Learner managed learning: Practice, theory and policy*, Leeds, HEC/WEF.

Boud, D. and Higgs, J. 'Bringing self-directed learning into the mainstream of tertiary education', in Graves, N. (ed.), *Learner Managed Learning: Practice, theory and policy*, Leeds, HEC/WEF.

Bourner, T. (1996) 'What can be learned using action learning?', *Organisations and People* 5(4), 18–22.

Cairns, L. (1993) 'Learner managed learning: A metaphor for educational revolution', in Graves, N. (eds.), *Learner Managed Learning: Practice, theory and policy*, Leeds, HEC/WEF.

Entwistle, N. and Waterson, S. (1988) 'Approaches to studying and levels of processing in university students', *British Journal of Educational Psychology*, 58, 258-265.

Gibbs, G. (1981) *Teaching Students to Learn*, Milton Keynes, Open University Press.

Graves, N. (ed.) (1993) *Learner Managed Learning: Practice, theory and policy*, Leeds, Higher Education for Capability/World Education Fellowship.(HEC/WEF).

Hodgson, V., Mann, S. and Snell, R. (1987) *Beyond Distance Teaching – Toward open learning*, Milton Keynes, Open University Press.

Marton, F. and Saljo, R. (1976). Symposium: Learning processes and strategies – I, On qualitative differences in learning – II, Outcome as a function of the learner's conception of the task, *British Journal of Educational Psychology*, 46, 115–27.

McGill, I. and Beatty, L. (1992) *Action learning: A practitioner's guide*, London, Kogan Page.

Pask, G. (1976). 'Styles and strategies of learning', *British Journal of Educational Psychology*, 46, 128–48.

Richardson, J. T. E. (1994) 'Mature students in higher education: I. A literature survey on approaches to studying', *Studies in Higher Education*, 19.

Stephenson, J. (1993) 'The student experience of independent study: Reaching the parts other programmes appear to miss', in Graves, N. (ed.), *Learner Managed Learning: Practice, theory and policy*, Leeds, HEC/WEF.

Further reading

Biggs, J. B. (1985) 'Metalearning and study processes', *British Journal of Educational Psychology*, **55**(3)185–211.

Harper, G. and Kember, D. (1989) 'Interpretation of factor analyses from the approaches to studying inventory', *British Journal of Educational Psychology*, **59**, 66-74.

Kolb, D. A. (1979) *Organizational Psychology: An experiential approach*, London, Prentice-Hall.

Miller, C. M. L. and Parlett, M. (1974) *Up to the Mark: A study of the examination game*, London, SRHE.

O'Reilly, D. (1996) 'Competence and incompetence in an institutional context'. Unpublished draft. Proceedings from Expert Seminar: *Competence, Capability and the Learning Society*, York, Higher Education for Capability.

Percy, K. and Ramsden, P. (1980) *Independent Study: Two examples from English higher education*, Guildford, SRHE.

Revans, R. W. (1980) *Action Learning: New technology for management*, London, Blond Briggs.

Robbins, D. (1988) *The Rise of Independent Study*, Milton Keynes, SRHE and Open University Press.

Stephenson, J. (1989) 'The experience of independent study at North East London Polytechnic', in D. Boud (ed.) *Developing Student Autonomy in Learning*, London, Kogan Page.

Part Three

Assessing Capability

Chapter 8

Competence and capability: from 'confidence trick' to the construction of the graduate identity

Len Holmes

Summary

The context of this chapter is the current wisdom that higher education has become a mass system geared to preparing graduates for employment through the development of transferable intellectual and social skills. Len Holmes proffers a critical discussion of the concepts of capability and competence, exposing a lack of consensus about their respective theoretical and terminological trappings. This leads to 'a substantive positive critique of the currently dominant model of the capability curriculum'.

He identifies some of the obstacles to progress posed by traditional academia and proposes a way of balancing the academic and vocational through reframing the notion of capability and its delivery models. This solution is underpinned by reconsidering the nature of assessment, and 'reintroducing the agency of the student'.

The rise of competence and capability

There is no doubting the major shift in the discourse of higher education over recent years. The move towards a mass rather than elite system, structural changes in the labour market, and a political and economic regime that emphasizes the (purported) links between education and economic competitiveness, have all played a part in the increased focus on higher education as, at least in part, preparation for employment. The terms 'competence' and 'capability' are clearly part of this changed discourse. They are now mainly associated with particular types of approaches, linked with particular institutionalized initiatives. 'Competence' is a key term in the development of National Vocational Qualifications (NVQs); 'capability' is the term adopted in 1980 by the RSA (Royal Society for the Encouragement of Arts, Manufactures and Commerce) in its 'capability manifesto' for education in general and which was developed in 1988 to the Higher Education for Capability initiative. But beyond the specific association with institutionalized initiatives, the same issues have been articulated through a range of other terms. In 1984, the funding agencies for higher education issued a joint document asserting that

the abilities most valued in industrial, commercial and professional life as well as in public and social administration are the transferable intellectual and social skills. (NAB/UGC, 1984)

The Enterprise in Higher Education initiative (EHE), funded by the (former) Employment Department, was established to promote curriculum development that would enable students to develop 'enterprise skills'; most institutions of higher education undertaking projects under the initiative appeared to have interpreted these to be the 'transferable skills' referred to by the NAB/UGC document.

The relationship between NVQs and higher education awards is currently under examination (CVCP, 1994; Employment Department, 1995; HEQC, 1995). There is general recognition that, except in courses that are intended to prepare students for specific occupations, the way that NVQs operationalize the notion of 'occupational competence' would create difficulties for undergraduate programmes. In brief, an NVQ is intended to be a 'statement of competence', and is awarded only after an individual has demonstrated performance to nationally prescribed standards, in a full set of activities for the particular occupation, in a wide range of situations. The primary form of assessment is to take place in the workplace, preferably in 'naturally occurring' situations.

So although it may be possible in some programmes to provide for credit towards an NVQ, the notion of 'occupational competence' has had less influence in recent developments in the higher education curriculum than the notions of 'transferable skills', 'personal competence', 'core skills' and similar terms.

Generally speaking, the term 'capability' has been interpreted as referring to broader personal characteristics, in the same way as terms such as 'transferable skills', etc. These personal characteristics are deemed to be valuable to individuals personally and to society more widely:

Capable people have confidence in their ability to (1) take effective and appropriate action, (2) explain what they are about, (3) live and work effectively with others and (4) continue to learn from their experiences, both as individuals and in association with others, in a diverse and changing society. (Stephenson, 1992, p 2)

The Association of Graduate Recruiters (AGR) has recently published its own contribution to the debate, emphasizing the need for graduates to be 'self-reliant':

The self-reliant graduate is aware of the changing world of work, takes responsibility for his or her own career and personal development and is able to manage the relationship with work and with learning throughout all stages of life. (AGR, 1995)

The conventional manner in which the notions of 'capable people' and the 'self-reliant graduate' are interpreted is through the production of a set of 'transferable skills' or 'capabilities' (or, in the case of the AGR, 'self-reliance skills'). Thus the overall term 'capability' is disaggregated into a set of purported 'capabilities' which, it is claimed, can form the basis of a revised curriculum – what might be termed a 'capability curriculum'. (For simplicity, I shall use the term 'capability' and 'capabilities' to refer to the other terms also in common usage, including 'personal competence', 'transferable skill(s)', 'core skills', 'self-reliance (skills)' and 'enterprise skills'.)

This relates not only to the content of the curriculum (and the educational process) but also to the form that assessment takes. Increasingly, there have been attempts to develop alternatives to the traditional methods for assessment used in higher education, and the recording of performance in terms of overall marks or grades and degree classification. Various ways have been tried to assess performance in workplace settings, often involving workplace assessors in addition to or instead of academic staff. 'Profiles', 'portfolios' and 'records of achievement' have been promoted as superior to traditional coursework and end of unit examinations. Stephenson (1993) argues that interest in records of achievement has grown, not only because they are able to convey more detailed information about the range of abilities and interests of a student, but also because they enhance the student's education through their monitoring, reviewing and recording of their own learning. Whilst profiles and records of achievement are also used in assessment of subject specific knowledge and skills, they appear to be most used in documenting assessed transferable skills or capabilities. This will enable the student to have a record of their achievement in these capabilities. As such capabilities are what employers look for in graduate recruits, it is argued, such records of achievement, or profiles of personal competence, can attest to the suitability of the individual for employment, that is, their 'employability'.

Searching for 'capabilities'

Despite the apparent widespread agreement on the importance of such generic capabilities, by whatever term they are known, there has been a notable lack of agreement on how they may be identified. A variety of attempts has been made to determine these supposed abilities. Lists and models abound, of greater or lesser length and complexity. NAB and UGC expressed them in simple terms:

The personal or non-academic skills of students, which higher education is expected to develop, include the general communication, problem-solving, teamwork and inter-personal skills required in employment. (NAB/UGC, 1986, p 3)

In a study of employers' stated perceptions of the 'transferable employment skills' needed by graduates, a list of 20 such 'skills' was produced (Smith, et al., 1989). A project by Nankivell and Shoolbred at Birmingham Polytechnic on staff perceptions of 'personal transferable skills' was based on the view that:

there is a general consensus on the major groups of skills – written and oral skills, interpersonal and teamwork skills, problem-solving skills and information handling skills. (Drew, et al. 1992, p 11)

Drew's report, in the same paper published by the Standing Conference on Educational Development, concerned students' perceptions of 'personal skills and qualities' (PSQ), as identified in a project at Sheffield City Polytechnic. She states that it was decided not to specify PSQ, regarding this as unhelpful because:

different PSQ seemed relevant to different subject areas and individuals... It seemed more helpful to encourage staff and students to themselves identify relevant PSQ.' (Drew, et al. 1992, p 39)

An action research project at Sheffield University led to a list of 108 'skills', which were placed into eight categories. This was later refined to produce a model that was intended to represent how these 'skills' related to 'zones', in terms of increasing complexity (Allen, 1993).

Of course, various institutions participating in the Enterprise in Higher Education initiative have similarly attempted to develop 'skills models', two of which are reported by the CVCP (1994). The Business and Technology Education Council has a framework of seven Common Skills, and students on all Higher National Diploma and Certificate courses must be assessed on these. The Quality in Higher Education research report listed a set of 'generic or core skills and attitudes', which employers and academics appeared to agree should be demonstrated by graduates. These include:

willingness to learn, teamwork, problem-solving and a range of personal attributes including commitment, energy, self-motivation, self-management, reliability, co-oper-

ation, flexibility and adaptability, analytic ability, logical argument and ability to sum-
marise key issues.' (Harvey and Green, 1994, p 7)

The then Employment Department has developed a Personal Competences
model, and NCVQ (now QCA) has developed Key Skills units. The notion of
'self-reliance skills' discussed in the recent report from the Association of
Graduate Recruiters (AGR, 1995) is disaggregated into a set of 12 'career management skills and effective learning skills'. In addition, we might also consider the increasing number of employers developing and using their own (ie
different) competency frameworks in graduate recruitment (IRS, 1994).

This plethora of lists raises doubts about the feasibility of putting into practice the apparent agreement about the general notion of 'capability' in terms
of such disaggregated 'capabilities'. Moreover, there are serious conceptual
difficulties with the notion, whatever term is used. The various lists contain
very different sorts of notions, some referring to skills, others to apparent personality characteristics, yet others which may depend heavily on the specific
social context for their realization (eg motivation, teamwork). Moreover, no
attempt is made to explain how such varied capabilities result in the desired
performance.

Bridges (1992) distinguishes between 'cross-curricular skills' and 'transferable skills' in terms of the domains between which transfer is deemed to take
place. The former relate to cognitive domains, or subject areas; the latter
relate to social contexts. Clearly, the notion of 'capabilities' and the like relates
to the latter, concerned as it is with 'transfer' between the context of study (or
'learning') and post-graduation performance, in employment and other
social contexts. Unfortunately, Bridges points out, we lack a 'theory of social
domains', which would make the notion of such skills intelligible and practical. He goes on to make a further distinction between 'transferable skills' and
'transferring skills'; the former are those supposed abilities that may be
deployed in various social contexts with little or no adaptation, whilst the latter are those involved in adaptation. 'Transferring skills' are:

as it were the metaskills, the second order skills which enable one to select, adapt,
adjust and apply one's other skills to different situations, across different social contexts and perhaps similarly across different cognitive domains (Bridges, 1992)

Such analysis raises severe questions about the conceptual validity of the
frameworks of capabilities that are usually presented as self-evidently appropriate bases for making assessment decisions, which purportedly will significantly affect the employment chances of students and also affect the
performance of organizations that employ them (or decide not to employ
them).

Given such doubts about both the practical and the conceptual soundness
of the dominant approach to the capability curriculum, ie in terms of the disaggregation of capabilities, it seems reasonable to re-examine the whole

notion of 'capability' and, if possible, to reframe it. In order to do this, we need to reconsider the nature of assessment in higher education, and its relationship to the educational process and to the processes of graduate recruitment.

Assessment

Underlying the claims made for the dominant (ie disaggregational) approach to the capability curriculum is a model of the links between education, assessment and selection for employment (and other post-qualification activity, including advanced study). In simple terms, this model regards education as a process through which the student acquires or develops, as an individual, certain characteristics (such as knowledge, understanding, skills, competences and capabilities). Assessment is the process for judging or measuring the extent to which the individual has acquired or developed these; the judgement/measurement is then inscribed in the form of a grade or mark if the programme of education is incomplete, or if it is completed, certificated in the form of an award, possibly with some rating, eg degree classification. Selection is the process of using these measures or judgements, along with other relevant information about the individual, when making the decision whether or not to employ the graduate. If the selection process is undertaken properly, the graduate recruit will then perform as required (given that other factors are right). In principle, it is assumed, it is possible to ensure that all stages in this education–assessment–selection process are set up and operated in such a way that the links between the educational process and competent work performance is one of smooth and effective transition. Because in practice this is not happening, then repair is deemed necessary, hence the various initiatives in respect of graduate 'employability'.

This model of assessment is widely, albeit implicitly, held and is not a special feature of the capability approach:

assessment in education can be thought of as occurring whenever one person, in some kind of interaction, direct or indirect, with another, is conscious of *obtaining and interpreting information about the knowledge and understanding, or abilities and attitudes of that other person.* (Rowntree, 1977, p 4, my emphasis)

No matter who controls examinations, and for what purposes, the immediate object of an examination is to assess *some attributes of the students; it is an instrument of measurement.* (Mathews, 1985, p 52, my emphasis)

The issues that are usually addressed in debates about assessment and attempts to develop 'better' approaches to assessment are mainly methodological – how can we measure more effectively (and efficiently, fairly, etc)? It is a 'folk psychology' model where a person's performance is assumed to be caused by, the result of, some 'internal' dispositions, ie personality, attitudes, preferences, using some instrument or tool-like entity, such as knowledge, understanding, skills, capabilities – a sort of 'homunculus with a toolkit' model. For example, the leaflet publicizing a workshop on 'developing students' transferable skills', run by the Oxford Centre for Staff Development, states that:

Transferable skills are the skills such as those *involved* in communication, organization, teamwork and problem-solving, which students will *take with them* to their careers. (my emphasis)

As neither the dispositions nor the 'instruments' can be observed directly, it is usually assumed that they can be inferred from the performances of the individual in various situations. Whether a student is assessed by means of the essays written in response to questions in a traditional unseen examination or by undertaking some form of 'real work' whilst on placement with an employer, the assumption is that it is possible to gain access to such causal and instrumental entities. Moreover, these are treated as being very stable (though capable of development) so that predictions can be made about likely performance in other situations. So the main principle for ensuring effectiveness is that of validity, ensuring that the methods of assessment do actually measure those qualities and characteristics in question.

This 'homunculus with a toolkit' model is not explicitly used in discussions about the link between capabilities and performance is taken for granted, regarded as 'common sense'. Indeed, it is not restricted to the (dominant version of the) capability curriculum, but is also commonly seen in discussions about education in general, especially in terms of students using their knowledge and understanding. When we ask how the term 'use' is being used, we usually find no coherent alternative to the instrumental meaning, ie knowledge being used like a tool. Whilst few may believe in a real homunculus, a ghost in the machine, proponents of the dominant version provide no explanation of how the self motivates, manages, promotes, relies on, and is aware of self.

Recent developments in social psychology provide conceptual and theoretical bases for rejecting such a simplistic model of human action and behaviour. Notions of causality in human activity have been well explored and demolished by writers in the discursive approach to psychology (eg Gergen, 1985; Harré *et al.*, 1985; Potter and Wetherell, 1987; Edwards and Potter, 1992; Harré and Gillett, 1994). Drawing on the philosophical work particularly of Wittgenstein and Austin, such writers focus on how the actions of humans take place in social settings, within which their meaning is established through discursive interaction. What an individual does is not intelligible through an examination of causes; rather it can only be understood in terms of the discursive explanation of the individual's intentions in relation to some explicable rule, 'normative accountability'. So a student's performance in an assessment activity cannot be taken as a vehicle for discovering some inner ability that causes the performance. Rather, it can be understood only in terms of the student's attempt to influence the actions of the assessors, by following some (implicit or explicit) rules about how one does this. This is illustrated by the frequent complaint by examiners that students 'failed to answer the question set'; assuming the students did not intend to fail, we must conclude that they interpreted the examination setting, and the specific task set in the form of an examination question, in a way that was different from that interpreted by the examiner. What cannot be inferred from the students' (inappropriate) performance is how they would or might have performed if they had interpreted the situation and the task in the required manner.

Conventions of assessment

An alternative approach starts by recognizing that assessment is a socially structured process involving a number of different actors engaging in different actions, within a context that has dimensions of time (and space). The usual focus in debates about assessment is on what the students should be required to do. The assessor is treated as making judgements about what the student has done, and what this purportedly shows about the student. The assumption about chronicity is that of the continuing present; the student 'has' knowledge, ability, etc, or 'is' capable, competent, confident, etc. Yet when we consider the full socially structured process of education–assessment–selection, we can see more clearly its diachronic nature. In particular, we see that the purposes to which assessment is put are clearly future-orientated. Assessment within a degree programme is concerned with whether or not the student will get a degree, and with what classification. Within academia, the award of a degree and its classification play a key part in the selection for advanced study, particularly for research degrees. Within the arena of graduate employment in professional–managerial–scientific occupations, a degree has an important role in recruitment and selection by employers. The gatekeepers to these social arenas, advanced study and graduate employment, are not primarily concerned with past performance, but rather with future performance. Implicitly or explicitly, the award of a degree is addressed to such gatekeepers; the outcomes of assessment in higher education are signals about the judgement about anticipated future performance.

However, the future performance can be only anticipated, not known (or even predicted, in the strong sense of that word). Judgements about future performance are inherently subject to the risk of being wrong. Moreover, the immediate consequences of being wrong are usually borne by others, ie those in the situations in which performance is not as anticipated. The reputation and status of the assessors and of the assessment process is therefore crucially dependent on gaining and maintaining the confidence of those who make use of assessment judgements, what we might call a 'confidence trick' (Holmes, 1994b). This is achieved by the use of conventions of warrant (Gergen, 1989), ie discursively based rationales or justifications for the assessment judgements. The whole chain of processes, linking assessment activities in educational settings, through the inscription of some 'verdict' on the individual (such as class of degree), to the use of such inscribed verdicts for other purposes, including graduate recruitment, may be thus seen as a 'convention of assessment', whereby the links in the chain are warranted.

The discourse of capability, and also the discourse of competence, may thus be seen in terms of such warranting conventions. 'Capability' does not refer to some internal characteristic or attribute of an individual, but is a discursive element within the social-discursive process by which an individual is constituted as one who may be admitted to those social arenas into which graduates normally enter. One social arena is that of employment, typically in terms of occupations referred to as 'professional', 'managerial', or 'scientific'. The implication of this is that 'employability' must also be seen, not as a personal characteristic, but as a discursive element in the education–assessment–selection process. Employability is not the result of developing and demonstrating capability; employability is a facet of capability, the expression of assessors' warranting activity orientated towards the gatekeepers to graduate employment. When orientated towards the gatekeepers to advanced study, the warranting activity would use a different vocabulary, eg 'suitability' for a taught masters or for a research degree.

Capability, employability and suitability (for advanced study) are, then, not individual characteristics, identifiable and measurable from performance. They are the discursive warrants for the assessment–selection decisions, inescapably risky judgements about anticipated future performance in social conditions where the attainment and maintenance of confidence in the decision-makers by others is of paramount value. Indeed, it may well be the case that the development of the discourse of capability has enabled employers and their (often self-appointed) representatives to contest the previous conventions of warrant. It is certainly noticeable that the sophistication of 'capability talk' has increased over the past decade or so (eg compare NAB/UGC, 1984 with CVCP, 1994). Little account is taken of research on the actual practices of employers of graduates, particularly in respect of the degree to which these involve processes of ascription rather than assessment of achievement (Brown and Scase, 1994). Contrary to the claims of proponents of the capability curriculum, rather than helping students to gain employment as graduates, profiles of personal competence and records of achievement may serve to stigmatize them as 'less capable'.

Recharting the capability agenda

Critiques of the currently dominant formulations of the capability curriculum are unlikely to affect significantly the widespread attempts at its introduction. The current context, in which academia is structurally dependent on state funding and in which there is political consensus on the 'need' for a mass higher education system, places high value on the vocabulary of employment-related skills. Any attempt to displace current formulations of the capability curriculum must seek legitimacy within the current social and political context. However, attempts at introducing the capability curriculum must engage with the traditions of academia, or face the prospect of being undermined by covert if not overt resistance. The danger is that this will also undermine those very traditions valued in academia, espousing disinterested pursuit of knowledge, its production and dissemination, for its own sake. We might therefore look at ways in which the critique above may form the basis not only for interpreting the world, but for changing it. After all, academia has, arguably, always been concerned with 'practical' affairs of society, including the occupational (eg see Silver and Brennan, 1988; Barnett, 1990). Moreover, typical presentations of the calls for the capability curriculum adopt the rhetoric of valuing 'traditional academic' education (although the sub-text is often anti-academic).

I have suggested that assessment in higher education is a convention of warrant, whereby the award of a degree is taken as warranting entry into the graduate occupational arena, typically into professional, managerial and scientific occupations. It also warrants entry or re-entry to advanced study, particularly for a higher degree by research. We might therefore say that a degree carries a double warrant (Holmes, 1994a). Now normally, attempts to introduce a capability curriculum have been based on the assumption that the requirements for each of these social arenas, occupation and academic, are isomorphic. That is, that there are certain transferable skills (eg problem-solving) which may be 'used' in either arena, and so a single, common framework of such capabilities can and should be developed and adopted. Such attempts are mistaken, and the plethora of attempts with little sign of sustainable success may be taken as indicators of the underlying error.

If we take the occupational arena and academia as two separate though connected generalized 'communities of practice' (Lave and Wenger, 1991), albeit the two are highly varied, we can begin to focus on the typical practices in each. Rather than look for the supposed attributes and 'mental tools' that underlie these practices, it is the practices themselves which should concern us. Thus, instead of being concerned with students' 'skills of written communication' we can begin to consider how we get students to produce papers (as for a conference or journal), book reviews, research reports and other sorts of documents that academics produce for other academics, and also (management) reports, memos, briefing papers, etc as used in the occupational arena. By engaging in such practices as a form of 'legitimate peripheral participation' (Lave and Wenger, 1991), the students will be engaged in the social process of education, moving from novice to accepted practitioner.

The graduate identity

Such an approach might be developed by considering higher education as a process by which an individual may develop their identity as a graduate, as one who is highly educated. However, it is important to use the term 'identity' as it has come to be understood and used within the social sciences over recent years. The notion of identity as a 'fixed' entity is rejected in favour of the idea of the process of identity formation and re-formation. The process involves a dynamic relationship between the individual's personal sense of self and the social processes which to a significant degree determine what count as the criteria for being ascribed a particular identity. Thus an identity cannot be decided on solely by an individual, as a personal act of choice and will, but must always be subject to affirmation (or dis-affirmation) by others.

Harré's concept of identity project (Harré, 1983) may be used as an approach to reconsidering the process of becoming a graduate. An identity project is the continuing process by which a person seeks to attain and maintain uniqueness and individuality (personal being) whilst also being socially recognized (social being). This involves the 'appropriation' by the individual of the characteristics of socially and culturally (and therefore discursively) legitimated identities. From this follows a stage of 'transformation', making personal sense of the socially acquired understanding, in terms of personal experience. The 'publication' of the actor's claim to the identity, the public expression of the characteristics associated with the identity leads, if successful, to 'conventionalization' into the personal biography and social order. So the 'moral career' (Goffman, 1968) of the graduate is one achieved by means of transition through a set of hazards, leading to esteem, reputation and self-worth, or loss of these – 'spoiled identity' (Goffman, 1963). In this way we can reframe the educational and assessment process, or more properly the education-assessment–selection process, as that of an identity project of becoming a graduate, someone who is highly educated. This would link with Vygotskian-influenced approaches to education (eg Daniels, 1993), and Lave and Wenger's (1991) notion of 'legitimate peripheral participation' in communities of practice.

A key aspect of the identity project approach would be the reintroduction of the notion of agency on the part of the student. Despite the rhetoric about 'student-centredness' in the conventional approach to the capability curriculum, it is essentially a socialization model, one of role-taking rather than role-making. The student's identity is formed by the inscription process involved in recording achievement. The more that the capabilities are specified, and especially where the assessment criteria are specified, the less that the student can engage in a creative transformation of the socially given attributes associated with a graduate. If the education–assessment process is one in which the student is enabled, through opportunities to engage in tasks and activities that are representative of those which graduates do, as professional workers and as academics, then the student can represent these as part of her or his personal claim on the identity as a graduate. The essential element is that the student must make the claim, and along with it, assert his/her claim on the right of entry to the social arenas associated with 'being highly educated'.

It is also essential to emphasize the notion of the double warrant. In order to succeed in the claim on the graduate identity, the student must gain acceptance from key parties whose recognition is important. In the assessment–selection phase, the student must engage with gatekeepers to the desired social arenas. As these may be broadly distinguished into the academic and the occupational, the student will have to make the claim doubly, within the languages of the two social arenas. We might therefore extend the sociolinguistic notion of code switching to this process of claiming the graduate identity. Rather than search for a generic vocabulary of capabilities, or even a vocabulary of generic capabilities, we might focus on helping students represent the activities in which they have engaged in the separate languages of academia and the occupational arena. This is more than 'selling oneself' (a rather ominous phrase to apply to job seekers); it is at the heart of the claim on the graduate identity, and is truly student centred.

If we reconsider some of the ways that the notion of capability and other cognate terms have been introduced, we can see how these support the idea of focusing on the graduate identity. Stephenson (1993) talks about 'capable people' and the AGR's report refers to the 'self-reliant graduate'. That is, they start with some general notion of what sort of person a graduate should be. Furthermore, the various lists of supposed abilities and characteristics that have been produced by various agencies may be regarded more as semantic elaborations of how we might expect to recognize capable people and self-reliant graduates, in terms of what they do and the way they do it. The variety of terms used may be seen as indicators of the rich vocabulary that is available to engage in descriptions of what we would expect to see in such persons – and also for individuals to use of themselves in laying claim to be such persons (Holmes, 1995). What these terms do not do is refer to some internal qualities and skills, capabilities, which are used in or result in desired performance.

Putting it into practice

One feature of the rhetoric around the supposed need for graduates to be more 'employable' leaves the foregoing necessarily conceptual and theoretical critique open to the accusation of being 'academic', a term which in Britain often has the force of an insult. I therefore offer below some examples from the teaching practice I and colleagues have begun to develop. In themselves these may be seen as not particularly novel. Indeed, I believe that excessive emphasis on novelty may inhibit rather than encourage curriculum change. Rather, the examples are presented here in terms of the rationale on which they are based, ie the emphasis on helping students to lay claim to the identity to which they aspire, particularly in terms of the 'double warrant'. The examples relate to undergraduate programmes in the Business School at the University of North London.

ACADEMIC WORK AT PRELIMINARY LEVEL

The Employment Studies pathway on the modular degree scheme was introduced in 1994/95. 'Work, Employment and Society' is a core module at preliminary level, the content of the module being primarily the sociology of work. The module is organized around students exploring chosen topics about current issues in relation to work and employment. The coursework assignment requires each student to produce three items of written work. First is a short paper discussing the theoretical frameworks and models that might be used to examine the issue. This is limited to a maximum of 1,200 words, the emphasis being on producing a 'map' of the theoretical issues rather than a discussion of them. Second, the student is required to produce a full bibliographic listing of 20 relevant items from a literature search, presenting this in a standard form and including at least ten journal articles. Third, the student must write a review of two relevant journal articles. Although the written submissions must be individual work, the students are encouraged to work in groups on their chosen topics. Groups make an oral presentation of their analysis of the conceptual and theoretical issues to the other members of the class; although compulsory for completion of the module, the presentations are not assessed for module grades.

These activities are discussed with the class in the first week, and represented to the students as examples of the types of activities in which academics typically engage. They choose an issue of concern or interest and then relate this to the existing scholarship. To do this, a literature search must be undertaken and the bibliographic details of items noted. Academics write papers, reviews, books, etc in which they usually discuss the literature with which they have engaged. They present their views and arguments to an audience of peers, in conferences, seminars, symposia, etc.

It is made clear to the students that the emphasis is upon their engagement in the activities typical of academic workers rather than those in professional–managerial occupations. Other modules will provide for opportunities to engage in activities representative of professional–managerial workers.

TRAINING AND DEVELOPMENT AS PROFESSIONAL PRACTICE

The Human Resource Management electives in the final year of the BA Business Studies includes a module on training and development. The module covers the theory and practice of training, within work organizations and in the wider public policy arena. The coursework for the module focuses on the practice of training within work organizations, and particularly on the generally accepted principle that such practice should be based on the training cycle model. Two elements of this model, analysing training needs and designing the training programme, provide the basis for coursework assignment. Using one of a selection of case-studies made available to the students, each student must produce a proposal for analysing the training needs in a particular area, and design an outline training programme for another specified area of need. The proposal for analysing the training needs must be presented in the form of a report, addressed to the relevant member of senior management. The proposed design for the training programme must be presented in the form of outline documentation, as this might normally be presented by training practitioners.

In discussing the coursework briefing with the class, it is made clear that the students must not engage in discussion of theoretical and conceptual matters. Rather, they are required to show through practical application that they have a sufficient grasp of the principles involved. The emphasis on the particular forms of documents to be presented is to provide for the students to engage in the type of activities in which a personnel and training practitioner would engage. Thus the report is part of the way that the practitioner would seek to gain the support of the senior manager, gaining and maintaining legitimacy in the identity of a professional practitioner. Students are encouraged to use the active voice and personal pronouns in the report, which must be clearly addressed to a specified senior manager. That is, the student must write as if they were the practitioner.

Conclusion

This kind of approach may thus provide a substantive positive critique of the currently dominant model of the capability curriculum. Simplistic attempts at developing models of capabilities have failed to yield acceptable and generalizable pedagogic practices. The recognition of the inherent conceptual flaws should lead us to seek an alternative model, which reframes assessment as a social process based on conventions of warrant. The award of a degree constitutes a double warrant, orientated towards anticipated future performance in two possible social arenas, academia and the 'world' of graduate employment. Reframing the education–assessment–selection process as an identity project for the student 'becoming a graduate' enables us to reintroduce the agency of the student, asserting her or his right of entry into desired social arenas through the claim on the identity as graduate. By maintaining the distinction between the social arenas, we can perhaps enable the call for 'parity of esteem' between the academic and the vocational to be achieved in a positive and progressive manner. Practical applications of this within the undergraduate curriculum can be readily identified, providing contexts and activities through which students move towards being able to make an effective claim of the graduate identity.

References

AGR (1995) *Skills for Graduates in the 21st Century*, Cambridge, The Association of Graduate Recruiters.

Allen, M. (1993) *A Conceptual Model of Transferable Personal Skills*, Sheffield, Employment Department.

Barnett, R. (1990) *The Idea of Higher Education*, Buckingham, Society for Research in Higher Education/Open University.

Bridges, D. (1992) 'Transferable skills: A philosophical perspective', *Studies in Higher Education*, Summer.

Brown, P. and Scase, R. (1994) *Higher Education and Corporate Realities*, London, UCL Press.

CVCP (1994) Strategy paper on vocational higher education, London, Committee of Vice-chancellors and Principals.

Daniels, B. (ed.) (1993) *Charting the Agenda*, London, Routledge.

Drew, S., Nankivell, M. and Shoolbred, M. (1992) *Personal Skills: Quality Graduates*, SCED Paper No. 69.

Edwards, D. and Potter, J. (1992) *Discourse Psychology*, London, Sage.

Employment Department (1995) *A Vision for Higher Level Vocational Qualifications*, London, Employment Department.

Gergen, K. (1985) 'Social pragmatics and the origins of psychological discourse', in K. Gergen and K. Davis (eds), *The Social Construction of the Person*, New York, Springer-Verlag.

Gergen, K. (1989) 'Warranting voice and the elaboration of the self', in J. Shotter and K. Gergen, *Texts of Identity*, London, Sage.

Goffman, E. (1963) *Stigma: Notes on the management of spoiled identity*, Englewood Cliffs, NJ, Prentice Hall.

Goffman, E. (1968) *Asylums*, Harmondsworth, Penguin.

Harré, R. (1983) *Personal Being*, Oxford, Blackwell.

Harré, R., Clarke, D. and De Carlo, N. (1985) *Motives and Mechanisms: An introduction to the psychology of action*, London, Methuen.

Harré, R. and Gillet, G. (1994) *The Discursive Mind*, London, Sage.

Harvey, L. and Green, D. (1994) *Employee Satisfaction Summary*, Birmingham, Quality in Higher Education Project.

HEQC (1995) *Vocational Qualifications and Standards in Focus*, London, Higher Education Quality Council.

Holmes, L. (1994a) 'Knocking on the door and ringing the bell: Higher education, graduate employment and the double warrant', paper presented at *Recording Achievement* conference, University of North London and Higher Education for Capability, March.

Holmes, L. (1994b) 'Is competence a "confidence trick"?', keynote address to the first Competence Network conference, University of Leicester, November.

IRS (1994) *Graduate Recruitment Survey 1994: Vacancies, salaries and prospects*, London, Industrial Relations Services.

Lave, J. and Wenger, E. (1991) *Situated Learning*, Cambridge, Cambridge University Press.

Mathews, J. (1985) *Examinations: A commentary*, London, George Allen & Unwin.

NAB/UGC (1984) *Higher Education and the Needs of Society*, London, National Advisory Board for Public Sector Higher Education/University Grants Council.

NAB/UGC (1986) *Transferable Personal Skills in Employment: The contribution of higher education*, London, National Advisory Board for Public Sector Higher Education/ University Grants Council.

Potter, J. and Wetherell, M. (1987) *Discourse and Social Psychology*, London, Sage.

Rowntree, D. (1977) *Assessing Students: How shall we know them?*, London, Harper & Row.

Shotter, J. and Gergen, K. (eds) (1989) *Texts of Identity*, London, Sage.

Silver, H. and Brennan, J. (1988) *A Liberal Vocationalism*, London, Methuen.

Smith, D., Wolstencroft, T. and Southern, J. (1989) 'Personal transferable skills and the job demands on graduates', *Journal of European Industrial Training*, **13**(8).

Stephenson, J. (1992) 'Capability and quality in higher education', in J. Stephenson and S. Weil, *Quality in Learning: A capability approach in higher education*, London, Kogan Page.

Stephenson, J. (1993) Preface to A. Assiter and E. Shaw, *Using Records of Achievement in Higher Education*, London, Kogan Page.

Chapter 9

Assessing the self-managing learner: a contradiction in terms?

Stan Lester

Summary

This chapter explores the need for change in systems of student assessment in the context of teaching and learning methodologies designed to promote capability.

Stan Lester recognizes that, although the ethos of the self-managed learner is becoming more widely accepted in higher education, it is frequently undermined by inconsistent approaches to assessment. He argues that if educational programmes are to support genuinely self-managed learning, there is a need to move away from content- or outcome-based assessment systems to a recognition that evaluation of content and outcome are the responsibility of the learner.

Once these implications are recognized any external assessment becomes problematic, although an acceptable solution may be achievable through basing assessment on activities or processes of learning such as enquiring, creating, reflecting and evaluating.

Introduction

Within higher education, traditional approaches to teaching and learning have tended to emphasize the content-based dimension represented by subject matter, theories and bodies of knowledge, at the expense of developing capability in overarching processes such as enquiry, reflection, creative synthesis and self-managed learning. Although institutions often espouse these latter as desirable if not fundamental aims (Allen, 1988), the reality can be a focus that develops them in a limited and haphazard way and encourages a relatively narrow kind of academic competence (Barnett, 1994). The recent introduction of approaches based on functional competence offers little more in this respect, as knowledge-based content simply becomes replaced or supplemented by content in the form of competence standards, dominating the learning process through their focus on predefined objectives and outcomes (Lester, 1995a).

In contrast, the majority of learning that occurs in daily life is not driven by a syllabus or competence framework, but identified and managed by people in accordance with their own objectives. This form of learning may not always lead to outcomes that would be recognized for accreditation, but particularly when the learner's objective is a compelling one it is usually extremely effective.

The importance of intrinsic motivation of this type for educational settings has long been recognized, for instance by Lindeman (1926) and Dewey (1938) among others. In higher education it has gained ground through structures such as negotiated learning contracts and design credit accumulation awards, and through approaches to development that respect learners' self-direction and ability to manage their learning actively. The latter include, for instance, reflective practice (Schön, 1983; 1987), action learning (Revans, 1980) and action research (Carr and Kemmis, 1986), which now underpin a considerable number of programmes and have gained academic credibility as well as demonstrating their relevance to practice. There are convincing rationales for their use, both from the perspective of learning effectiveness (see for instance Knowles, 1990; Evans, 1992) and socioeconomic considerations (eg Ackoff, 1974; Reich 1991).

However, a significant problem that can occur when introducing these approaches in higher education environments is that they become accepted at a surface level, but fail to become deeply embedded. Operationally, reflection/action and self-managed approaches can remain as methods within a traditional programme methodology, working at what Cunningham (1994) terms a tactical level as opposed to a strategic one. Conceptually, and more insidiously, they can be embraced as methodologies but without any real acceptance into the academic culture of their underlying epistemologies and values. In both situations learners receive conflicting messages – explicitly in the first where there are indications as to where self-managed learning is permissible and where it is not, and implicitly in the second, where a surface-level message is contradicted by a deeper one.

Assessment

One of the most revealing indicators of underlying academic theory-in-use is assessment practice. Assessment also tends to have a disproportionate influence on learners because of the perceived value of certification, so the values implicit in how assessment is carried out can easily undermine espoused philosophies of learning. This point is illustrated by the following examples, from programmes claiming to be based in reflective practitioner and action learning approaches respectively.

The first concerns a student on a full-time vocationally orientated degree, who was completing an account of his work placement. He had developed an innovative approach to the project he was involved in, discussed its relative merits and its relationship to relevant contextual issues, and thought through quite carefully how it would work in practice. However, he was having a lengthy and unproductive argument about it with a tutor, who disagreed with the logic behind it and suggested it was inadequately referenced. The student was twice referred to books that backed the tutor's point of view and, despite including a well-argued critique of these, the account was eventually given a mediocre pass accompanied by comments about needing to relate practice to theory.

The second involves an experienced manager and business owner following a postgraduate management programme. The programme explicitly aimed to develop practice, but for reasons of external prestige and apparent validity clung to a system of written examinations to supplement action learning projects and a learning portfolio. After the first year he commented that there appeared to be two types of knowledge about management – the practical knowledge, which he learned (through various means) out of necessity to run his business, and the type of knowledge tested by exams, which sounded good but didn't actually work.

These scenarios illustrate two not very useful lessons. One is that while it's acceptable to think about what you are doing, experiment and develop your own theories, the results are practical, situational and subjective rather than real knowledge. The first student was being trapped in a double-bind in which the tutor had tacitly accorded his own theories an objective status without making his standpoint clear. The student was developing personal knowledge and using it effectively, but his tutor was demanding that it conformed or at least had a clear relationship with more 'objective' knowledge. The converse lesson is that while theory is good for passing courses, it doesn't help get things done in the real world. The manager was beginning to see around the schizoid nature of the assessment system, but at the same time learning to bracket the 'formal' theory rather than critically engaging with it to develop his own models. In both cases, the result is divergence between the theories students think of as valid for qualifications and those that they actually use to guide their action.

More generally, the principle being applied is that of a set of orthodox or 'accepted' theories (those of the expert community, whether they are authors, teachers or standard setters) being held up as correct or at least as a necessary starting point, while others (particularly those of the learners) need either to conform or to be argued convincingly in terms of the orthodox theories if they are to be taken seriously. The principle applies equally whether the theories are expressed in academic terms or are theories of practice articulated as behavioural objectives or competence statements. In all cases, the problem is that the learner is presented with an external definition of what is right or acceptable, in a way that encourages referential or atomistic learning (cf Ramsden, 1986) and discourages critical thinking, creativity and self-managed learning.

The challenge of self-managed learning

Moving beyond this normative or discourse-based approach to assessment is a key prerequisite to enabling educational programmes to support genuinely self-managed learning. It is also problematic, as while the epistemologies which underpin self-managed approaches are gaining acceptance from the viewpoint of learning practice, they pose a fundamental challenge to much current assessment practice and in some respects to the idea of external assessment *per se*.

For instance, Schön describes a constructionist (sic) epistemology of practice in which 'our perceptions, appreciations, and beliefs are rooted in worlds of our own making which we come to accept as reality' (1987, p 36) and where learners are involved in 'worldmaking' as much as taking the world for granted. Not dissimilarly, Cunningham (1990) advocates a Post-Modern (sic) ethos that acknowledges there are no right and wrong answers to be found 'out there', but emphasizes a reflexive approach requiring value judgement and wisdom. The idea of 'worldmaking' is also reflected in the work of Korzybski (1958), Bateson (1971) and Bandler and Grinder (1975), who identify the difference between the 'territory' or external reality, which we cannot know directly, and our personal maps of it.

The implication is not only that 'there is a necessary difference between the world and any particular model or representation of [it]', but that 'the models of the world that each of us creates will themselves be different' (Bandler and Grinder, 1975, pp 7–8).

From an assessment viewpoint, these ideas suggest that to assess learning by reference to what it is expected will be learned is doing no more than imposing one interpretation or model of the world on another. This is perhaps acceptable in a pragmatic sense when learning is framed as a process of acquisition and accumulation, but it is completely inadequate for learning that is purposive, self-managed, critical or creative. If the learner is recognized as a map-maker or participant in 'worldmaking' rather than as just a map-reader and interpreter, it is contradictory to expect him or her to work within and be assessed against logics, theories and discourses of others' making: the results will at best be a form of gameplaying and deception where espoused theories are set up at divergence with theories-in-use, and at worst a chronic disability with regard to independent and creative thinking, learning and action.

Validating personal theory

The dilemma, then, is that recognizing the learner as a self-managing world-maker or map-maker contradicts the notion of assessment at least as commonly practised. This perspective or epistemology of personal knowledge generates particular challenges for assessment, as it starts from the position that knowledge and theory are constructed by the individual in the process of mapmaking or worldmaking. Not only does this make any direct assessment of knowledge and theory nonsensical, it suggests that because individual knowledge and practice is unique, it is also intrinsically valid through the fact of its being known and done. (This is not the same as its being useful, something that I will revisit shortly.) Whereas from a normative or discourse-based stance there are reference points from which to judge understanding or performance – the map is either assumed to be the territory, or the best representation of it – from a personal knowledge perspective these are revealed as no more than subjective maps, even if for many purposes successful ones.

To offer theories, curricula or competence frameworks or similar maps as guidelines that might be treated as matters for reflection and enquiry is completely congruent with self-managed learning (see for instance Lester, 1995b), but to insist through assessment that they are followed or used as a basis for judging validity is not. According these maps a pseudo-objective validity also dictates an orientation towards the past, as it points to working rationally from a pre-existing base rather than working intuitively and imaginatively as well as rationally towards a future direction or outcome.

A self-managed, personal knowledge perspective frees learners from the constraints of having to work from a starting point of conventional thought, and enables them to focus – critically and creatively – on the future. However, at first sight it also leaves the door open to a solipsistic latitude in which the learner can self-validate any outcome without rigour or creativity. On the other hand, as soon as validation is asked for, it is tempting to fall into the trap of holding up one model of the world as superior to another, or at least providing justification based on already familiar (or accessible, eg published) theory.

Introducing rigour and validation to personal theory is nevertheless achievable through the idea of 'fitness for purpose'. In practice, we tend to review our ideas in terms of their effectiveness in leading towards a purpose, or set of purposes, which we have defined; we are responsible for deciding whether, in our own terms, our ideas are sensible or not, even if part of the validation process involves consulting written material, entering into a dialogue or gaining an expert opinion. This test of fitness for purpose is an everyday, practical one, as well as being essential to any form of effective self-managed learning or reflective practice. It is equally applicable to practical outcomes and more purely theoretical ones (developing understandings of ...), and because the purpose is internally defined, it respects the learner's map or worldview and remains congruent with it. Because it is purposive rather than based on precedent (cf Schutz, 1970), it is also future orientated and allows room for lateral and creative approaches as well as more incremental and rational ones.

The limitation of fitness for purpose is that it operates within the boundaries set by the purpose itself, and so is totally dependent on how well the latter has been framed or constructed. In practical terms, this can often translate to blinkered thinking, 'firefighting', or pursuing aims regardless of their wider consequences, as well as offering scope for unethical, unjust or criminal behaviour. While critical, lateral and creative thinking can all be employed within these bounds, learning is ultimately limited because the whole learning system is controlled by the purpose and how it has been framed; fitness for purpose is essentially a single-loop test of validity, which in itself has no ethical, moral or spiritual dimension, but can be as narrowly pragmatic or instrumental as the learner wants it to be.

To move beyond this limitation points to considering the fitness *of* the purpose, or how well it has been framed in terms of wider contexts and issues. Fitness of purpose represents a double- or multiple-loop test of validity, as it asks the learner to consider the congruence of his or her objectives in broader contexts and question the assumptions on which they are based; effectively, to move out of the logic or frame or reference in which the purpose is based, and question its congruence in a wider context. Clearly this can be a process of many loops or levels as the learner considers successively bigger pictures and wider perspectives, and identifies and questions assumptions embedded in both the purpose itself and the theories and actions associated with it. Fitness of purpose is still based within a personal knowledge epistemology, as it avoids imposing external definitions of congruence and asks the learner to consider assumptions reflexively, making judgements of value and exercising wisdom. However, it has moved from within-frame, single-loop thinking to a without-frame, double- or multiple-loop approach, which is unbounded by predefined frameworks and where learning is ultimately unlimited. It respects the learner's map of the world, but enables the map to be extended and redrawn, including previously unexplored dimensions.

Extending fitness of purpose conceptually leads into the idea of systemic wisdom, and to a state of systemic congruence in which wisdom becomes holistic and intuitive as something akin to Bateson's Learning III or perhaps IV is attained (Bateson, 1971). However, for the purposes of assessment it is likely that fitness of purpose is adequate at the level of anything currently deemed to be assessable, and it is sufficient to be aware that there are levels of learning that go beyond consciously uncovering and questioning assumptions and developing contextual congruence, and that also transcend the limitations of language and perhaps conscious thought.

Assessment revisited

Although the model outlined above – personal knowledge, fitness for purpose and fitness of purpose – provides a framework for testing and questioning personal models and maps, it does not directly solve the issue of assessing the self-managed learner. It is essentially a self-assessment model intrinsic to self-managed learning, incorporating both a pragmatic, practical perspective and one of higher level, critical thinking. However, it is not a model for external assessment, for its integrity and effectiveness depends on the learner managing the process; the presence of an assessor deciding for the learner how well a theory serves its purpose or what assumptions are being made defeats the object of self-critical evaluation and undermines the value of the learning process.

Assessing the self-managing learner does then appear to be a contradiction in terms. The learner has no intrinsic need for assessment, for part of the process of learning involves gathering feedback, reviewing it and acting on it in a reflexive cycle of enquiry and action. Feedback and advice may be offered actively to learners, but there is a difference between feedback as a statement of observation or personal opinion provided as a resource for the learner to use according to his or her own judgement, and assessment, which assumes to make some form of external judgement. Assessment is in itself problematic, and it has been argued that assessment commonly views people 'through a filter of assumptions denying much of their potential, dignity and creativity' (Daley, 1971, p xiii), something which is hardly consistent with the concept of self-managed learning.

Despite this, the perceived need for external assessment and validation is unlikely to disappear even with a wider appreciation of self-managed learning; there are still reasons for assessment that are broadly (if not unproblematically) seen as educationally and socially desirable. Traditionally, these have included:

- motivating learners to cover or consolidate a syllabus or set of standards;
- identifying further learning needs;
- validating a level of knowledge, understanding or competence expected for a qualification or 'licence to practice';
- selecting for further education, training or employment;
- providing feedback to learners about their progress;

- providing feedback about the effectiveness of a teaching, training or learning process.
(cf Atkins *et al.*, 1993, pp 6–7)

Of these, most can be achieved by other means. The only one that is particularly problematic is qualifications, and current trends suggest that assessment issues will increase in intensity as on the one hand there is growing pressure from governments and to some extent employers both for qualifications and for explicitly rigorous assessment processes, and on the other there is an increasing need for self-managed learners who are adept at going outside conventional boundaries.

Overcoming this conflict depends on assessment methodologies that uphold the 'potential, dignity and creativity' of the learner, and ensure that learning that goes 'outside the box' is supported, rather than being constrained within perspectives and logics of others' making. These methodologies will not be found at the level of attempting to assess knowledge and understanding, or theories of practice about what constitutes competent work performance, but will need to enable learners themselves to develop and test personal theory and practice through the model discussed, or something akin to it. In effect, assessment needs to move from assessment of 'content' or conformance to an expected outcome (vertical assessment, Lester, 1995a), to assessment of the learner's processes in developing and evaluating their personal models, maps and theories-in-use (horizontal assessment, Lester, 1995a).

A methodology for 'horizontal' assessment might consider the learner's actions in enquiring, creating (whether in a creative or process-based sense), reflecting and evaluating. Within this, personal knowledge, fitness for purpose and fitness of purpose provide a series of levels that can be used in defining criteria, so that while at a basic level the processes of enquiring, creating and reflecting may relate to fairly self-contained and purposive personal referencing, at higher levels they will involve greater exploration of underlying assumptions and location in contexts and contexts of contexts.

Within this type of assessment there needs to be room for negotiation, as the assessment system will still be the product of a map or worldview, even if at a more overarching and less restrictive level than with a content or outcome-based model. Basing assessment on a small number of principles rather than on rules or criteria will assist this flexibility, as well as assisting learners to move beyond closed paradigms of thought. For instance, there are many methods of enquiring, based in different methodologies and epistemologies and emphasizing different directions of thought, and equally, creating can be an imaginative leap in which the result just seems to materialize, a planned journey from current state to planned state, or a creative process using a mixture of logic and imagination.

Conclusion

If self-managed learning is to be assessed, it requires an approach to assessment that respects the learner's model of the world while providing a framework for testing it from within and encouraging further critical and creative development. In the model I have proposed, the focus of assessment moves from a 'vertical' or content-based dimension where what has been learned is compared with a model of what it is expected will have been learned (whether this is a syllabus, outcome or set of standards), to a 'horizontal' or process-based dimension, where value is attached to development from unvalidated personal theory through fitness for purpose towards systemic wisdom. For the individual learner, there is now an infinite horizon rather than the invisible ceiling of my first student's double-bind, and the lessons become ones of freedom, responsibility and wisdom.

A model of this type has several advantages. It respects the uniqueness and individuality of knowledge and action, while requiring that theories and actions are challenged and developed in a wider context than that of the individual's personal outcomes. It respects creative right- and whole-brain thinking and learning (Sperry, 1969) as well as the logical, left-brain processes, which typically dominate assessment outside of the creative arts. Finally, it encourages testing against current contexts and future needs, rather than dictating historic models and discourses as starting points. Although it is still necessarily the product of a particular perspective and therefore not unproblematic, it is more consistent with supporting the learner to be self-managing: confident as an explorer and a creator of theory and action, contextually aware, and developing towards systemic wisdom.

References

Ackoff, R. L. (1974) *Redesigning the Future: A systems approach to societal problems*, New York, John Wiley.

Allen, M. (1988) *The Goals of Universities*, Buckingham, Society for Research in Higher Education/Open University Press.

Atkins, M. J., Beattie, J. and Dockrell, W. B. (1993) *Assessment Issues in Higher Education*, Sheffield, Employment Department.

Bandler, R. and Grinder, J. (1975) *The Structure of Magic I*, Palo Alto, Science & Behavior Books.

Barnett, R. (1994) *The Limits of Competence: Knowledge, higher education and society*, London, Routledge.

Bateson, G. (1971) *Steps to an Ecology of Mind*, New Jersey, Jason Aronson.

Carr, W. and Kemmis, S. (1986) *Becoming Critical: Education, knowledge and action research*, Lewes, Falmer Press.

Cunningham, I. (1990) 'Beyond modernity: is postmodernism relevant to management development?', *Management Education and Development*, 21(3), 207–18.

Cunningham, I. (1994) *The Wisdom of Strategic Learning: The self-managed learning solution*, Maidenhead, McGraw-Hill.

Daley, A. (1971) *Assessment of Lives: Personality evaluation in a bureaucratic society*, London, Jossey Bass.

Dewey, J. (1938) *Experience and Education*, New York, Macmillan.

Evans, N. (1992) *Experiential Learning: Assessment and accreditation*, London, Routledge.

Knowles, M. (1990) *The Adult Learner: A neglected species*, 4th edn, Houston, Gulf Publishing.

Korzybski, A. (1958) *Science and Sanity*, 4th edn, Lakeville CT, The International Non-Aristotelian Publishing Company.

Lester, S. (1995a) 'Professional pathways: A case for measurements in more than one dimension,' *Assessment and Evaluation in Higher Education*, **20**(3), 37–49.

Lester, S. (1995b) 'Beyond knowledge and competence: Towards a framework for professional education,' *Capability*, **1**(3), 44–52.

Lindeman, E. C. (1926) *The Meaning of Adult Education*, New York, New Republic.

Ramsden, P. (1986) 'Students and quality', in G. C. Moodie (ed.), *Standards and Criteria in Higher Education*, Guildford, Society for Research in Higher Education/NFER-Nelson.

Reich, R. B. (1991) *The Work of Nations*, London, Simon & Schuster.

Revans, R. W. (1980) *Action Learning: New techniques for management*, London, Blond & Briggs.

Schön, D. A. (1983) *The Reflective Practitioner: How professionals think in action*, New York, Basic Books.

Schön, D. A. (1987) *Educating the Reflective Practitioner*, London, Jossey-Bass.

Schutz, A. (1970) (ed. H. R. Wagner), *On Phenomenology and Social Relations*, Chicago, Chicago University Press.

Sperry, R. W. (1969) 'A modified concept of consciousness,' *Psychological Review*, **76**, 532–6.

Chapter 10

Practice-based assignments: social work education as a case-study

Dave Evans and Jackie Langley

Summary

As many of the chapters in this volume testify, assessment plays a pivotal role in professional education and accreditation. This chapter explores in depth the problems posed by assessment in practice-based settings and evaluates some solutions attempted in a social work context.

The authors locate their discussion firmly within wider current debates about the nature and assessment of professional competences, yet they also acknowledge the constraints of the requirements of professional bodies and higher education institutions, which do not always coincide. A strength of their evaluation is that it gives voice to the student social workers who experienced the placement methods, and to their concerns, insights and critical reflections.

Dave Evans and Jackie Langley note in their concluding remarks, 'higher education institutions will need to prepare themselves for an acceptable work-based assessment strategy for professional education that includes the use of a knowledge, skills and value base – learning skills as well as practice performance.' Their chapter suggests some ways forward.

Introduction

Professional education has become increasingly associated with institutions of higher education during this century, an association which would seem to have had several advantages. It has enhanced the process of professionaliza-tion sought by a number of occupational groups, ensured a critical perspective on current work practices, and secured the development of a research tradition in policy and practice development. Unfortunately, it also would appear to have brought with it a number of disadvantages, including the inheritance of an assessment system developed for academic and not professional competence. In this chapter we argue for the development of assessment methods that seem appropriate to professional education, using our experiences in social work education as a case-study.

The issue of assessment of competence

Rowntree (1987) argues that assessment systems should be congruent with the aims of the educational programmes. Brown and Knight (1994) make a similar point in suggesting that there has been a shift away from reliability and toward validity in assessment systems. Thus a concentration on double-blind marking of theoretical essays or examinations can only be seen as unhelpful if the essential heart of the social work enterprise is largely missing from the assessment schedule.

Hayward (1979) reports, with regret, a reliance on essays and examinations in the social work qualifying course assessment schedules of the late 1970s. More recent consumer studies (Wright and Davies, 1989; Evans, 1991) suggest that assessment methods in the 1980s were still falling short of eliciting and evaluating the professional competence that programmes sought to ensure. Evidence is still lacking whether assessment in social work qualifying education accurately predicts performance in future employment, although there has been some (Taylor et al., 1965) suggestion that it did not in medicine. However, before assessment methods can be shaped to elicit professional competences, a clear understanding of professional competence is first necessary.

What, then, is the nature of professional competence? The Central Council for Education and Training in Social Work's (CCETSW) functional analysis of social work, undertaken in 1995, revealed six core functions and a taxonomy of increasingly specific competences. However, this analysis fails to indicate the relationship between the core functions. 'Developing professional competence' (our emphasis) is surely of a different order to 'promoting, enabling, assessing and planning'; the latter comprising a repertoire of demonstrable tasks, the former the conceptual abilities to develop that repertoire (Evans, 1991).

Schön (1987) and Winter (1992) propose a two-part model of professional competence: practice and the reflection upon practice. This analysis, however, underplays particularly the acquisition in qualifying programmes of the knowledge, skills and values needed to prepare for subsequent practice in an unpredictable range of future employment settings. It also ignores the changing nature of competence that practitioners develop through their careers and that Benner (1984) outlined in nursing.

We therefore propose a model of professional competence which has four components:

1. a base of knowledge, skills and values;
2. practice;
3. learning skills that can generate new practices and changes in the base;
4. career progression through time during which the interrelationship between the other three will develop.

The challenge for the assessment system in professional education is to develop assessment methods that elicit and evaluate all four components of this model. Two versions of the Diploma in Social Work (CCETSW, 1989; 1995) have attempted to specify methods that elicit practice. The requirement in 1989 for 'direct and systematic observation' has been further refined to three direct observations in each of the two assessed placements. These require-ments were doubtless a response to the low level of direct observation reported initially in Morrell (1980) and largely confirmed nearly a decade later by Williamson *et al.* (1989). Walker *et al.*'s (1995) finding that 90 per cent of placements include direct observation offers some confidence that CCETSW's strategy has borne fruit. However, their analysis did not reveal how often direct observation was being employed in any given placement.

Learning skills comprise, in our view, a range of conceptual abilities, including analysing and evaluating practice processes and outcomes, using supervision and peer learning processes, as well as the more usually cited 'transfer of learning', 'relating theory and practice', 'critical appraisal' and 'study skills'. These learning skills are particularly difficult to elicit since they are largely conceptual and not behavioural processes and therefore not amenable to observation.

One method of eliciting these processes is to encourage students to talk and write about the ideas they bring in preparing for their practice, the effec-tiveness of their practice and why their practice changes through time. Sometimes assessors will only be able to infer learning by observing the changes in students' practices. Williamson *et al.* (1989) report the interesting finding that practice teachers were more likely to give an indication of student development and less likely to give an indication of absolute level of performance. Whilst this finding was interpreted as suggesting a deficiency it could also have reflected a considerable strength in focusing on learning skills.

Methods that elicit changes in professional competence throughout a career are beyond the scope of qualifying programmes, although they could be developed in post-qualifying and assessment. However it is reasonable to expect some progress between the intermediate and final assessment stages of qualifying programmes, notably in students' ability to transfer learning and to evaluate critically the relevance of theory to their particular practice context, as well as in an improvement in practice performance and a broad-ening and deepening of the base.

The structure of professional education requires learning and assessment to take place in two very different settings: an academic institution and a practice agency. The impact of differences in ethos, service aims and traditions, has been compounded by their differential power in the assessment system. This has encouraged a somewhat dichotomous assessment system (see Table 10.1).

Both settings have developed strengths and weaknesses. The system of sampling work in academic settings, for example, empowers students to make specific efforts at certain times without the stress of constant assessment and has been advocated for practice settings, too (Doel, 1987; Evans, 1991). Likewise the direct access of academic internal assessors to students' knowledge base is a strength yet to be achieved in practice settings for practice skills. Practice settings, however, have developed the strengths of consistency in assessment judgements through the central role of the main practice teacher. Moreover, the predominant focus on oral evidence in practice settings is not only congruent with the predominance of oral communication in social work practice but is also an anti-oppressive strategy, since there is some evidence that predominantly written assessment methods discriminate on grounds of ethnic origin and class (Evans, 1991; de Souza, 1991).

Table 10.1 Assessment in academic and practice settings

Assessment procedure	Academic setting	Practice setting
Staff registered as teachers and internal assessors	Mainly	Still the minority, although numbers are increasing through accreditation and the CCETSW award
Internal assessors' access to student performance	Direct	Much indirect through students' reports of practice
Selection of students' performance assessed	Sample (eg written work)	Nearly total (eg whole placements)
Consistency of assessor	Fragmentary (due to different subject specialists)	Considerable (due to central role of main practice teacher
Assessment methods	Mainly written	Mainly oral
Standard setting	Double marking	Single judgement (the norm)
External assessors' access to student performance	Direct	Indirect (through practice teachers' and students' reports)

Developing practice-based assignments

It is our opinion that practice-based assignments offer methods that can develop strengths from both traditions. We conceive practice-based assignments (see also Doel and Shardlow, 1989; Evans 1991) to be discrete assessment events in which practice, the knowledge, skills and values base and learning skills are all three elicited, thus producing a major congruence with professional competence and a high level of validity. Practice-based assignments can also be designed to elicit progression in competence through time. We conceive practice-based assignments to be central assessment events, which are contained within the programme assessment schedule and are thus available to the External Assessors, the Assessment Board and the Practice Assessment Panel, if considered appropriate. Doel and Shardlow (1989), however, conceive them more as events that are organized within practice placements and are not directly accessed by anyone beyond the practice teacher. Typically, a practice-based assignment will include:

- a practice event;
- the students' thinking about that event.

The practice event will often comprise one specific interaction either with service users or colleagues. The students' thinking can include both *prospective* thoughts (such as theoretical ideas that may be relevant, transferred learning from past contexts, plans for the interaction) as well as *retrospective* thoughts (critically evaluating the practice and the theory, transfer for future contexts and explanations of why plans are not fulfilled). The practice event is most likely to be recorded on tape (audio or video) although certain aspects of the practice event such as many of the social work students' and the other person's thoughts and feelings will be private and will require other methods such as process recording or service user feedback mechanisms. The students' thinking can be recorded in writing or on tape. The traditional method in teacher training for assessing lessons on teaching practice entailed separating out the prospective lesson plans from the retrospective lesson evaluation. Such a distinction could be usefully explored in the education of other professionals.

The two Diplomas in Social Work (East Sussex and Suffolk/Essex) that we have been involved in planning and implementing have developed a number of practice-based assignments, with the aims of placing professional competence at the heart of the assessment system. We have selected four to present in this article, two of which focus on specific interactions while the other two target placement settings.

Specific interaction assignments

The Suffolk/Essex programme has developed an assessment method called the 'taped assignment'. This assignment comprises four different phases: a specific interaction on placement, which is taped (audio or video); the student's written or spoken (recorded) thoughts about the interaction; discussion about the interaction and the students' thoughts between the student and the two internal assessors, their practice teacher and their personal tutor; evaluative feedback from internal assessors both oral and written. The particular value of the dialogue phase (Phillips *et al.*, 1994) is that students can be further questioned about their work to seek a justification for certain behaviours or to elicit evidence not included in the taped interaction or their thoughts about the interaction. Two of these assignments are required in different semesters of each year of the programme (four in total), thus giving the potential of assessing development; within the one year both practice teacher and personal tutor can assess development. Typically, only the personal tutor is in a position to assess development from year 1 to year 2.

Students identify a number of strengths in this assignment. Mostly they identify the value of reflecting upon their own practice, of examining the detailed processes of that practice and identifying its strengths and weaknesses:

allows analysis of self and the relationship with the client

and

listening to what you said exactly as opposed to what or how you think you said or approached something.

Some students also value the opportunity to receive specific feedback about their detailed practice from their practice teacher and personal tutor. Several students judge that the assignment has a beneficial future impact on their practice.

It encouraged me to plan interviews and interventions more carefully

and

I listen more carefully about what is said by client.

Some students also commented on how the assignment actually became part of the work with service users. For one student the tape had an immediate beneficial impact on service delivery, by helping break down power differentials when the service user agreed to allow the tape to assist the student. Other students made use of the tape outcome, linking it in one case with a service user's interest in photography and in another case replaying it for a severely disabled service user's sense of self-image.

However, the assignment also has attendant difficulties. These can be divided into the practical and the ethical. Practical difficulties include the availability of tape recorders for all students at different times in the placement, the quality of tape recording and learning how to use tapes as student, internal and external assessors. Students were particularly concerned about the first difficulty and external assessors about the second, both particularly in the early development of the programme. Programme partners have generously responded by making audio (and video) recorders more available. Students are now requested to edit the tape by identifying a key passage for the Practice Assessment Panel and External Assessors. They are also required to ensure acceptable playback quality. Students receive initial training in the use of tape recorders in college role plays and often on placement.

The ethical difficulties stem principally from the process of including service users or other colleagues in the students' assessment process. Issues of confidentiality have largely been resolved through the use of an informed consent form and the programme's undertaking to wipe tapes after the assessment process has been completed, unless permission not to do so is granted.

Less easy to resolve, however, has been the issue of how students choose who to ask to participate in the tape. The programme attempts to suggest that:

- it is best to tape interactions that occur naturally in the course of the placement rather than contrive one for the assignment;
- most service users are likely to welcome this reciprocal activity on behalf of the student, providing they have genuine choice and understand why it is occurring (see Evans, 1987a).

However, these messages do not always reach all students and internal assessors (especially practice teachers) although some students discover it for themselves:

I found the idea of taping interviews difficult on ethical grounds at first, although most clients were very helpful and did not have any difficulty with taping.

The East Sussex programme has developed an assignment, which similarly focused on specific interactions, entitled the Practice Record. The Practice Record covers two interactions, one near the start of the placement and the other after half-way. At least one interaction must be with a service user, although the other may be with a colleague. The assignment includes an extract from a process recording for both interactions, a tape (audio or video) for one and the student's written reflections on the two interactions. Although the two stages of the assignment are commented on separately, they are assessed as one assignment. The one internal assessor is the practice teacher.

Students identify strengths similar to those identified by Suffolk/Essex students: the opportunity to reflect on the detailed strengths and weaknesses of their own practice and some recognizable influence on their future practice.

Some value the opportunity to reflect, particularly on more subjective aspects of practice:

encourages me to examine my own feelings and attitudes.

Some students also value the opportunity to relate theory to specific practice contexts:

making the theory real and workable, or not as the case may be.

One practice teacher for this programme sums up these strengths:

It enables the student to closely link feelings, actions and theory in a practical format.

Practice teachers also identify the value of a two-stage assignment in assessing progress.

The two stages of the assignment can, however, prove problematic for students. One student identified a tendency to build on the first rather than to give both equal weight. One practice teacher and an external assessor also identified the difficulty of providing one compromise assessment for the two parts of the assignment, which may differ in quality of student performance and which do differ in the quality of evidence available, with a tape for only one part. One possible development might be to separate out the two parts into two discrete assignments, each with a tape and a process recording and to add an assessment criterion about the student's development to the second assignment.

A second major difficulty identified by several students and one practice teacher was the word limit for the assignment. Students identified similar difficulties to Suffolk/Essex students in adjusting to tapes and had the additional difficulty of learning how to record processes.

Placement settings assignments

One central element of professional competence in social work as in other professions is the ability to work within an organization, being aware of its potential and its restrictions in order to optimize these for the benefit of service users. This element has been recognized both in the wider literature (Hugman, 1991; Evans and Kearney, 1996) and also in successive requirements for social work qualifying education (CCETSW, 1989) culminating in its recognition as one of the six core social work competences (CCETSW, 1995).

Both the East Sussex and the Suffolk/Essex programmes have sought to elicit this ability for assessment through two different methods. Neither method seeks to focus on a specific recorded interaction but rather on the students' ability to understand the setting as a whole.

The Suffolk/Essex programme's method is called the 'oral presentation' wherein first year students present to the two internal assessors – their practice teacher and their personal tutor – their understanding of their placement organization. This assignment has three phases: an oral presentation including such visual material as the student requires, which lasts 15–20 minutes; questioning by their practice teacher and tutor and discussion; evaluative feedback and future learning. The whole assignment should take no more than an hour. The assignment occurs towards the end of the first term, some two to two and a half months into the student's first placement on the programme and at the end of a college learning sequence on organizational theory. It thus has the potential to enhance the usual induction processes of placements.

Students speak strongly of the assignment's value in increasing their understanding of their placement organization and its context, not only for their own sakes but also to the advantage of service users and colleagues.

helped me to know what I am talking about with clients/colleagues

and

it has raised my awareness of how practice has to be within the limitations of statute and hierarchy.

Several students also indicated the value of the oral assessment mode, with visual materials to aid understanding:

oral presentation allows more creativity/variety – is a welcome change from written assignments

and

looking for different, more visual ways to demonstrate learning built up my confidence.

Students indicate few difficulties with this assignment but include: arranging three-way meetings between tutor, practice teacher and student, particularly when tutors have a number of tutees to assess in the same period; little standardized preparation for the assignment, relying on individual tutors and practice teachers; compressing their understanding of their placement agency into 15–20 minutes. Programme staff, however, were aware of the difficulty of external assessors' accessing this assignment. After discussion between the programme and its external assessors, it was agreed not to tape these presentations, possibly by analogy with assessment in medicine, whereby a small proportion of the assessment schedule can take place live and is not accessed by external examiners.

The East Sussex assignment occurs at the beginning of year 2, following a four-week mid-programme placement. The assignment method is seminar presentation, whereby each student presents their evaluation of their placement to half the year group for three-quarters of an hour, using other visual material as they decide. Students participate in a half-day workshop on presentation skills as preparation. The presentation is video-recorded, for students to be able to assess themselves, for internal moderation and for external assessors' access. The internal assessor is one of the social work tutors.

While the Suffolk/Essex assignments focus on getting to know the organizational setting of a nine-month placement by way of a more rigorous induction process, the East Sussex assignment concentrates on using research skills to enter a short observational placement and evaluate its functioning in relation to its stated aims.

The East Sussex students report very similar strengths and weaknesses to the Suffolk/Essex assignment. They particularly value the oral presentation mode in the seminar:

[the presentation] made me aware of the importance of clarity and organization of thought.... when presenting

and

it allows people who are not so articulate in writing another way to present their abilities.

They also reported a similar difficulty in compressing considerable information about a setting into one assignment:

sheer overwhelming vastness of information gathered

and

selecting what to present and what to leave out.

Additional strengths in this assignment are the peer learning that takes place and the recognition of the relevance of research skills.

Watching presentations expands knowledge of what's outside

and

research is interesting as it is 'live', as well as reading.

Ways forward

Although Doel and Shardlow (1989) and Evans (1991) were advocating practice-based assignments at the beginning of the development of the Diploma in Social Work, it is unclear how much this type of assessment method has found its way onto Dip SW assessment schedules. There would appear to be a number of reasons for delays in such developments.

Whilst many people in social work education, both in academic and practice settings, have radical views about social work practice, they often have fairly conservative ideas about social work education. This is scarcely surprising since few, particularly in the academic setting, receive any formal training in professional education or are well acquainted with the growing body of research and theory about professional education in general or social work education in particular. The very conservatism that is decried for students' learning from restricted models tends to pervade educationalists' learning.

One corollary of this conservatism is the somewhat cosy familiarity with which many students, internal assessors (particularly in the academic setting) and external assessors view written modes of assessment. All three participants in the assessment process will undoubtedly need to learn new skills in order to prepare and/or evaluate oral communication, whether it be live or recorded. Clearly all three participants could be usefully aided in that process, through student coaching, staff induction, external assessor conferences and other forms of development.

Another corollary of this conservatism is an understandable caution about developing new assessment methods. Assessment is an important activity, which, if undertaken lightly or irresponsibly, could place future vulnerable service users at risk. However, the security of traditional methods such as double-blind marking of essays, which are relatively strong in reliability, may be open to that very criticism if they are also relatively weak in validity.

Another obstacle to the development of practice-based assignments has probably been the processes of territoriality in social work education. One such concern over territory occurs between the practice and academic settings (Sheldon, 1978; Richards, 1984; Evans, 1987b). Academic staff who are confident in the literature but have become out of touch with practice may be reluctant to assess the details of practice. However practice staff may be confident in their ability to recognize good practice, but inclined to leave the theory assessment to the academic staff. Practice-based assignments require both staff to leave their more comfortable territory in order to grapple with the totality of professional competence.

Practice itself is at the heart of the debate about reliability and validity in assessing students. Specific interactions between students and service users will vary not only according to the ability of the student but also according to characteristics in the service user, such as whether they are voluntary or involuntary service users, aspects of the match between student and service user in terms of age, gender, ethnic origin, sexual orientation and class, and the response of both student and service user to being taped. All these variables threaten reliability in order to gain validity.

Practice can also be somewhat problematic to record accurately for the assessment process. Standard setting processes (Evans, 1991) surely require that more than one internal assessor as well as external assessors can have direct access to practice. CCETSW (1995) specifies two ways of accessing practice for assessment: direct observation and video-tape recording. While relatively unobtrusive in some practice contexts, observation is often not preferred by students (Evans, 1987a) and does not open the access beyond one internal assessor. Video-taping clearly captures both visual as well as auditory information. However it is a highly obtrusive mode of taping to use in service users' own homes, including day and residential care settings, as well as being quite expensive. Audio-taping, which CCETSW regrettably neglects, is far more portable, unobtrusive and inexpensive. It also loses less information than is often imagined, since extra-linguistic features such as volume, pitch and rate convey much of the information conveyed by non-verbal communication (Evans, 1991).

Several of the improvements in quality to be gained from practice-based assignments have already been alluded to above: the focus on the totality of professional competence; the potential to minimize some discrimination; the potential for student learning. There is also a political incentive in the growing influence of the National Council for Vocational Qualifications (NCVQ, now incorporated into the Qualifications and Curriculum Authority). This Council's remit has been extended to include professions as well as vocations and it seems set to expand. Not only does it seem to attract all-party support, but the NVQ framework is receiving a warm welcome from academic institutions. A survey conducted by the *Times Higher Educational Supplement* (Tysome, 1995) found that NVQs were seen as 'beneficial' three times more frequently than 'damaging' by higher educational institutions. NVQs rely heavily on work-based assessment strategies. Higher education institutions will need to prepare themselves for an acceptable work-based assessment strategy for professional education that includes the use of a knowledge, skills and values base, learning skills as well as practice performance.

References

Benner, P. (1984) *From Novice to Expert*, New York, Addison Wesley.
Brown, S. and Knight, P. (1994) *Assessing Learners in Higher Education*, London, Kogan Page.
CCETSW (1989) *Rules and Requirements for the Diploma in Social Work*, London, CCETSW Paper 30.
CCETSW (1995) 'Assuring quality in the Diploma in Social Work' in *Rules and Requirements for the Diploma in Social Work*, London, CCETSW Paper 30.
de Souza, P. (1991) 'A review of the experiences of black students in social work training', in CCETSW (eds) *One Small Step towards Racial Justice*, London, CCETSW, 148–79.
Doel, M. (1987) 'Putting the "final" in the final report', *Social Work Today*, 2 February, p 13.
Doel, M. and Shardlow, S. (1989) 'The Practice Portfolio: A research report', University of Sheffield, Department of Sociological Studies (unpublished).
Evans, D. (1987a) 'Live supervision in the same room: A practice teaching method', *Social Work Education*, 6(3), 13–17.
Evans, D. (1987b) 'The centrality of practice in social work education', *Issues in Social Work Education*, 7(2), 83–101.

Evans, D. (1991) *Assessing Students' Competence to Practise*, London, CCETSW.

Evans, D. and Kearney, J. (1996) *Working in Social Care: A systemic approach*, Aldershot, Arena.

Hayward, C. (1979) *A Fair Assessment: CCETSW Study 2*, London, CCETSW.

Hugman, R. (1991) *Power in Caring Professions*, London, Macmillan.

Morrell, E. (1980) 'Student assessment: Where are we now?' *British Journal of Social Work*, **10**, 431–42.

Phillips, T., Bedford, H., Robinson, J. and Satastak, J. (1994) *Education Assessment and Dialogue: Creating partnership for improving practice*, London, ENB Research in Education Series.

Richards, M. (1984) 'Pulled in all directions', *Community Care*, 18 October 18–21.

Rowntree, D. (1987) *Assessing Students: How shall we know them?*, 2nd edn, London, Harper & Row.

Schön, D. (1987) *Educating the Reflective Practitioner*, San Francisco, Jossey Bass.

Sheldon, B. (1978) 'Theory and practice in social work: A re-examination of a tenuous relationship', *British Journal of Social Work*, **8**, 1–22.

Taylor, C. W., Price, P. B., Richards, J. M. and Jacobson, T. L. (1965) 'An investigation of the criterion problem for a group of medical general practitioners', *Journal of Applied Psychology*, **49**, 399–406.

Tysome, T. (1995) 'NVQs pass tough admissions test', *Times Higher Education Supplement*, 30, June 6.

Walker, J., McCarthy, P., Morgan, W. and Timms, N. (1995) *In Pursuit of Quality: Improving practice teaching in social work*, Newcastle-upon-Tyne, Relate Centre for Family Studies.

Williamson, H., Jefferson, R., Johnson, S. and Shahbang, A. (1989) *Assessment of Practice: A perennial concern?* University of Wales College of Cardiff, Social Research Unit.

Winter, R. (1992) 'Outline of a general theory of professional competence', Chelmsford, Anglia Polytechnic University (unpublished paper).

Wright, A. and Davies, M. (1989) *Becoming a Probation Officer*, Norwich, University of East Anglia Social Work Monographs.

Part Four

Professional Bodies
and the
Needs of Employers

Chapter 11

Professional capability: requirements and accreditation in the legal profession

Diana Tribe

Summary

This chapter surveys recent developments in professional preparation in law in the United Kingdom. Professor Tribe points to the lack of commonality in approaches at different stages of legal education, both in the requirements of professional bodies and in the modes of provision by different institutions.

Despite the various rhetorics of reflective practice, competence and capability and lifelong learning, tensions remain between the 'academic' and the 'vocational', discernible most clearly in the way different elements are assessed. Close analysis of several empirical studies illustrates the difficulties in defining and assessing skills so that:

- professional bodies and institutions of higher education can be assured of standards;
- each student is prepared for practice in law or other employment;
- the requirements of employers are recognized and satisfied.

International comparisons may suggest possible ways forward, but they provide no ready-made solution within the UK context.

While this chapter is engaged with developments in the law professions, it deals with issues of relevance to education in the professions generally.

Introduction

If a broad approach to the definition of competence-based education is taken, then it can be said that contemporary legal education at all stages is marked by a proliferation of statements of competency, learning outcome statements and skills guides which provide a specification of performance against which skills might be judged. (Jones, 1994)

The 'ultimate aim' of a legal education, as described by the Lord Chancellor's Advisory Committee on Legal Education and Conduct, a body which gives statutory approval to training regulations for both branches of the legal profession, is 'to produce humane, reflective, all-round lawyers' (1995a, b). How this is to be achieved, through the four stages of a lawyer's training – the undergraduate or 'academic' stage; the postgraduate or 'professional' stage; the professional skills or training contract stage; and the continuing professional development stage – is made less than clear, however, in the Advisory Committee's Consultation Papers.

An analysis of the various stages of legal education referred to above illustrates that although the training of lawyers is firmly controlled by the relevant professional bodies at each stage, there appears to be no common approach to the different stages.

Definition of skills and competences that form part of each stage of legal education and training

The undergraduate stage

The Law Society (the regulating body for solicitors) and the Council of Legal Education (which regulates training for the Bar) have long been involved in a common debate about the objectives of undergraduate legal education. The influence of these bodies is considerable, since they must approve the undergraduate courses that are run by English universities and professional providers, if those courses are to achieve the exempting/qualifying status required by most students.

In their *Joint Announcement on Qualifying Law Degrees* (1995), which was approved by the Lord Chancellor's Department in 1994, the Law Society and the Bar not only outlined the academic content required to be taught at the academic stage of training (the seven foundation areas of legal study), but also identified the competences with which students should be equipped at the academic stage: these are defined as 'the intellectual and practical skills needed to research the law... to apply it to the solution of legal problems and to communicate – both in writing and orally – the results of such work'. It is interesting to compare this analysis of the skills to be taught at the undergraduate stage with that of the Lord Chancellor's Advisory Committee on Legal Education, which reported in the same year and defined the aim of the initial stage of legal education as being 'to get students to think like lawyers, constructively but critically'. In neither case, however, have these bodies attempted to explain through what mechanism these objectives should be achieved.

The emergence of law degrees early in this century was marked by a struggle to achieve academic acceptance of the subject as one fit for study at university level, followed by the definition of relevant subject areas, the development of 'new' subject areas and new methods of delivering their content. It is only over the past 15 years that elements of what has been described variously as 'clinical' skills or competence teaching have been widely incorporated into law teaching at the undergraduate level. The content of such courses varies widely between institutions but seems generally to be influenced by notions of reflective practice and 'capability'. They may include the following:

- vocational skills for the legal profession (sometimes referred to as clinical legal education)

Here students are involved in training in a law centre (or simulated law centre) context, to develop the specific practitioner skills employed by legal professionals. The aim of this activity is to prepare students for their eventual employment as solicitors or barristers. Skills commonly included in such programmes include:

- legal analysis;
- professional/ethical responsibility;
- advocacy;
- litigation management;
- legal advice;
- legal document drafting;
- general professional skills (developed for general employment purposes).

Skills such as these are designed to prepare students for all types of professional occupational contexts. Training in some or all of these employment skills is often incorporated into undergraduate law courses (and in some universities students can study a modern language or business practice as an integral part of their law degree). The rationale behind the integration of general professional skills into law degrees is that not all students will necessarily enter the legal profession at the end of their undergraduate training; indeed, the evidence suggests that a decreasing number will actually do so. However, the large majority will eventually enter into employment of some kind, for which these more general professional skills will be appropriate. The type of skills normally included in programmes such as this will include:

- time management;
- case management;
- chairmanship;
- negotiation ;
- client interviewing;
- document drafting;
- advanced information technology skills;
- foreign language skills.

- life skills (for personal development purposes)

This is training that aims to help a student to maximize his/her future potential, not simply in relation to employment, but also in personal life. It is claimed that these are skills that all undergraduate students need to develop as a fundamental basis for personal intellectual development, regardless of subject or occupational context, and include:

- oral and written communication;
- self-management;
- information retrieval;
- word processing;
- research/study skills.

The introduction of skills teaching to undergraduate programmes has presented serious teaching problems and in some cases no attempt is made to teach the skills. Rather, reliance is placed on student-centred learning where students are given tasks to complete, which it is assumed will inculcate those skills thought desirable and necessary. Legal skills are also notoriously hard to assess and although the subjective element of assessment can be reduced through the development of standards, checklists, criteria and the like, these are perceived by critics as reductionist and simplistic, and in practice are often ignored, assessment being carried out, initially at least, on the basis of personal preference.

Universities vary in the extent and manner in which skills and competences are integrated into the undergraduate curriculum. In some cases freestanding compulsory modules (often in the foundation year of study) are offered, which contribute to the overall assessment of each student. These modules are sometimes taught by members of the law staff and sometimes by communications/study skills experts from within the university.

In other cases, a more adventurous approach has been developed in which skills/competences are integrated across the curriculum as a whole; here they form a subset of the objectives for each subject studied, and subject tutors take responsibility for ensuring that these areas are covered in each subject. Thus, for instance, a Land Law tutor would ensure that the teaching of his/her subject included the development of communication skills (both oral and written), the making of presentations, working in groups and the development of research skills.

The professional/post graduate stage

The most significant changes over the past decade have occurred however at the post graduate stage of legal training. In 1989 the Council of Legal Education, which provides training for the Bar, developed a new 'skills-based' course to prepare prospective barristers for pupillage in response to criticisms from the profession that the old Bar Finals course produced students with technical knowledge but without the practical skills required to be competent barristers.

In 1993 the Law Society followed this lead by introducing the Diploma in Legal Practice to replace the old Law Society Finals course for those who intend to qualify as solicitors. This diploma is based around a set of 'competence'-based standards that provide an integrated model for a competence-based approach to learning. The dominant mode for the course is one year of full-time training, although there are alternatives (eg it may be integrated within a four-year degree, as at the University of Northumbria, or run part time over a two-year period, or studied by distance learning or even on a sandwich basis).

Jones (1994) indicates that the standards are based on:

- knowledge and tasks that are assessed through coursework and end of session examinations.
- lawyering skills in five key areas (drafting, research, advocacy, interviewing, negotiation) which are not defined by the Law Society but rather stated in the form of outcome statements. There are no detailed guides to the assessment of these skills; course providers are expected to formulate their own detailed assessment criteria that specify in some detail the behaviours that need to be demonstrated to show competence in each skill.
- professional practice skills – these are made up of a core set of generic skills that are common within the range of professional activities referred to above and include for instance communication skills, client relationship skills, office practice skills, personal work management skills, IT skills and personal development skills. No criteria for the assessment of the performance of these skills are provided by the Law Society and it would appear that most course providers do not assess them as such.

Students on the Diploma in Legal Practice are assessed on their ability to complete the steps and procedures involved in certain key transactions, and on their ability to perform a range of lawyers' skills. If successful they will be assessed as being 'competent' to move on to the next stage of legal education – supervised practice within a training contract..

As Maughn *et al.* (1995) suggest:

there seems to be quite a contrast between what is happening at the academic stage and the vocational stage. Some of the progressive initiatives shown by the Law Schools at the academic stage are influenced by notions of reflective practice and capability and seek to go beyond the old paradigm of knowledge and skill. At the vocational stage the programme rests firmly on the knowledge and skills divide... the substantive law components are tested through coursework and examination... the skills are assessed separately. Such a separation serves only to solidify attitudes about the academic/vocational hierarchy.

Neither the Bar Vocational Course nor the Legal Practice Course has been without its critics. The Bar has had well-publicized difficulties with claims that a skills-based course discriminates against candidates from ethnic minorities, and it has been alleged that the skills basis for the Legal Practice Course has had the effect of diluting the provision of necessary legal technical knowledge for legal practice.

The Lord Chancellor's Advisory Committee in its June 1995 paper sought responses from interested parties to the question 'Is the current balance at the vocational level between skills and knowledge appropriate?', whilst at the same time indicating the view that students 'should be equipped with up-to-date skills for professional practice in the context of rapid and radical changes to the provision of legal services' and that they should be inculcated with a 'professional attitude' and the notion of 'lifelong learning'.

The professional skills course and continuing professional development

For new recruits to the profession, the Professional Skills Course takes place during the training contract and the training contract itself incorporates a set of standards for the skills that trainees are to have developed during the training contract. 'This provides a carefully structured set of standards that provide an integrated approach to post-degree professional education' (Jones, 1994).

The Lord Chancellor's Advisory Committee reporting in 1995 defined the objectives of training for those solicitors for whom continuing professional development courses are now mandatory (almost the entire profession) as follows:

The broad aim of continuing professional development should be to develop practice management skills as well as to enable qualified practitioners to update their expertise and widen their horizons. At a deeper level this kind of education should inculcate the notion of 'lifelong learning' as being at the heart of lawyering. All lawyers must recognise the need to expand or update their proficiency, knowledge, skills and attitudes.

In practice, however, the continuing professional development programme is only nominally controlled by the Law Society and individual practitioners have considerable latitude as to the type and quality of further training undertaken provided that they acquire the requisite number of training 'points'. Some attend courses offered by educational or commercial providers; others acquire the necessary 'points' by certifying that they have used one of the training videos currently produced for that purpose. What this means is that the practitioner tends to concentrate on acquiring further information which she/he believes will be useful in expanding her/his expertise into new areas and away from those areas where there is perceived to be a declining market.

It would be surprising if practitioners showed more than a superficial interest in courses aimed at developing skills and competences, and this tends to be borne out in practice (except perhaps for those larger firms who employ in-house educational trainers).

How can these qualities be assured?

Quality assurance goes beyond the mere written definition of aims and outcomes and tends to be centred around the assessment process. For that reason it is of some interest to consider the methods of assessment used in the development of skills and competences for lawyers.

A survey of law degrees carried out by Tribe and Tribe (1989) showed that the methods used for the assessment of skills varied very much from skill to skill within institutions, as well as between institutions. In some cases there was no formal assessment; all that was required for students to pass was their attendance. In others, assessment was based upon a mixture of attendance and written work, whilst in yet others this was combined with, or an alternative to, more innovative techniques such as filmed presentations, tribunal representation, or a comparison of the outcomes of negotiation exercises. In most institutions several methods were combined in use, and in at least three there was a schedule of component subskills which was used as a basis for the allocation of marks.

What was clear from the survey, however, was that there was a fundamental conceptual problem associated both with the delivery of skills teaching and with its assessment, in that there was a shortage of objective criteria by which to judge students' performance.

Put simply, the problem was perceived thus: if we assume that it is, for example, appropriate to teach the skills of interviewing to law students, we must identify the skills that make a good interviewer and then identify the behaviours (or subskills) that combine to make up those skills. These behaviours (or subskills) will then form the basis for a teaching programme and for subsequent student assessment.

We may argue, for instance, that in order to perform an interviewing task effectively, a student must be a competent listener, but this means that we must then identify the behaviours or subskills that will indicate this. Thus a breakdown of desirable listening behaviours might be as follows:

an effective student interviewer

- shows interest in the person who is speaking;
- shows interest in the subject under discussion;
- continues to listen when the subject becomes boring;
- does not allow prejudice to reduce attention;
- does not permit enthusiasm to carry them away;
- is not critical of the other person's speech or method of delivery;
- regularly summarizes what is heard;
- checks for understanding;
- does not allow emotional reactions to affect understanding;
- concentrates when difficult ideas are being expressed;
- creates the right environment for listening;
- allows sufficient time for full understanding before reacting;
- makes a final review of understanding of facts.

Even if such subskills can be conceptualized in this way, the problem is still short of solution, since each subskill remains capable of further breakdown into component low inference behaviours. For instance, the subskill 'shows interest in the person who is speaking', may be identified by such behaviours as:

- intermittent eye-contact;
- head nodding;
- smiling;
- avoiding looking at watch;
- avoiding interruptions from phone/colleagues.

In any case it may be the balance between the subskills when they are combined together which is most important in the carrying out of the overall interviewing task.

If one cannot identify with sufficient clarity exactly what students should achieve, it is difficult to assess whether, and to what extent, they have achieved it. The unarticulated, idiosyncratic model 'I cannot define it but I know it when I see it' works in only a very limited way.

Not surprisingly, although there are many skills training programmes within law courses in the UK, it is rare to find that their objectives have been clearly defined in the way suggested above. The study of Cort and Sammons (1980) attempted such an analysis based not upon empirical study of what it is that professional lawyers do, but rather on an observation of student attempts to carry out lawyer operations. This resulted in the identification of six major competences. The Antioch Competency Based Model took this approach considerably further: here 53 lawyering tasks are defined, each of which is then split down into approximately ten observable behaviours per task. Each of these is then in turn divided into several subsets with marks specifically allocated to each subset on a ten-point scale. Individual ratings are eventually combined to give a score for each student. A variation on this method has been used at Mercer University, where some of the original 53 competences are identified as being essential for students to acquire, whilst others are only desirable, thus providing additional complexities in an already complex system.

Whilst such systems appear to be systematically based, the identification of a set of subskills representing low inference behaviours is a difficult and time-consuming task; moreover, there is no provision for assessing the manner in which the subskills are combined to produce the total competency in question. The production of written standards is frequently assumed to lead to a systematic basis for assessment, but there are in fact no objective criteria for the allocation of marks, which still proceeds on a subjective basis. Finally, written accounts of competences tend to be linear in form and provide only two-dimensional models for what are essentially 'three-dimensional' activities.

Another fundamental problem related to the actual grading of skills activities by staff. Even supposing that skills can be identified and defined, what criteria should be used in allocating marks to their performance? What is the basis for distinguishing between 60 per cent and 70 per cent in a negotiation exercise when so much depends on context (ie the strength of the other negotiating party) that it is only possible to make rough numerical judgements about individual performances? Additionally, academic staff need extensive training to be able to use a skills schedule such as the Antioch model, and the whole system is time consuming and expensive; it seems extremely unlikely that such a method would recommend itself to British academics.

The difficulties referred to above in defining and assessing skills have meant that for many colleagues in the UK a written form of assessment, in which students are asked simply to reflect on their acquisition of skills, was the natural and preferred method. Thus students might be asked to present a case book outlining negotiation planning, tactics used and outcomes achieved as a basis for assessment; it is argued that although this may indicate something about an individual student's self-appraisal, it is not an objective test of his/her actual negotiation skills. It is understandable that staff prefer assessment based on written work, however, since it can be assessed by more than one member of staff, it can be repeated if unsatisfactory, and sent to the external examiner in cases of doubt. Furthermore, there is a feeling among lecturing staff that such written assessment is in some way more 'objective' and 'reliable' than the assessment of practical work.

However, with the advent of the Legal Practice Course, which was introduced in some institutions in September 1993, law teachers at last began to move towards more universal and formalized practices. The Legal Practice Course requires students to demonstrate 'competence' in the skills of drafting, research, advocacy, interviewing and negotiation before they can be awarded the Diploma necessary for entry into a training contract with a firm of solicitors. In some universities the teaching and assessment of these skills is integrated into the subject content that runs alongside. Thus the skill of interviewing may be assessed as an integral part of the conveyancing course, and the skill of advocacy as an integral part of the litigation course. This 'transactional' approach is one originally favoured by the Law Society on the grounds that it is the nearest approximation to the reality of a solicitor's practice. In other cases exemplars of skilled behaviour are video-taped to assist assessors in determining whether an individual student has displayed 'competence' in a particular skill or not. Exemplars are certainly helpful when used to illustrate written standards, but exemplars themselves cannot be used as an alternative. Different assessors will view the same exemplar differently and perceive different aspects of the same exemplar as being critical (Wolf, 1993).

The needs of employers

It would seem reasonable to assume that the needs of employers of law graduates would vary depending on whether they enter the legal profession or some other employment context. However, a small study carried out by staff at the University of Hertfordshire showed that the type of questions asked of referees by potential employers were relatively consistent regardless of the eventual employment context.

The questions listed below occur very regularly:

- What degree classification do you expect/did this candidate achieve?
- Is this candidate trustworthy?
- Does this candidate have good interpersonal skills?
- Does this candidate have good research skills?
- Is this candidate a 'clock watcher'?
- Is this candidate hard working/conscientious?
- Has this candidate a good level of literacy?
- Is this candidate 'flexible' in approach?

The questions listed below appear regularly:

- Has this candidate usually been able to hand work in on time?
- Has this candidate usually been a regular attender at classes?
- Would this candidate be a suitable person to work in a large city firm?
- Would this candidate be a suitable person to work with legal aid clients?
- Can this candidate write a concise and accurate account of a set of facts?

- Did this candidate suffer from regular periods of absence due to ill health when a student?
- Does this candidate possess basic IT skills?

Some potential employers tend to phrase their questions more obliquely, but on the whole seem to be searching for the same kind of competences. They appear to take for granted the academic ability of graduates and to be unconcerned about the details of the curriculum studied. What even a superficial analysis of these questions suggests is that the type of graduates sought by potential employers (whether within the legal profession or otherwise) are those who possess the skills/competences described variously as generic, transferable, personal, or professional practice, ie:

- general communications skills, which permeate communications outside and inside the office environment;
- client relationship skills;
- internal office practice skills, including those involved in working with others, for example, delegation, team building and group leadership;
- the personal work management skills of time management, task priority setting, meeting deadlines, diary keeping and punctuality;
- IT skills both generic (the ability to use general computerized tools) and specific (the ability to use legally specific tools and applications);
- personal and professional development skills – the ability to determine personal priorities, seek out new forms of learning that maintain and advance personal expertise, learn through self-reflection and respond flexibly to change.

These 'core' or generic skills are the ones that universities have been urged to develop by a series of governmental initiatives over the past two decades (the Enterprise in Higher Education initiative, the Royal Society of Arts capability movement and the NAB/UGC statement) (Barnett, 1990). The intention is to produce a range of skills that will be of value in a variety of employment contexts.

As indicated above, these skills are frequently, though not universally, incorporated to a greater or lesser extent within the undergraduate stage of a lawyer's training. Their existence is inferred from the standards defined by the professional bodies for students at the post graduate stage, although they are not directly addressed at this stage. Nonetheless potential employers still seek assurance that individual applicants possess these skills.

References

Barnett, R. (1990) *The Idea of Higher Education*, Buckingham, SRHE/Open University Press.

Cort, H. R. and Sammons, J. L. (1980) 'The search for "good lawyering"': A concept and model for lawyering competences' 29 *Clev. St L. Rev.*, 397.

Jones, P. (1994) *Competences, Learning Outcomes and Legal Education*, Legal Skills Working Paper, Institute of Advanced Legal Studies, University of London.

Law Society and the Council of Legal Education (1995) *Joint Announcement on Qualifying Law Degrees*, London.

Lord Chancellor's Advisory Committee on Legal Education and Conduct (1995a) *Review of Legal Education: The vocational stage* (Consultation Paper), June 1995.

Lord Chancellor's Advisory Committee on Legal Education and Conduct (1995b) *Review of Legal Education: The foundation stage* (Consultation Paper), June 1995.

Maughn, C., Maughn, M. and Webb, J. (1995) 'Sharpening the mind or narrowing it? The limitations of outcome and performance measures in legal education', *ALT International Journal of Legal Education*, **29**(3), 255.

Tribe, D. and Tribe, A. J. (1989) 'Assessing law students', *Assessment and Evaluation in Higher Education*, **13**(3), 195.

Wolf, A. (1993) *Assessment Issues and Problems in a Criterion Based System*, London, Further Education Unit.

Chapter 12

Professional capability: a case-study bridging vocational, academic and professional frameworks

Geraldine Doherty and Rachel Pierce

Summary

Tensions between different interest groups are by no means uncommon in the arena of professional education. This 'insider' account of the review of a professional qualification in social work addresses those tensions and their possible resolution.

In attempting to build bridges between academic, professional and vocational interest groups, those revising the award needed also to find conformability between methodologies with apparently contradictory tendencies – the 'reductionist' approach of functional analysis of competencies and the 'holistic' approach of reflective practice.

To what extent these epithets hold true, the reader may gauge from this and other chapters that wrestle with this problem. To what extent the solution offered here will be successful must await evaluation in the professional field. As to whether it is transferable to other professions, the reader must exercise professional judgement.

Introduction

This case-study concerns the recent review of the Diploma in Social Work (DipSW), the professional qualification in social work. It locates the review in context, by identifying the statutory mandate of the professional body, the Central Council for Education and Training in Social Work (CCETSW), and the range of other vocational and academic interests involved. We set out the resultant incorporative approach, which seeks to bridge the three frameworks – professional, academic and vocational – as a model for other professions to consider.

The second part of the chapter explores in more detail the contribution of functional analysis and its transformation at the professional level. We identify the principal focus of the DipSW as the holistic assessment of the competent reflective practitioner and we put forward a definition of competence as the integration of knowledge, skills and values.

The context

Background context

Responsibility for the DipSW lies with the statutory body, CCETSW. The DipSW was approved by CCETSW as the social work qualification in 1989, after major consultations with all the key education, professional and employment interests and agreement on a Statement of Requirements for Qualification in Social Work, which identified the knowledge, values and skills required to achieve competence in social work practice. This was in advance of the 'competence' movement, but with the knowledge that it was on the horizon.

Together with all the key interests, CCETSW also undertook to review the DipSW Statement of Requirements at intervals to keep it up to date with current and future professional and service needs. However, the timing of the review in 1994 and the timescale for it were government decisions and unfortunately prevented the opportunity to review the DipSW with other related professions in the health and care fields, hindering consideration of interprofessional aspects and joint exploration of the interface between vocational, professional and academic awards.

The current context: general

In the five years between 1989, when CCETSW first approved the DipSW, and 1994, when it was reviewed, major changes had taken place. The government was challenging the monopoly of the professions and the preparation of professionals by higher education, eg the replacement of college-based teacher training by class-based provision. More significantly, the government's National Standards Programme, which established the National Council for Vocational Qualifications (NCVQ) and Lead Industry Bodies, had been extended to higher levels, thus bringing professional training and qualifications within its remit and within government targets.

The previous unchallenged authority of the then Department for Education (DfE) and higher and further education to provide education and training for professionals, with its emphasis on inputs, was being replaced by the former Employment Department (ED) and employment interests, by national competence standards and assessed outcomes.

These challenges were not just politically inspired. They sought also to answer legitimate concerns about qualified professionals – what did qualifications guarantee about the holders? What were they competent to do in practice?

But such a swing to employment interests and assessment in the workplace also generated its critics, questioning the efficacy of the assessment process, particularly in relation to underpinning knowledge, especially as this approach was broadened to the development of General National Vocational Qualifications (GNVQs) and to higher level National and Scottish Vocational Qualifications (VQs).

Work at the higher levels of VQs still remains at an early stage. The Qualifications and Curriculum Authority (formerly NCVQ) now has the remit, but exercises it voluntarily. There have been a range of Higher Level Projects, several seminars with professional and statutory bodies, a Committee of Vice-chancellors and Principals working party, and a Higher Levels Steering Group which has carried out a consultation on its 'Vision Paper'. But as yet there has been no serious engagement with VQs by any of the 'older' professions or any with regulatory bodies.

Meanwhile, the emergence of the vocational qualifications, and particularly the GNVQs, accelerated debates within education about broader access to university education, to the provision of vocational as well as 'A' level routes, and to their potential bridging. These debates were paralleled by higher education debates about a national credit framework for further and higher education, articulating academic, professional and vocational qualifications and extending access to higher education, in which CCETSW had played an active role.

Although these proposals are not yet fulfilled in practice, these various initiatives have led recently to the logical merging of the DfE and the ED in the Department for Education and Employment.

The current context: specific

This general context informs the specific context for education, training and qualifications for social work and the personal social services.

DipSW education and training is provided by higher education institutions (HEIs), in partnership with social service agencies, and the HEIs confer an academic qualification alongside the CCETSW professional qualification, thus bridging the professional and academic frameworks and making higher education and social service agencies major interested parties to the review. But by 1994 there was a new interested party, a newcomer since the approval of the DipSW in 1989 – the Care Sector Consortium (CSC) – the Lead Industry Body for the sector, with a remit to develop National Occupational Standards as the basis for National Vocational Qualifications within the progressive national vocational framework, based on competency and the use of functional analysis methodology.

The CSC was initially established as a Lead Industry Body and graduated later to an Occupational Standards Council when its remit was extended to the higher levels. It covers all the health and social care personnel throughout the UK, the majority of whom had no education, training or qualification structure. There were a number of initiatives, such as CCETSW's two social care awards, an in-service one and a preliminary one for 16–19 year olds, but no progressive career structure or training continuum for this wide range of staff, not even any linking of these qualifications as access to the social work qualification. The situation was no better on the health side.

The CSC, with its constituent members – employers, unions and statutory bodies (including CCETSW as a lead member) – therefore welcomed this employment initiative and worked hard to establish VQs at levels 2 and 3, covering a wide range of occupational areas in the sector. CCETSW played a key role in producing a Working Model of a Progressive Continuum Qualification Structure, which linked the VQs to the DipSW and on to CCETSW's Post-Qualifying Award (PQSW) and Advanced Award (AASW). In this progressive continuum a VQ at level 3 provided an entry requirement for the DipSW and a relevant VQ at level 4 would provide credit towards the DipSW. Although this Working Model was not formally adopted by the CSC it remained an explicit guide.

But with the extension of the remit to the higher levels, some of the CSC interests on the social care side were keen to take VQs ahead to the higher levels, thus threatening to move into the professional social work arena. The risks were real, with the comparative weakness of social work as a profession – with no qualification requirement for appointment as a social worker, thus no protection of title, not a fully graduate profession and with no social work regulatory body. Any such move on the health side would have been stifled at birth. But on the positive side these moves illustrate the significant contribution that VQs are making to the sector which, by being extended to the higher levels, would provide further opportunities to this important mature workforce.

CCETSW's strategy

So what was CCETSW's strategy? It was not an auspicious context for the 1994 review. It was too soon on all counts, and not least because the DipSW was not fully implemented until 1994 and there had been some eight years of debate and consultation before it had been approved in 1989. But more importantly there was no blueprint for professional qualifications in relation to the competency debate and higher level VQs, and a real threat on the horizon for a weak professional area such as social work.

Our analysis of the context led us forward – to explore and identify the strengths and contribution from each of these developments – rather than backward into protecting our previous position. We recognized that the competency movement was here to stay, but was capable of further development, and even transformation at the higher levels. The context had changed and we therefore adopted an incorporative approach, which confirmed CCETSW's statutory role, with its remit for the qualifying and post-qualifying social work awards and the standards of education and training leading to them, but recognized the remit of the CSC for developing national occupational standards for the sector and the value added of employment endorsement of the qualification itself and of its place in the continuum of qualifications.

This analysis led CCETSW to offer partnership in the review project to the Care Sector Consortium, on terms that recognized each other's remits, to work together under a joint steering group, with four representatives each from CCETSW and the CSC, one of the authors of this paper (Rachel Pierce) as chair, and the other (Geraldine Doherty) as the CCETSW appointed project manager. This partnership was not welcomed by higher education interests, which were concerned to see that the knowledge component and the importance of research were not eroded and that the qualification would remain both an academic and a professional award. However, these commitments were also those of CCETSW.

The agreed aims of the project were:

- to develop draft national occupational standards for new social workers, one year into practice. The period of one year into practice was chosen as representing a general point when a new social worker should be confident to demonstrate in practice what she/he has learned during training;
- to review and revise the Statement of Requirements – the knowledge, values and skills required for the award of the DipSW – based on the draft national occupational standards.

CCETSW's aims in this partnership were:

- to defend social work education and training and the DipSW – as the professional qualification, a base for a career in social work, and firmly rooted in higher education (thus continuing to bridge the professional and academic frameworks) – against the potential threat of the Care Sector Consortium and employers bypassing the DipSW and developing a separate higher level Vocational Qualification for social workers;

- to secure the DipSW within the progressive continuum of qualifications – Vocational Qualifications, the DipSW, Post-Qualifying and Advanced Awards – and particularly to articulate the bridge with the emerging level 4 Vocational Qualifications in Care, thus also bridging the vocational framework;
- to establish more consistent standards at the outcome from the DipSW;
- to promote more flexible opportunities for access to the DipSW education, training and qualification;
- to achieve its contemporary relevance in the context of changing needs, legislation and service delivery throughout the UK, particularly taking into account the major changes in children's services following the recent and impending children's legislation, in adult services following the Community Care changes and in probation following the Criminal Justice Acts, 'National Standards' and 'Punishment in the Community', etc.

The review process confirmed this partnership decision and CCETSW's aims, and the outcome we believe provides the best opportunity for meeting the education and training needs of social workers within the constraints of a two year education and training period. We also believe that this partnership and incorporative approach provides a model that could be explored further by other professional groups, particularly in the health and care sector.

The review process

There were two distinct stages to the review process:

1. the identification and agreement of what constitutes the key purpose of social work and the main functions essential to its achievement;
2. the establishment of revised rules and requirements for the award of DipSW based on the assessment of the knowledge, skills and values required to undertake these main functions.

Stage one

The first functional analysis stage of the review process involved two rounds of workshops and postal consultations around the UK. The consistent points of debate were:

What is meant by professionalism? what can and should be expected from the newly qualified social worker?

How can professional practice be responsive to a changing legislative and organizational context that requires a focus on the management of budgets and the development of cost-effective packages of care, while continuing to address the interpersonal aspects of people's lives and the communicating, enabling and empowering work that has always been central to the purpose of social work?

The final outcome, after much debate, was that there are six core functions of social work and it was decided that a student should be required to show evidence of possessing them all before being awarded the DipSW and essentially a licence to practise.

This confirmed that it was not the functions, but the depth and breadth of experience and the increased self-management that differentiated social workers with a year's practice from the newly qualified social worker.

In finalizing the outcome of the functional analysis it was decided to move away from the language of the functional analysis process – functions, units, elements and performance criteria – for two reasons:

1. concern that such language would fuel fears that the use of functional analysis would reduce the complexities of social work practice to a mechanical list of functions;
2. the recognition that the level of disaggregation for a professional two-year education and training programme could not and should not be the same as that required for S/NVQs, ie more holistic assessment was required.

Therefore a new terminology was developed – that of core competences, practice requirements and evidence indicators. The six core competences identified are shown in Table 12.1.

One of the important things to say about the competences shown in Table 12.1 is that they contain complex concepts such as rights, risks and change. It is clear from the start that we are not talking about straightforward or

Table 12.1 The six core competences of social work

Communicate and engage	Communicate and engage with organizations and people within communities to promote opportunities for children, adults, families and groups at risk or in need to function, participate and develop in society
Promote and enable	Promote opportunities for people to use their own strengths and expertise to enable them to meet responsibilities, secure rights and achieve change
Assess and plan	Work in partnership to assess and review people's circumstances and plan responses to need and risk
Intervene and provide services	Intervene and provide services to achieve change, through provision or purchase of appropriate levels of support, care, protection and control
Work in organizations	Contribute to the work of organizations
Develop professional competence	Manage and evaluate own capacity to develop professional competence

simplistic activities but about core tasks which, because of their very nature, require a reflective analytical approach, incorporating a highly developed level of interpersonal skills and professional judgement.

PRACTICE REQUIREMENTS

A number of practice requirements were developed for each core competence, which further defined the elements of practice that would be required to achieve the competence. For example, to achieve the core competence *Assess and plan* – work in partnership to assess and review people's circumstances and plan responses to need and risk – students would have to be able to meet the following practice requirements:

- work in partnership to assess and review people's needs, rights, risks, strengths, responsibilities and resources;
- work in partnership to identify and analyse risk of harm, abuse or failure to protect;
- work in accordance with statutory and legal requirements;
- work in partnership to negotiate and plan responses to assessed needs, rights, risks, responsibilities, strengths and resources;
- work in partnership to develop packages of care, support, protection and control.

Stage two

The second stage of the review process was to build a set of assessment requirements for the DipSW that would be standard in expectation, in that the set would be based on the six core competences and require an integration of knowledge, skills and values, and which could be realistically completed and achieved within a two-year full-time training programme, as well as being capable of flexible delivery.

Throughout the review process, care was taken to avoid any move to mechanistic assessment. Many of those consulted had experience of, and valued, the introduction of S/NVQs but were concerned about the requirements related to the collection and presentation of evidence; and feared that a revised DipSW drawn from a functional analysis exercise would be bound to result in students hunting for evidence of meeting assessment specifications rather than having time to learn and reflect. At the same time the government, CCETSW and DipSW programme providers were concerned about achieving greater consistency of outcome standards for the award of DipSW. Therefore it was important to make the best use of the detail of competent practice provided by functional analysis.

It was decided that the way forward was to base assessment on the achievement of practice requirements – 26 in all – for the six core competences.

EVIDENCE INDICATORS

It was decided next that the further breakdown of competent practice should be provided only as evidence indicators of the type of activities that students would normally undertake in order to provide evidence that they had met the practice requirement.

Taking, as an example, the first practice requirement for the core competence *Assess and plan*, the evidence indicators outline (for the guidance of students and their practice teachers) the types of activity that students might undertake to achieve competence in this practice requirement – *Work in partnership to assess and review people's needs, rights, risks, strengths, responsibilities and resources*:

- identify and evaluate the context and purpose of assessment;
- gather, record and evaluate information to make an assessment;
- work with service users, carers and other professionals to evaluate and review actual and potential needs, strengths, responsibilities and resources;
- establish rights, statutory requirements and organizational responsibilities and priorities;
- identify available resources within own organization, other agencies and support networks;
- formulate and present an assessment and options for action;
- refer people to other agencies as necessary.

Competent practice

The guiding principle of the review was that competence is an integration of knowledge, skills and values and that it is only practice that is founded on values, carried out in a skilled manner and informed by knowledge, critical analysis and reflection, which is competent practice.

It was essential that this guiding principle underlay the development of the assessment requirements for the award, including the values and knowledge requirements and the mandatory 'reflective practitioner' task.

The values requirements

The whole issue of values and how they should be assessed was keenly debated throughout the review and the final outcome was the identification of six value requirements. It was decided that in order to achieve the award of the DipSW, students must demonstrate in meeting the six core competences that they:

- identify and question their own values and prejudices, and their implication for practice;

- respect and value uniqueness and diversity, and recognize and build on strengths;
- promote people's rights to choice, privacy, confidentiality and protection, while recognizing and addressing the complexities of competing rights and demands;
- assist people to increase control of and improve the quality of their lives, while recognizing that control of behaviour will be required at times in order to protect children and adults from harm;
- identify, analyse and take action to counter discrimination, racism, disadvantage, inequality and injustice, using strategies appropriate to role and context;
- practise in a manner that does not stigmatize or disadvantage either individuals, groups or communities.

The approach taken to the assessment of the value requirements was that, since values are integral to rather than separate from competent practice, evidence that value requirements have been met must be drawn from and refer to specific practice undertaken in relation to the six core competences. This was to ensure discrete evidence of the application of values in practice rather than academic pieces of work or students providing evidence through consideration of hypothetical situations. It is also clearly stated in the requirements that students must show clear, consistent and thoughtful integration of values in all assessed work.

Knowledge

A general knowledge base was identified in relation to each of the core competences and it was recognized and required that students would develop a deeper and more extensive understanding of knowledge particularly relevant to the service user group and context of their practice learning opportunities.

The rules and requirements state that students must be assessed on their understanding of relevant knowledge and theory in the context of its application to social work practice and their ability to apply it.

The reflective practitioner

To be effective practitioners, capable professionals, social workers must be able to conceptualize, reflect, analyse and critically evaluate underpinning knowledge and their own practice. They must be strategic thinkers able to weigh up the advantages and disadvantages of proposals and to anticipate the possible consequences of decisions or actions. They should be able to explain in a coherent, comprehensive and convincing manner how their practice is informed by their knowledge base, and be able to apply their knowledge and learning to new situations through appraising what is general and what is particular in each situation. Hence, to achieve the DipSW, students are required to demonstrate transferability of knowledge, skills and values in practice and for final assessment all students must provide evidence of their capacity to reflect on their practice, transfer knowledge, skills and values in practice and understand their responses to change, including their personal learning styles.

Review outcome

In summary and conclusion, we believe the DipSW review achieved all of CCETSW's aims:

- the strength of the innovative partnership with the Care Sector Consortium achieved employment endorsement for the revised DipSW by:
  - keeping the DipSW as the professional qualification, a base for a career in social work and firmly rooted in higher education (thus continuing to bridge the professional and academic frameworks);
  - defining the competences – knowledge, values and practice requirements – for the DipSW from draft national occupational standards, and so ensuring their employment relevance;
  - securing the DipSW in the progressive continuum of qualifications, particularly articulating the bridge with the emerging level 4 VQ awards (thus also bridging the vocational framework).
- the functional analysis (necessary for the development of draft National Occupational Standards) provided a disciplined framework for analysis, and it proved possible to develop and transform it to meet the needs of complex social work, reflective professional practice and holistic assessment of students.
- the competences – knowledge (including the law component), values and practice requirements:
  - ensure the qualification's relevance to changing needs, legislation and service delivery;
  - provide a framework for consistent standards at outcome, to be monitored by external assessors.
- the six core competences provide a model for more flexible modular programmes including open and distance learning provision, and the bridge with level 4 and the removal of any APEL (Assessment of Prior Expereatial Learning) restrictions increase opportunities for access with credit to education, training and qualification, and hence more cost-effective provision.

Finally, and of special relevance to the debate on professional capability, we believe the innovative partnership and incorporative approach provide a model – a case-study – for linking vocational, professional and academic awards, which could be explored further by other professional groups, particularly in the health and care sector.

Chapter 13

Professional competence development: the internal audit experience

Alex Dunlop, Trevor Hassall and Maggie Challis

Summary

The authors of this chapter report from their ongoing study of the nature of professional competence, focusing on the internal audit profession. They deal particularly with the influence of assessment on curriculum content and design.

The chapter reviews the educational process of new members of the internal audit profession both in this country and in the USA, highlighting recent attempts by the American profession to identify essential competencies and to incorporate an assessment of these into the examination process.

The chapter goes on to consider the concept of metacompetence and the use of the two-dimensional approach to assessment developed by Winter (1995). It concludes by recommending greater use of the case-study approach and examines its potential for more effective teaching and assessment.

Introduction

Our earlier work on professional competence in the internal audit profession led us to conclude that there was an ill-advised reliance on the seeking of a well-defined, discretely bounded route to the educational and formative process by which a practitioner might attain professional competence. In order to meet the expectations of all the stakeholders involved, it merited greater initial analysis, particularly longitudinally, in terms of identification and clarification of the point in the novice/expert continuum at which the practitioner presently resided and at which the next stage of development was aimed.

The situation was appropriately described by Eraut (1992) who posed the following questions:

- What is our professional knowledge base?
- What is best learned in higher education, what is best learned in professional practice and what is best learned through an integrated course involving both contexts?
- What has to be learned before qualification and what is best postponed until after qualification?

These are questions that need to be answered by all professional bodies when formulating their education, training and assessment programmes. Poorly planned curricula, focusing largely on the assessment of technical knowledge over a wide range of subjects perceived to be relevant have sought to create the impression of a competent professional, whereas the end result of a protracted shallow-learning process could easily be a less-than-knowledgeable professional. According to Eraut (1995), a major impact of the increasing presence of the National Vocational Qualification (NVQ) system (NCVQ, 1991) has been to place greater pressure on professional bodies to become more explicit as to what a member of a body should be expected to be able to do competently. The notion of explicit standards of competence would seem to fit the demands of modern society to an extent that no politician could possibly ignore.

The natural corollary of such a proposition is for professional bodies to move from the concept (albeit implicit) of a unitary competence level to one of disaggregation and that of 'threshold competence', with stages of progression explicitly delineated. Such a process would be likely to extend beyond what we currently regard as the 'qualification' stage and to continue well into the established career situation.

The internal audit profession provides an effective model for the examination of this process, operating as it does in an international, market-led environment, subject to continuous change and under pressure from users to produce an ever more effective and efficient service. The profession on both sides of the Atlantic has recently, or is currently, reviewing its educational, training and assessment processes. The methodologies used to determine the desirable outputs from these systems provide useful insights into the range of problems likely to be encountered in attempting to strike an acceptable balance between what is optimally desirable (as evaluated) and what is reasonably attainable.

If we attempt to answer the first of Eraut's questions and identify the knowledge base of a profession, to what extent is the way in which practitioners describe this consistent with the way in which it is assessed? Rowntree (1987) notes that assessment shows what is valued within a curriculum. Is assessment effectively exerting control on the curriculum? To what extent does curriculum content become what can be practically assessed rather than what is important?

Eraut (1995) also notes the potential of assessment to influence the rest of the curriculum. Assessment is recognized as being one of the major factors that influence the way in which students approach their learning (Ramsden, 1992). As an alternative to the currently used (and perhaps ultimately most costly in the long term) solution of transferring the real assessment of professional competence to clients/employers, the use of an appropriately structured case-study approach to the teaching and assessment of prospective and developing internal auditors is proposed.

The professionalization process

A useful contribution is made by Johnson (1972, 1984) who suggests that instead of trying to define a profession, it is more useful to consider 'professionalism' as an ideology and 'professionalization' as a process by which an occupation seeks to advance its status and progress in terms of social and economic recognition in a manner consistent with that ideology. One of the first steps in this process is to take responsibility for a prescribed body of knowledge, which the profession concerned must identify. This accords with Moore (1970), who suggests that there are two primary bases for specialization; first, the substantive field of knowledge that the specialist professes to command and second, the application of that knowledge. The internal auditing profession, particularly in the USA, but also in the UK, has made substantive attempts at codifying and implementing these aspects in recent years and these will be referred to later in the chapter. The profession then notionally attempts to enter into a contract with society that allows it exclusive use of this body of knowledge. The basis of this contract is that in order to be able to practise, some guarantee must be given that this practice will be used in a socially responsible way.

This contract is often fulfilled explicitly by a code of ethics that the profession will use to control its members. In the case of the internal audit profession in the UK, members of the Institute of Internal Auditors are required to comply with an official code of ethics, which sets out in detail the standards of conduct expected of them. In describing its purpose, the code states that a distinguishing mark of a profession is acceptance by its members of responsibility to the interests of those it serves. Members must maintain high standards of conduct in order to discharge this responsibility effectively.

One of the ways in which the profession suggests it will facilitate this is to allow only those whom it deems professionally competent to practise. Much will depend on the perceived quality of this professional competence that the profession is seeking or has developed. The question therefore for each profession is, what is this professional competence in their particular case and how should it be identified, developed and assessed?

Pressures for change

The current commercial and political climate has forced all professions to maintain a constant review of the continuing relevance of their perceived realm of activity and the ways in which they address the needs and expectations of the users of their services; none more so than the internal auditing profession.

The American arm of the profession (IIA Inc.) is by far the largest body and dominates the scene internationally. The UK body (IIA UK), was established a few years after the American one, in the 1940s, and has a membership of around 4,000, with currently some 1,000 students. In the UK, the institute largely dominates the educational provision for student members, by means of its own distance learning programme (75 per cent of the total).

In announcing its new examination structure and content (which was subsequently revised), the Institute of Internal Auditors (IIA UK) stated that the new syllabus was designed to meet two important objectives (Radford, 1994). First, it must ultimately be capable of producing a qualification that will be recognized internationally, and second, it must be capable of satisfying NVQ (National Vocational Qualification) level 5 requirements. In addition, current market demands are addressed by the proposals to establish a two-tier qualification, by the introduction of a technician level qualification (subsequently retitled practitioner level), with NVQ level 4 equivalence, which would be a discrete professional qualification in its own right.

In a subsequent article, Izzard (1995) establishes several different objectives for the syllabus review:

- to design a syllabus that reflects the needs of internal auditors;
- to design a package that will attract experienced practitioners and managers as well as the relative novice;
- to market a package that employers will support;
- to design a syllabus that is within IIA UK capability, both professionally and financially.

These are forthright attempts to react to the changing nature of both internal and external demands on the services provided by the profession. The reference to the attainment of NVQ level 5 requirements is further evidence of the desire to move in line with changing market perceptions, in that level 5 is currently the aspirational classification for professional qualifications.

In the last few years in the UK, as elsewhere, there has been an increasing awareness of the role within organizations of systems of corporate governance, a fact which inevitably impacts on the internal auditing profession. The recommendations of the Committee on the Financial Aspects of Corporate Governance (Cadbury Committee) (1992), included the strengthening of systems of internal control, including internal audit, and that boards of companies should report on the effectiveness of these control systems (subsequently altered to a confirmatory review process).

These proposals are still working their way through the development and implementation processes of governance systems, but there can be no doubt as to the fact that the profile of internal audit as part of the control system of organizations has been considerably heightened.

The pressures for change from both within and outside the internal audit profession are giving rise to the demand for a competent internal auditor. This leads us to the question – what is competence?

The concept of competence

Internal audit, as with many other professions, has had its proposed future development in terms of education and training focused by the development of NCVQ and the competence approach. However, the competence approach to professional education and training is not uncontested (Eraut, 1995; Barnett, 1994; Ashworth and Saxton, 1990).

The professional education and training process is concerned with the movement from novice to professional. This movement takes place in a wider environment that is by no means static. The changing expectations in terms of the services offered by the professions and those demanded by the users will mean constant change for the other parts of the model.

An important consideration in terms of the professions is exactly what level of competence is being considered. Studies of the progression from novice to expert such as Dreyfus and Dreyfus (1986) indicate that there are five stages: novice, advanced beginner, competent, proficient and expert. At what stage should someone be allowed to practise independently? Similar concerns also exist concerning the level of student entry and the progression to the ultimate level of expertise.

This movement from novice to expert defines the overall model in terms of depth; the parameters concerning breadth will also be important. In this area the questions concern how general or specific the approach to the area studied needs to be. This will to an extent be determined by decisions made about how this whole area of professional competence is defined.

In trying to identify and measure this we could take the functional approach adopted by NCVQ, which identifies units of competence within an occupational framework. If this approach is taken does it exclude the possibility of synergy, that the sum of all the individual competencies may be greater than the individual parts? This holistic versus atomistic debate is important when defining the factors that come together and are collectively identified in the action, behaviour or outcome that is performance. Competence is concerned with performance, this performance can be evidenced and is therefore capable of assessment. If competence is an ability to do and this is what is being assessed, what does one need to know before one can do and to what extent should the underpinning elements be identified?

What then are the factors that underpin performance and therefore competence? Within the definitions of competence there is mention of several factors. Jessup (1991) in his definition identifies skills, knowledge and understanding. Other taxonomies, notably Carter (1985), extend these headings by the inclusion of one further category, that of personal qualities or attributes. The definitions of these various factors overlap to some extent. For example, Wolf (1990) argues that in a vocational context knowledge and understanding are the same thing.

A major change is evident here in that competence approaches measure performance. It is not acceptable to infer competence by direct measures of knowledge and understanding. This is indicated by Debling and Hallmark (1990), who state that whilst effective performance may depend on ownership of knowledge, such ownership does not guarantee effective performance. The change in approach is also indicated by Jessup (1991), who states that in an ideal world no form of assessment would be needed other than direct observation of performance under normal operating conditions in the workplace. However, in practice it may be too difficult or costly to do this. In this case it is accepted that knowledge might provide supplementary evidence in specific cases. In these instances it is suggested knowledge is assessed in a manner that reveals the potential to transfer competence within the required range and cope with future variations that might occur. This contrasts strongly with the traditional model in which knowledge is assessed and the result is used to predict the likelihood of future competent performance.

If the skilled behaviour of professionals is largely cognitive and is exhibited in complex decision-making, then the inference is that this is a combination of knowledge and cognitive process. The performance of this competent behaviour will be in context and it is vitally important that it is developed in the relevant situation.

Here thinking in terms of capability rather than competence may be useful. Stephenson (1992) indicates this in describing capability as:

not just about skills and knowledge. Taking effective and appropriate action within unfamiliar and changing circumstances involves judgements, values, the self-confidence to take risks and a commitment to learn from the experience.

The competence/knowledge interface in internal audit

As part of the continuing effort to identify the desirable components of the educational and training process of internal auditors, the Institute of Internal Auditors Inc. commissioned a study, completed in 1992, of what was to be called 'A Common Body of Knowledge for the Practice of Internal Auditing' (CBOK). It is in fact the latest in a series of systematic updates that began with the study compiled by Robert Gobeil (1972) and which was continued by Barrett *et al.* by means of an updated version in 1985.

This latest version of the CBOK results from extensive consultation and evidence collection. The study authors were able to make use of the data included in the questionnaire responses from 1,163 practising internal auditors of various levels of operational responsibility. The responses yielded interesting information. The subject areas most frequently selected as being important for internal audit practitioners included several areas conventionally regarded as skills-based or judgmental, such as reasoning, ethics, communication and organizations.

The CBOK study team identified a range of competencies for each subject area and asked respondents to grade these according to their perceived importance to the practising internal auditor. The grading levels ranged from 1 (not important) through to 4 (thorough understanding, ability to make quantitative and qualitative judgements and to apply them to a range of situations), an approach which indicates substantial parallels to the NCVQ approach mentioned earlier.

The ranking of the subject areas used in the study findings used a system based on the percentage of competencies for each subject area, which had a mean greater than 2.5 (with a minimum requirement of two competencies in this range). This approach could be inferred to favour those subject areas with fewer competencies, into which category fall reasoning and ethics, hence the use of the system preferred by Albrecht *et al.* (1993) shown in Table 13.1. Their approach ranks the straightforward arithmetical means of all the competencies in each subject area, thus attempting to give greater effect to the range of competency gradings in each one, producing a remarkably similar result – reasoning, communication and ethics still make up three of the top four subjects.

As could be expected, auditing competencies featured highly on both rankings and, as there were 43 competencies identified with it, this gives a good indication of its importance. In rankings such as the CBOK one, there can be a tendency to downgrade the importance of some of the lower rated subject areas. This would be wrong and dangerous, as any ranking above two indicates, according to the descriptors used in the study, a requirement for the auditor to have an appreciation and an awareness of these areas and they are, in any event, part of the generally accepted CBOK. This would cover areas

Table 13.1 Identification of internal auditor requisite competencies based on the Common Body of Knowledge study of the Institute of Internal Auditors Inc. (1992)

Subject area	Average of all competencies in subject area	Number of competencies in subject area
Reasoning	3.37	4
Communication	3.13	18
Auditing	3.10	43
Ethics	2.96	6
Organizations	2.71	17
Sociology	2.62	11
Fraud	2.58	17
Computers	2.49	39
Financial accounting	2.34	35
Data gathering	2.31	13
Managerial accounting	2.28	16
Government	2.11	9
Legal	2.08	14
Finance	1.96	23
Taxes	1.96	4
Quantitative methods	1.94	12
Marketing	1.91	14
Statistics	1.88	10
Economics	1.82	17
International	1.63	12
Total		334

Source: Albrecht *et al.* (1993), p 57

such as economics, statistics and quantitative methods, which are traditionally associated with internal audit education and receive considerable emphasis in higher education courses and professional examinations.

It was generally agreed that a common body of knowledge for internal auditing does indeed exist, but that the perceptions and needs of individual practitioners change as their position within the organization changes, with areas such as leadership and management becoming more important to those in senior positions.

These findings provide support for the stance taken by the Accounting Education Change Commission (AECC) (1990) in its Position Statement Number 1 on the Objectives of Education for Accountants, when it specified as one of its goals an intention to change the focus in accounting education from knowledge acquisition to one of 'learning to learn'. The latter approach was described as developing in students the motivation and capacity to continue to learn outside the formal educational environment.

The Commission considered that for an academic programme to use a learning to learn approach, it must address three issues:

1. **Content**: this should create a base upon which continued learning can be built, by developing both an understanding of underlying concepts and principles and the ability to apply and adapt them in a variety of contexts and circumstances, both of which are essential to lifelong learning.
2. **Process**: this should focus on developing the ability to identify problems and opportunities, to search out the desired information and to reach a well-reasoned conclusion. To understand the process of inquiry in an unstructured environment is an important aspect of learning to learn.
3. **Attitude**: most importantly, an attitude of continual enquiry and lifelong learning is essential for learning to learn. An attitude of accepting, even thriving on, uncertainty and unstructured situations should be fostered. An attitude of seeking continual improvement, both of self and of the profession, will lead to lifelong learning.

As part of its Statement, the Commission incorporated a composite profile of capabilities needed by accounting graduates. These comprised a series of eight groupings covering both knowledge aspects (eg accounting knowledge) and skills/competency aspects (eg interpersonal skills). Unlike the CBOK study, however, no attempt was made to weight these in any order of perceived importance and so its impact is somewhat diffused.

Possible ways forward – a case-study approach

The implications of the CBOK findings, considered in conjunction with the earlier suggestions as to the nature of professional competence and of the AECC study must be seen to be important for the professional development and assessment processes of internal auditors.

The weightings given in the study to competencies in the nature of skills, rather than discrete or specific knowledge support the conclusions of Jessup (1991) and of Schmidt et al. (1990), in that assessment of performance will best be carried out in relevant situations, which could be the workplace or simulated scenarios. In instances where knowledge assessment has to be used as a surrogate for performance assessment, the process would benefit from the use of techniques such as case-studies (which could even be pre-seen), which would provide some evidence of ability to apply competencies over a range of issues.

The case-study approach to professional education and assessment has been used for several years by the Institute of Chartered Accountants of Scotland (and more recently by the Institute of Chartered Accountants in England and Wales). Allison (1993) maintains that such a case-study-based test of professional competence should be related to the kind of experience obtained from the working environment, which leads to the postulate that experience will result in an improvement in the student's performance in a related examination.

These assertions fit well with the conclusions reached in recent research on the effectiveness of the use of case-studies in accounting education. Hassall *et al.* (1994) provide a detailed review of the potential learning and skills development outcomes that can be derived from the use of case-studies and identify several possible directions for further development and refinement of the medium, including those identified by Easton (1992), who considered case-studies at a non-discipline specific level:

- knowledge;
- analytical skills;
- application skills;
- creative skills;
- decision-making skills;
- communication skills;
- social skills;
- self-analysis skills;
- attitudes.

Argyris (1980) considers the use of case-studies in the business and management area and outlines some of the benefits of case-studies as being:

- hearing others' views;
- confronting differences;
- making decisions;
- becoming aware of the complexity of reality;
- realizing that there are rarely right or wrong answers.

Libby (1991), whose research is in the specific area of accounting education, has identified the benefits of case-studies to students and instructors as follows:

- affective benefits to students:
  - motivation;
  - interest in material;
  - development of confidence.
- skill development of students:
  - oral communication skills;
  - written communication skills;
  - group interaction skills.
- cognitive benefits to students:
  - development of problem-solving skills;
  - development of judgement skills;
  - development of ability to solve problems addressing multiple issues;
  - development of ability to deal with ambiguity;
  - development of an understanding of the real world;
  - comprehension of material.

- affective benefit to instructor:
  - interest in material.

Writing on the potential for the use of case studies in the teaching of accounting, Wines *et al.* (1994) comment on the necessity for accounting courses to be characterized by the important dimension of realism, which is considered to be provided by case-studies. Their use provides the student with a better understanding of the role and limitations of the subject in the modern, dynamic and complex business environment.

The findings of the foregoing commentators indicate that case-studies are most successful at producing learning outcomes, which, in terms of a learning taxonomy calibration, would be considered to be at an advanced level. This is consistent with Romm and Mahler (1991) who argue that case studies and the different types of learning outcomes they produce could fit with professional progression and the different cognitive skills and qualities needed at various stages.

Having identified the potential usefulness of case-studies in the professional development and assessment process, it would be beneficial to attempt to identify a suitable methodology for integrating this with the profile of a competent practitioner, as identified by the professional body involved. We have reviewed the process developed by the Institute of Internal Auditors Inc. in attempting to retain relevance with professional practice, but it was noted that its atomistic approach could give rise to an unstructured and less than synergetic outcome.

A more satisfactory approach might be the two-dimensional process for educational assessment described by Winter (1995) as used in the ASSET (Accreditation and Support for Specified Expertise and Training) programme relating to a competence-based degree in social work. The first dimension to be constructed is a set of 'core assessment criteria', which serves as a framework to ensure that professional practice aspects of the educational process are kept under continuous consideration and act throughout as a guiding and quality control mechanism. The core assessment criteria developed in the particular case instanced by Winter are as follows:

- commitment to professional values;
- continuous professional learning;
- affective awareness;
- effective communication;
- executive effectiveness;
- effective grasp of a wide range of professional knowledge;
- intellectual flexibility.

These criteria were developed following empirical studies of the characteristics of successful academic work and of the categories used by social work practitioners to indicate the qualities required for successful professional practice. Also incorporated were the findings from a theoretical study of the nature of the professional role, with particular reference to interpersonal professional work.

The second dimension is the construction of functional analyses, following discussions with practitioners, to ensure coverage of the requisite units of competence as identified. The competence statements thus developed are similar to the NVQ 'elements of competence' methodology, but differ in the area of evidencing performance. In this case, evidence of competence must be specifically related to at least one of the overriding core assessment criteria, thus ensuring that requisite professional standards are attained throughout.

Attempts to ensure, however, that these broader competences are also embedded within NVQs have been made by means of the personal competence statements in management NVQs and by the Unit 'O' in the field of Health Care. Guidance from NCVQ suggests that these metacompetences should be represented in all NVQs and should be addressed at the initial stages of writing occupational standards.

The recognition of the relevance and role of the metacompetence accords with the contentions of Berman Brown and McCartney (1995). They explain the rationale behind the choice of terminology, in that the prefix 'meta' means 'above' and metacompetences are those abilities, skills and capacities that exist above and beyond any competence which an individual may develop, guiding and sustaining them, and from which they originate. They can be defined as the higher order abilities upon which competencies are based and which have to do with being able to learn, adapt, anticipate and create, rather than with being able to demonstrate that one has the ability to do.

The arguments in favour of a new model of professional development advanced by Velayutham and Perera (1993), whilst making extensive use of the approaches previously delineated by Schön (1983) in *The Reflective Practitioner: How professionals think in action*, are entirely consistent with those of Winter (1995) and Berman Brown and McCartney (1995). Schön (1983) describes reflection-in-action as a process of continual experimentation in the framing of a problem situation and the application of prior knowledge and experience to achieve favourable results. The practitioner is thus constantly having a reflective conversation with the problem situation.

Conclusion

Recognizing the constraints that exist in the case of education and assessment in the internal audit profession (employer disparity, physical distance, commercial pressures), it is suggested that appropriately developed and structured case studies, as an integral part of the assessment process of internal auditors, could play an important part in meeting the full range of competences and in underpinning the quality assurance aspect of the system. The knowledge and competence elements that could most appropriately be assessed via the case-study medium could be identified and form the framework around which the requisite case-study might be developed. These would also form the basis for the preparation of the standard marking and grading approach for student responses to the case.

There would also be an important role in this process for an element of workplace-based assessment. As with most professional bodies, the Institute of Internal Auditors (UK) insists on a three-year practical experience period before a candidate, successful in the conventional examination process, can be admitted to membership. Students are required to maintain a logbook of their work experience, which must be submitted to the Institute for consideration before membership is approved. This process (which commonly coincides with the examination study period), on the part of the student and employer, can largely be unstructured, but it need not be so.

In tandem with the analysis of the elements of knowledge and competence allocated to the case-study method of assessment, an appropriate range can be designated for workplace assessment, with the requirement that, through the medium of the logbook (appropriately structured), the student provides evidence of competence, related always to the relevant core assessment criteria, which will encourage and demonstrate reflection in and on practice and the resulting learning being applied. This procedure will result in there being a more structured and relevant approach to the process of workplace learning and will assist both the student in identifying the place of the workplace experience in the educational process and the employer in structuring work and training programmes in a manner most effective to the student and to the organization.

The writers have begun work on the next stage in their research programme, which is the carrying out of an ethnographic study of internal audit practitioners in the UK, with a view to identifying the range and elements of knowledge and skill that they consider to be necessary to enable an internal auditor to perform effectively and competently; this will facilitate the construction of a framework of requisite knowledge and skills and meta-competences, and should inform future developments in the education and assessment process.

References

Accounting Education Change Commission (1990) 'Objectives of education for accountants: Position Statement Number 1', *Issues in Accounting Education*, Fall, 307–12.

Albrecht, W. S., Stice, J. D. and Stocks, K. D. (1993) 'What do internal auditors need to know?' *Internal Auditor*, October, 57.

Allison, C. M. (1993) 'John Spencer and Co: Auditing as an integral part of a multi-discipline case study', paper presented to the *National Auditing Conference*, Stoke, UK.

Argyris, C. (1980) 'Some limitations of the case method: Experiences in a management development programme', *Academy of Management Review*, **5**(2).

Ashworth, P. D. and Saxton, J. (1990) 'On competence', *Journal of Further and Higher Education*, **14**(2), 3–25.

Barnett, R. (1994) *The Limits of Competence: Knowledge, higher education and society*, Buckingham, Society for Research into Higher Education/Open University Press.

Barrett, R. J. et al. (1985) *A Common Body of Professional Knowledge for Internal Auditors: A research study*, Altamonte Springs, FL, The Institute of Internal Auditors Research Foundation.

Berman Brown, R. and McCartney, S. (1995) 'Competence is not enough: Meta-competence and accounting education', *Accounting Education*, **4**(1), 43–53.

Cadbury, A (1992) Report of the Committee on Financial Aspects of Corporate Governance, London, Committee on Financial Aspects of Corporate Governance.

Carter, R. (1985) 'A taxonomy of objectives for professional education', *Studies in Higher Education*, **10**(2).

Debling, G. and Hallmark, A. (1990) 'Identification and assessment of underpinning knowledge in the context of the UK Government's Standards Programme', in H. Black and A. Wolf (eds) *Knowledge and Competence: Current issues in training and education*, Sheffield, Employment Department.

Dreyfus, H. L. and Dreyfus, S. E. (1986) *Mind over Machine: The power of human intuition and expertise in the era of the computer*, Oxford, Basil Blackwell.

Easton, G. (1992) *Learning from Case Studies*, 2nd edn, London, Prentice Hall.

Eraut, M. (1992) 'Developing the knowledge base: A process perspective on professional education', in R. Barnett (ed.) *Learning to Effect*, Buckingham, Society for Research into Higher Education/Open University Press.

Eraut, M. (1995) 'The role of standards in academic and vocational contexts: Current practice and future possibilities', paper presented at joint HEQC/NCVQ/SCOTVEC Conference, Birmingham, UK.

Gobeil, R. E. (1972) 'The common body of knowledge for internal auditors', *Internal Auditor*, Nov./Dec., 20–9.

Hassall, T., Lewis, S. and Ecclestone, K. (1994) *The Use of Case Studies in Accounting Education: Research papers in accounting no 1*, School of Financial Studies and Law, Sheffield Hallam University, UK.

Izzard, H. (1995) 'Council approves the new MIIA syllabus', *Internal Auditing*, January, 10–12.

Jessup, G. (1991) *Outcomes: NVQs and the emerging model of education and training*, Brighton, Falmer Press.

Johnson, T. J. (1972) *Professions and Power*, London, Macmillan.

Johnson, T. J. (1984) 'Professionalism: Occupation or ideology?', in S. Goodlad (ed.) *Education for the Professions: Quis custodiet?* London, SHRE and NFER-Nelson.

Libby, P. A. (1991) 'Barriers to using cases in accounting education', *Issues in Accounting Education*, **6**(2).

Moore, W. (1970) *The Professions*, New York, Russell Sage Foundation.

NCVQ (1991) *Criteria for National Vocational Qualifications*, London, National Council for Vocational Qualifications.

Radford, P. (1994) 'Syllabus review: into the next millenium', *Internal Auditing*, April, 22–25.

Ramsden, P. (1992) *Learning to Teach in Higher Education*, London, Routledge.

Romm, T. and Mahler, S. (1991) 'The case study challenge: A new approach to an old method', *Management Education and Development*, **22**(4), 292–301.

Rowntree, D. (1987) *Assessing Students*, London, Harper & Row.

Schmidt, H. G., Norman, G. R. and Boshuizen, H. P. A. (1990) 'A cognitive perspective on medical expertise: Theory and implications', *Academic Medicine*, **65** (10), 611–21.

Schön, D. A. (1983) *The Reflective Practitioner: How professionals think in action*, New York, Basic Books.

Stephenson, J. (1992) 'Capability and quality in higher education', in J. Stephenson and S. Weil (eds) *Quality in Learning*, London, Kogan Page.

Velayutham, S. and Perera, H. (1993) 'The reflective accountant: Towards a new model for professional development', *Accounting Education*, **2**(4), 287–301.

Wines, G., Carnegie G., Boyce G. and Gibson R. (1994) *Using Case Studies in the Teaching of Accounting*, Australian Society of Certified Practising Accountants.

Winter, R. (1995) 'The assessment of professional competences: The importance of general criteria', in A. Edwards and P. Knight (eds) *Assessing Competence in Higher Education*, London, Kogan Page.

Wolf, A. (1990) 'Defining the knowledge component', in H. Black and A. Wolf (eds) *Knowledge and Competence: Current issues in training and education*, Sheffield, Employment Department.

Chapter 14

Delivering relevant higher education to the workplace

Geoffrey W. Beeson

Summary

As in the UK, Australian higher education is developing stronger links with industry and more active involvement in continuing professional development. In this chapter Geoffrey Beeson describes the development of a flexible, work-based first degree in technology management. Positioned to assist technical employees in manufacturing to develop management abilities, it is designed to enable full-time workers to learn without major disruptions to work and personal commitments.

The programme makes use of varied learning materials coupled with tutor contact by telephone, fax and e-mail as well as workplace tutorials. A credit-based approach offers multiple entry and exit points as well as a facility to take prior learning into account. Initial evaluations from students and representatives of sponsoring companies are positive, with the ability of the programme to fit around work schedules and students' personal lives being particularly welcomed.

Introduction

I have tried a number of methods of study and my personal belief is that [this] is still the best one I have come across. I was doing night school at [a college of advanced education] and that used to drain me, and one of the reasons that I didn't complete the course there was because I was too tired going from work to lectures and spending until 10 o'clock at night just doing two subjects every six months... It wasn't flexible enough for me. (employee-student)

It's helped me to become more of a group learner than I was when I first started doing the certificate. I've learnt how to work in a group better and how a group works so that everyone pulls their weight and is not just a giver or a taker. (employee-student)

The concept of the course is fantastic in relationship to the training we require. . . we need to look at raising the technical competence level of our staff. . . (training manager)

These comments were made about an innovative bachelor degree programme designed to meet identified needs of manufacturing industry while conforming to the normal requirements of an undergraduate degree in applied science. The Bachelor of Applied Science (Technology Management) at Deakin University was designed in consultation with manufacturing industry to meet an expressed need for graduates with knowledge and skills in new technologies and management, integrated in a way which would reflect the way technological products were then and in the future would be manufactured, marketed and sold. There was a need for the course to be accessible to those in full-time employment with little or no disruption to their current work activities, and to take into account the wide variation in education, training, and experience amongst them, and in their further education and training needs.

The development of this new course reflected two emerging forces in education and training in Australia: a growing recognition of the importance of continuing professional development, and renewed pressure for a strengthening of links between higher education and industry. Wider acceptance of the need for continuing professional development has been stimulated by a relentless increase in the general rate of change, including changes in the nature and context of work (especially technological change), changes in employment patterns, and a recognition that most people in developed societies will experience several career changes during their working lives. An orientation toward ongoing and self-directed learning, and a capacity to deal effectively with changing and complex situations are key requirements of the capable professional practitioner.

This chapter outlines the initial implementation and evaluation of the Bachelor of Applied Science (Technology Management) and its further development and application, based on experience gained from the early programmes, to support more effectively the development of the capable professional practitioner.

A new programme to meet emerging needs

The technology management programme was based on results from a survey of the education and training requirements of local manufacturing and computing companies by the Faculty of Science and Technology at Deakin University and a subsequent needs analysis in two large automotive manufacturers. These identified a need for graduates with knowledge and skills in new technologies and management. There had also been persistent requests over a period of time for an undergraduate programme for technically orientated employees that would give them the necessary technological and managerial knowledge and skills to move into decision-making positions in the manufacturing industry. Key areas of need included the use of technically sophisticated equipment, quality control and product reliability, establishing and operating in world markets, technical documentation, and recruiting and retraining skilled workers. While not new or different in themselves, the existence of these collected needs demanded a new combination of knowledge, understanding and skills. The development of such a combination resulted in a new specialization, technology management, in the existing applied science degree.

Specializations in the established applied science degree already existed in environmental management, information management, health promotion and the management of hazardous materials. The new programme conformed to the basic structure of the existing degree, having foundation studies (knowledge and skills fundamental to the course), a science sequence (studies in the relevant specialization), and optional studies (complementary studies of students' choice). However, there were important structural differences in that the new programme was not built around the three years full-time or six years part-time completion schedule of the existing courses, and there was a planned availability of a sequence of awards. Three different, nationally recognized awards were available, at successively higher levels, depending on the number and combination of units satisfactorily completed (see Figure 14.1).

Nature of the programme

The key features of the programme, designed to meet the requirements outlined, are summarized below. The combination of these features resulted in the capacity to meet identified needs of students in a way in which other, more traditional higher education courses have not.

Industry-relevant content

The content of the course was significantly influenced by the needs of industry, and was tailored for the three specific award outcomes indicated in Figure 14.1. The certificate level studies were relevant to basic supervision and management in a technological environment, and provided students with the knowledge and skills to progress to the next award level. At the associate diploma level the employment focus was middle management. Consequently, the content was aimed at developing a mix of technical and

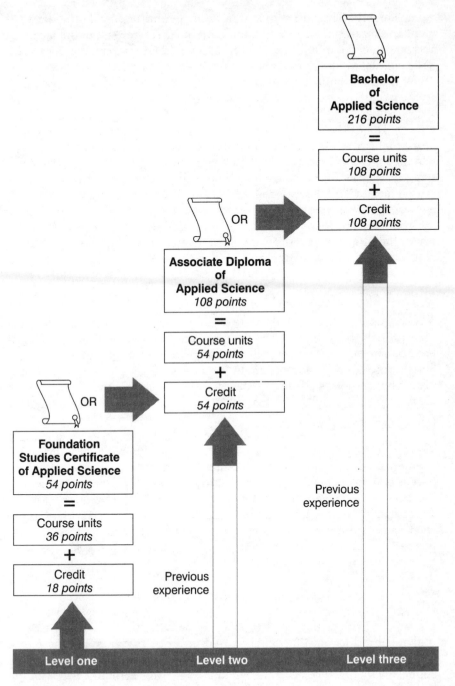

Figure 14.1 Awards available in the programme

management skills, especially in computing, and at managing the development and marketing of a technological product. The content of the technical and management units at the degree level was relevant to more senior management, with emphasis on project management and the role of new technology in the manufacture of a technological product.

Recognition of prior learning

Students had the opportunity of gaining credit for relevant prior learning – whether this learning was through formal education or training, in-house training, or uncertificated learning. In this project, the process used for determining what credit, if any, should be given for prior learning was originally developed using experience elsewhere as a starting point, and subsequently incorporating knowledge gained through assessing prior learning in the context of the project. The process involved the use of predetermined criteria, a questionnaire, and student interviews.

Multiple entry points

A consequence of giving appropriate credit for relevant prior learning was that students were able to enter the programme at different levels, dependent on their prior knowledge. Such an approach conserves resources and is less inclined to stifle students' motivation through the unnecessary reteaching of course content already mastered.

Workplace-based learning

The course was delivered to the workplace – initially two vehicle manufacturing plants. Students worked through the learning materials at their own pace and at times convenient to them; tutorial sessions were arranged in conjunction with the employer and were conducted on site by university academic staff. Apart from these tutorial sessions, which averaged two hours per week, time allowances for students were confined to introductory on-campus sessions at the start of the course and a mid-course feedback session of one hour involving students, lecturers, project managers and employer representatives.

Self-paced learning

Individualized learning materials, based on print, audio and video media were developed to allow for varying rates of progress. The materials were supported by the tutorials at the workplace, e-mail communication with the tutor, and computer-managed progression.

E-mail

Each student was provided with the use of a laptop computer and modem at the start of the course to enable 24-hour communication with the tutor and the project management via a university central computer. This enabled students to get queries answered and problems resolved as they proceeded and to deliver assessment material to the tutor by electronic rather than printed means.

Computer-managed learning (CML)

This application software running on a central university computer supported the management of both tutor-based and individualized learning. It provided objectives, directions for learning and assessment tasks. Students could attempt the relevant assessment tasks at any time, and proceed to new learning units once defined criteria had been met.

Nationally recognized award at each of three exit points

The BAppSc (Technology Management) course structure provided for a nationally recognized award – certificate, associate diploma, or degree – on completion of each major level of study.

The programme was first implemented with two pilot groups, consisting of 32 and 36 employee-students respectively, in 1990. Successive groups, with increased numbers of employee-students from a wide range of businesses and industries, followed in subsequent years. Progressive modifications and developments were made, based on feedback from evaluations and on the needs of the businesses joining the programme. Further details about the programme and its evaluation may be found elsewhere (Beeson et al., 1992; 1993).

Evaluation

Evaluations were carried out in three major phases. The first phase focused on the two pilot groups and their work at the certificate level. The 68 students in these two groups were employed in two vehicle manufacturing companies and consisted of 60 men and eight women. Their ages ranged from 20 to 52 with a mean of 34 years. Twenty of these had completed Year 12 of formal schooling, and a further six had a higher education qualification. Twenty-six had completed less than Year 10 of formal schooling. The main focus of the evaluation was on the extent to which the course and its methods of delivery satisfied the needs of the students and of the employers who were supporting their study. Data were gathered from three main source areas: course records and individuals in two groups – a primary group consisting of students and employer representatives, and a secondary group made up of course lecturers and programme managers.

The second phase examined the programme at associate diploma level in 1991, also with the two pilot groups. The third evaluation phase was more extensive, running from March 1992 to April 1993 and covering all levels of the programme. By this time the number of students had expanded to more than 500 from ten companies involved in manufacturing, distribution, packaging and service. A total of 163 students (139 male, 24 female), including 17 discontinued students, and representatives from eight companies, took part in this phase of the evaluation.

The results of the study showed that, overwhelmingly, students, client companies and Deakin University staff involved with the course endorsed the suitability and effectiveness of the delivery methods used. Students liked its flexibility in allowing them to study at times and places convenient to them. In the great majority of cases, study location was the home and study time was evenings and weekends. Many of the students who were successful in the technology management programme had previously attempted on-campus courses at a university or TAFE college but had dropped out before completing their courses. The need to fit in study requirements with work, family and personal or social commitments was clearly an important consideration.

The ability to study at their own rates was also strongly appreciated by the students. Despite some differences concerning the extent to which the programme allowed rates of working to vary, feedback indicated that this was a key component of the delivery method. The opportunity to gain credit for previous relevant learning, whether via a formal award or not, was also strongly endorsed.

The flexibility of time and place of study, together with the ability to work at their own rates and to have prior relevant learning credited, allowed many of the students to 'get back into study' towards a formal award. In several cases, this was initially attempted with some apprehension, but the mix of these four delivery features made it easier for these 'new start' students to try their hand.

Typical comments from students were:

The beauty of this course is that we don't have to do evening classes. That's one of the strongest points. You can sit down and do the course without being separated from the family, which is very important. It's a terrific way of doing it.

The self-paced aspect of the course is good. However, unless you are very hard on yourself it is easy to get sidetracked.

Overall, the students considered they had appropriate and sufficient contact with their lecturers and with other students, although, as might be expected, there was some variation from student to student and from lecturer to lecturer. Contact with lecturers was almost exclusively through workplace tutorials, telephone, fax and e-mail. Contact with other students was through the workplace tutorials and through other contacts at the workplace. In most cases the students arranged a semi-structured set of contact arrangements with their fellow students at the same workplace. The students valued the contacts with both lecturers and their fellow students, and considered both important in the context of the course delivery methods.

Company training managers and workplace supervisors also expressed strong support for the course delivery methods and for the programme as a whole. Lecturers teaching the course reported positive views of the course and its delivery methods. Not surprisingly, they held a wide variety of views about the various delivery features and their implementation, and made a number of suggestions for modification. Some lecturers found a considerable adjustment was needed in taking on a teaching role in the programme.

Comments made by company representatives included observations such as:

[The programme] is very beneficial to our company... For staff to go along to a... college, to pull them off the job is extremely expensive and ineffective... we have no control over that [on-campus] learning and we would have no input as to whether that learning was appropriate to the needs of the organization.

Because of the relatively short time the programme had been running when the evaluation data were collected, information concerning student rates of progression through the course were preliminary. However, the information that was available indicated progression rates that compared favourably with other undergraduate courses, especially off-campus courses. Nearly all the discontinued students interviewed reported favourable attitudes towards the course and a desire to complete it when their circumstances allowed.

Recent developments

Based on feedback from the major evaluations referred to above, including specific suggestions from students and company representatives, the technology management programme has continued to expand in the period to 1998. This expansion has been considerable and has involved both the number of employee-students and the number of participating companies, including government departments. Along with this expansion to a wider range of client companies and employees, there have been further developments and modifications to the way the programme is offered. Programme options at the lower levels (university certificate and diploma) have been expanded and tailored to meet the needs of specific client groups. These options include both generic and specialist studies. The generic programmes provide a framework within which the specialist programmes may be developed. The study materials can be adapted to suit the needs of the particular client groups and be given an enterprise slant, as appropriate.

The changes to the technology management programme have reflected the changes in employment and Australian industrial and business environments and research cultures, and in the use of new technologies in course delivery, that have occurred since the programme was first introduced in 1990. A significant feature of the programme is in providing articulated pathways for students from the certificate level, which may involve shop floor employees, through to a degree programme that provides access to tertiary education. At the lower levels, the course may be tightly structured in order for the company to achieve its training objectives, but as students progress through the awards, the emphasis shifts to their individual career and staff development.

At the university certificate level, students are accepted into the programme through a negotiated process with the relevant company and this is based on approved professional and/or work experience. Progression thereafter is based on academic performance. Most students enter the programme at the university certificate level and progress through the awards, following the articulated model.

Technology management programmes are now offered by both Deakin University through its award courses in science, engineering and technology, and through Deakin Australia, the University's commercial division, which provides education and training to large corporations, government departments and professional associations. The technology management programme complements the Deakin Australia offerings in management, education and training. Programme improvements, and an increased number of course delivery options have been introduced as new and improved technologies for supporting course delivery have become available. A range of methods of teaching are employed, including computer-mediated communication, small group tutorial sessions, computer-aided instruction, and audio and/or video teleconferencing. The optional studies and science major study can also be undertaken on campus if students choose. Units taught on campus utilize a range of teaching methods, including laboratory-based classes, lectures, tutorials and fieldwork, as appropriate. A comprehensive description of the changes, developments and outcomes of the technology management programme is being published separately.

Concluding comments

The technology management programme began, and has continued, as a coherent group of course options designed to meet the needs of industry employees, and the industries themselves, for relevant higher education.

These needs have been for the ongoing development of capable professional practitioners in a range of fields covering technology, science and management. Employees and companies have both identified the need for people who are not only competent in a particular job at a particular period of time, but who also have relevant knowledge, skills and dispositions that they are able to apply in ways which enable them to solve new problems and master new situations in a continually changing world. Employee-students and companies involved with the technology management programme have all shown they are willing to take action to meet these needs. The technology management programme has been, and continues to be, successful because it has focused on meeting identified needs – of employee-students, of client companies and of national higher education awards. It has taken advantage of new technologies to provide greater flexibility and a higher level of learning support for students than would otherwise have been possible. It has also been prepared to change, as companies' needs develop and change, as new and improved teaching technologies and methods become available, and on the basis of feedback from students and companies about the programme. Throughout, its focus has remained developing the capable professional practitioner.

Note
The first implementation of the programme was carried out in collaboration with Box Hill Institute of TAFE (Technical and Further Education), a regional college offering award courses to trade, technician, and paraprofessional levels, and non-award further education and training activities. Some of the early research, development of course materials, and the pilot group evaluation was supported by funds from the Victorian Education Foundation.

References

Beeson, G.W., Stokes, D.M., and Symmonds, H.C. (1992) 'An innovative higher education course to meet industry's needs', *Higher Education Research and Development*, **11** (1), 21–38.
Beeson, G.W., Stokes, D.M., and Symmonds, H.C. (1993) *Flexible Delivery to the Workplace of a Bachelor of Applied Science Course: An evaluation*, Canberra, Australian Government Publishing Service.

Chapter 15:

The skills of graduates: a small enterprise perspective

Mantz Yorke

Summary

This chapter presents the findings of a survey of 104 small enterprises in Merseyside, conducted by the Centre for Higher Education Development at Liverpool John Moores University and supported by the European Social Fund. The survey sought to discover what small businesses expected of graduates in the way of skills and attributes, and found a number of common expectations within a sample of diverse size and sectors, consistent with the notion of capability.

The outcomes of the survey are set against the intended outcomes of a sample of curricula operating in local higher education institutions. Although the curricula surveyed sought to inculcate transferable skills, the skills for the most part were those typically associated with academic work. The broader notion of capability figured only to a limited extent.

This generates discussion about the capability approach to higher education and the extent to which programmes should be designed to promote employability in graduates.

Graduates and small/medium enterprises

It is widely accepted that the small and medium enterprise (SME) sector is of high importance for national economies, and that it will recruit in fair measure from graduates and diplomates leaving higher education. Connor *et al.*

(1996) reported that one in four graduates are employed in small enterprises, and that graduates constituted 8 per cent of employees in enterprises with fewer than 25 staff, findings that were broadly replicated in a study of 1,000 graduates from the University of Sussex (Connor and Pollard, 1996).

The larger employers have a number of fora in which their expectations of graduates can be expressed, but smaller enterprises find – for obvious reasons of size and dispersion – some difficulty in joining in discussions of how they can draw on, and contribute to, the outcomes of higher education.

Surveys of expectations, such as that conducted by Harvey and Green (1994) in which only six of the 127 responses came from SMEs, underrepresent the SMEs' perspectives. Even when greater attention is given to SMEs the numbers tend to be small, reflecting the methodological difficulties inherent in approaching such a diverse and dispersed collection of enterprises. For example, Johnson and Péré-Vergé (1993) collected data from 23 enterprises, and Harvey et al. (1997) obtained responses from some 30 small enterprises.

Harvey and Green (1994, p 76) suggest that:

higher education institutions [HEIs] should:

- attempt to involve employers on a partnership basis at all stages of course development and subsequent monitoring rather than seeking *post hoc* reactions to course provision;
- facilitate pro-active approaches from employers by ensuring clear lines of communication via identified and accessible contact points;
- ensure that there is sufficient opportunity for academic staff to develop the appropriate skills to integrate and assess skills alongside knowledge;
- encourage a reflective and responsive approach to employer views and thus help to develop an approach that empowers students for lifelong learning.

Looked at from the point of view of the relationships between higher education institutions and SMEs, the practical difficulties are obvious. In any region there are many SMEs, ranging from a mere handful of employees to organizations employing quite large numbers of people. There are various organizations, such as 'Business Bridges', which bring institutions and SMEs together for purposes such as technology transfer. However, there are relatively few opportunities for the parties to get together to discuss the nature of curricula in higher education and how these reflect, or might reflect, the needs of SMEs.

A first step in the development of a dialogue of this kind was seen as the surveying of the expectations of a sample of such enterprises, together with some analysis of institutional curricula in order to determine the extent to which the enterprises' expectations might be reflected in them. A project of this sort was seen as having the potential to contribute to the following:

- the development of curricula in HEIs;
- improved liaison between HEIs and SMEs in the region (notwithstanding the existence of a Business Bridge and other initiatives); and possibly
- some improvement in the match between the outcomes of higher education and the needs of SMEs.

This chapter reports the outcomes of such a project, the bulk of the work of which was conducted in 1995.

Method

Small enterprise survey

It was decided, given the resources available, that it would be possible to survey around 100 small enterprises. An interview-based approach was chosen because it was felt that questionnaires would elicit a small number of responses. It was also recognized that participating enterprises would probably be able to devote only a limited amount of time to this survey, and hence a brief structured interview schedule was constructed, which sought some background information and invited them to indicate which skills and attributes from a provided list were 'very important' or 'important' to their operations. The lists of skills and attributes (see Table 15.1) were based upon the much longer list used by Harvey and Green (1994), which was deemed to be too lengthy for this project's purposes.

Six groupings of small enterprises were selected for the survey on the twin bases of relevance to the regional economy and likely relation to the 'output' from the three Liverpool HEIs. The match between the two bases for choice was not perfect: for example, none of the HEIs runs programmes explicitly linked to printing, or to hotels and tourism. The enterprises actually surveyed constituted an opportunity sample of those that were approached for assistance (see Table 15.2). Thirty-nine per cent of the approached enterprises took part in the survey.

Although the intention at the outset was to sample from enterprises with between 10 and 99 employees, thus concentrating on the category of 'small' enterprises (DTI, 1995), it proved necessary to approach some 'micro' enterprises because there were too few small enterprises available for survey in some of the selected groupings.

One or other of the two research assistants visited the people responsible for recruitment at each company and, after eliciting some brief background information (such as whether they employed graduates, were thinking of employing them, or had no particular intention of doing so), presented them with the lists of skills and attributes. Respondents were asked to indicate which five of each were very important to them and then which were

Table 15.1 The list of skills and attributes used in the project

Skills	Attributes
Ability to plan	Work under pressure
Organize events	Ambition
Handle own workload	Commitment to work
Handle finances	Get on with people
Manage others	Dependability
Computer literacy	Energy
Awareness of how organizations work	Work varied hours
Numeracy	Imagination/creativity
Present a case	Inventiveness
Individual problem-solving	Take the initiative
Group problem-solving	Cope with variety of challenges
Team-working	Self-confidence
Written communication	Willingness to learn
Oral communication	
Get to the heart of a problem	
Summarize key issues	
Critical analysis	
Foreign language skills	

Table 15.2 The sample of small enterprises surveyed

Group	Number approached	Number surveyed	Percentage surveyed
Communications/media	32	21	66
Hotel/tourism/leisure	48	13	27
Advertising/marketing/PR	55	16	29
Manufacturing	53	21	40
Information technology	40	15	38
Printing	42	18	43
Overall	**270**	**104**	**39**

(merely) important. There was an opportunity to add further skills and attributes to each list but, in the event, hardly any were added.

Curriculum analysis

A sample of curricula running in each of the three Liverpool HEIs was subjected to a content analysis. Particular attention was given to what was being assessed, since this – probably to a greater extent than programme aims or the expectations set for particular curricular units (as objectives or learning outcomes) – gives an indication of what the curriculum 'is really looking for'.

This work was conducted by staff in each of the institutions involved, and dealt with programmes – selected for at least a partial fit with the enterprises being surveyed – in the areas of visual and performance arts, humanities, science, information technology, engineering and business studies.

Results

Characteristics of the six groups

MANUFACTURING

Of the six companies interviewed, those which employed graduates did so in a variety of roles and hence their responses to the survey diverged. Most of the companies interviewed that employed graduates were well established and older in comparison to those that did not. They also tended to be larger.

INFORMATION TECHNOLOGY

Most of the IT companies in the Merseyside area tend to be either satellite offices of larger companies or small consultancy firms, with the larger companies having headquarters in London or Manchester. Of the free-standing enterprises, most were no more than 15 years old and most employed graduates. In IT-related enterprises there was a definite orientation towards the recruitment of graduates.

PRINTING

Companies in this category fell into two groups. The first group included many companies that offered only the traditional printing service and thus appear to have no need for graduate expertise: most of the processes used were automated and required limited semi-skilled attention. On the other hand, the development of IT was forcing companies to invest heavily; more skilled people were required, and there was a greater need for graduates in some of the companies. However, the sample contacted was heavily skewed toward the provision of the traditional printing service.

COMMUNICATIONS AND MEDIA

Due to the nature of the industry, it is extremely rare to find independent companies in Merseyside that employ ten or more people on a permanent basis. Hence it was decided that the study would include some companies that employed fewer than ten people. Amongst the sampled enterprises in this sub-category there was a strong bias towards those that employed graduates.

HOTELS, TOURISM AND LEISURE

It proved extremely difficult to find hotels on Merseyside that were both within the specified employee range and also independent. There was also difficulty in arranging appointments with those that did fulfil the project's criteria since the staff responsible for recruitment were often extremely busy.

ADVERTISING, MARKETING AND PUBLIC RELATIONS

There is within this sector a distinction to be made between those who are employed on the creative side and those who work on accounts. The skills and attributes highlighted by respondents depended very much on where they were located in the industry. The increased use of IT had, according to some, led to a decrease in the number of people being employed.

Expectations of the small enterprise

A rough and ready index of enterprises' perceptions of the importance of skills and attributes was completed by weighting 'very important' twice as heavily as 'important', and computing a mean importance score. A mean importance score of 60 per cent of the maximum was taken as indicating particular importance to that group of enterprises. Tables 15.3 and 15.4 summarize the main findings in respect of skills and attributes.

Table 15.3 The enterprises' perceptions of particularly important skills

Group	Communications/ media	Advertising, marketing, PR	Hotel, tourism, leisure	Manufac- turing	IT	Printing
Experience of graduates (some/none)	(16/5)	(10/6)	(5/8)	(11/10)	(10/5)	(4/14)
Skill						
Oral communication	✓	✓	✓(<)		✓(<)	
Ability to plan	✓(>)					
Handle own workload	✓(>)	✓(<)		✓(<)	✓(>)	✓(>)
Teamworking		✓	✓			
Manage others			✓(<)			
Get to heart of problem				✓(<)	✓(>)	
Critical analysis				✓(>)		
Ability to summarize					✓	
Group problem-solving					✓(>)	

Note: (>) markedly greater emphasis given by those with experience of graduates; (<) markedly greater emphasis given by those with no experience of graduates.

Table 15.4 The enterprises' perceptions of particularly important attributes

Group	Communications/ media	Advertising, marketing, PR	Hotel, tourism, leisure	Manufac- turing	IT	Printing
Experience of graduates (some/none)	(16/5)	(10/6)	(5/8)	(11/10)	(10/5)	(4/14)
Attribute						
Work under pressure	✓(<)	✓	✓(<)	✓(<)	✓(<)	✓
Work varied hours	✓(<)					
Commitment	✓	✓	✓(<)	✓(<)	✓	✓(<)
Dependability	✓	✓(<)	✓		✓(<)	
Imagination / creativity		✓				
Get on with people				✓		
Willingness to learn					✓(<)	✓(<)

Note: (>) markedly greater emphasis given by those with experience of graduates; (<) markedly greater emphasis given by those with no experience of graduates.

Curricular analyses

There is only space to provide a few brief findings from the analyses of the selected curricula that were running in the three institutions.

There was, in these institutions, a broad commitment to developing the capacity of students to act effectively in the wider world – in one case the Enterprise in Higher Education initiative had provided funding for relevant developments. Some of the programmes made explicit reference to the development of transferable skills through the pursuit of academic study.

An investigation of what was revealed by the assessment demands of the programmes showed that there tended to be a slippage between what programmes aimed to achieve and what was actually assessed. Transferable skills such as critical thinking, construction of an argument, working to deadlines, and so on are those that have normally been subsumed within academic studies. Other skills, such as teamwork and giving oral presentations, were less in evidence. Where, for example, oral presentation was assessed, it tended to count for a relatively small proportion of the marks available, and team-working tended to be implicit in the expectation of reports of periods of work experience. It is probable that a pattern such as this would be found quite widely in higher education.

Only one of the sampled programmes made a substantial reference to the needs of small businesses. As well as referring to the need to gain an understanding of large organizations and the variety of roles occupied by professionals, this particular programme expected students to gain the following:

- an awareness of how a small business is established and managed;
- an understanding of financial planning operations;
- an understanding of the methods of setting up a workshop;
- an awareness of the legal restraints and liabilities that affect the designer and manufacturer.

The problem with this study-unit was that its assessment related to the handling of various aspects of costs and the formulation of a business plan. Apparently missing were all those 'live dynamics' that play such a large part in organizational effectiveness.

Discussion

Tables 15.3 and 15.4 show that the surveyed enterprises generally desire a number of skills and attributes that are consistent with the notion of capability (Stephenson and Weil, 1992), in that they underpin effective performance; handling one's own workload, being able to work under pressure, commitment, dependability, and oral communication are valued strongly across the spectrum of the sample. In smaller enterprises it is particularly likely that employees will be expected to turn their hands to a number of activities, perhaps with relatively less support than their peers in larger organizations might receive. They will need to be flexible and – as the Association of Graduate Recruiters (AGR, 1995) suggests – adaptable and self-reliant. There would seem to be few, if any, 'easy rides' in the small enterprises sampled!

The survey of small enterprises revealed some marked differences between the groups regarding the employment of graduates: communications and media enterprises tended strongly to employ them whereas printing enterprises were much less likely to do so, perhaps because printing has fully to come to terms with the implications of developments on the information technology front and the decline of its traditional craft base.

It is important to acknowledge, of course, that the responses of enterprises that have little or no experience of graduates are necessarily hypothetical in character, and that what enterprises say they want may not be what they need. There is scope for more dialogue between such enterprises and higher education if mutual understanding and benefit are to be maximized. Given the diversity and dispersion of the former, this is obviously no easy task.

This admittedly limited survey nevertheless provides evidence of differentiation within the small enterprise sector, and that it would be a mistake to construe such enterprises collectively in monolithic terms. Even within the groups sampled here there is evidence of diversity (eg printing). The consequence is that it is presumptuous to seek to offer a definitive list of desired skills and attributes for small enterprises as a whole.

At first glance, there is quite a wide gap between the companies' expectations and what the selected higher education programmes seek to achieve. However, it is likely that a fair amount of learning relevant to the enterprises' expectations actually takes place as a by-product of students' experiences in higher education. The difficulty lies, perhaps, in making the 'capability' aspects of higher education more manifest through developments in curriculum design and assessment, which make no compromises with the notion of 'graduateness' (see HEQC, 1996). A fully worked-out implementation of a capability approach to higher education implies that some programmes of study would have to undergo a change that could be quite radical in nature, and that would need more than rhetorical support from the world of employment.

Conclusion

This limited study has highlighted the following:

- the well-known diversity of the small enterprise sector;
- that in this diverse sector there are some generally held expectations regarding graduates, and also some differences in expectation;
- that it appears, in a selection of higher education programmes, that relatively little attention is given to the development of capability in its full sense, although the development of a number of transferable skills related to academic work is featured;
- that there is probably some scope for greater harmonization between the expectations of small enterprises and the skills and attributes that programmes in higher education seek to foster.

This last point should not be taken as implying a narrow instrumentalism on the part of higher education. If writing on the labour market such as that of Reich (1991), the Association of Graduate Recruiters (AGR, 1995) and Harvey et al. (1997) is correct – and the recent quiet questioning by the government of the size of the UK's output of graduates sharpens the point – then success, for both graduates and enterprises, is likely to depend on the capacity to handle rapid and at times disturbing change. Higher education owes it to its students to ensure that they are as capable as possible of dealing with the challenges that they are likely to face.

Acknowledgements

The support of the European Social Fund is gratefully acknowledged. Thanks are also due to Phil Spruce and Wendy Stonefield who were the research assistants to the project, to Ian Taylor and Vicky Cartwright (University of Liverpool), and to Jill Armstrong and Michelle Verity (Liverpool Hope University College) who contributed to the curricular analyses undertaken in the project.

References

AGR (1995) *Skills for Graduates in the 21st Century*, Cambridge, Association of Graduate Recruiters.

Connor, H., Pearson, R., Court, G. and Jagger, N. (1996) *University Challenge: Student choices in the 21st century*, Report 306, Brighton, The Institute for Employment Studies, University of Sussex.

Connor, H. and Pollard, E. (1996) *What Do Graduates Really Do?* Report 308, Brighton, The Institute for Employment Studies, University of Sussex.

DTI (1995) *Small Firms in Britain 1995*, London, HMSO.

Harvey, L. and Green, D. (1994) *Employer Satisfaction*, Birmingham, University of Central England.

Harvey, L., Moon, S., Geall, V., with Bower, R., (1997) *Graduates Work: Organizational change and students' attributes*, Birmingham, Centre for Research into Quality, University of Central England.

HEQC (1996) *Graduate Standards Programme: Draft report and recommendations*, London, Higher Education Quality Council.

Johnson, D. and Péré-Vergé, L. (1993) 'Attitudes towards graduate employment in the SME sector', *International Small Business Journal*, **11**(4), 65–70.

Reich, R. B. (1991) *The Work of Nations*, London, Simon & Schuster.

Stephenson, J. and Weil, S. (1992) *Quality in Learning: A capability approach to higher education*, London, Kogan Page.

Part Five

Values and Models

Chapter 16

Conceptualizing competence and reflective practice: a feminist perspective

Mary Issitt

Summary

Drawing on the human service professions, Mary Issitt applies a feminist critique to developing professional capability in work settings.

While there are parallels between feminist and reflective practice approaches to professionalism, particularly through their rejection of positivist models of practice and development, there has been limited dialogue between them. A feminist reflective practice model is proposed, which highlights the need to be aware of power relationships and political dimensions in professional practice. Although reflective practitioner and feminist approaches are intrinsically concerned with competent practice, the current preoccupation in the UK with a model of competence purporting to reflect 'objective' task performance is a cause for concern: as well as being oversimplistic, it serves as a measure of social control that reinforces existing power relations and gender inequalities.

The chapter concludes by proposing that an integrated model of learning is needed, which goes beyond individualized, atomistic conceptions of competence and enables practitioners to develop the criticality and creativity central to feminist reflective practice.

Introduction

During the last decade or more a paradigm shift has taken place in professional education and training whereby the workplace has become promoted as the setting in which learning is demonstrated, assessed and developed. As this takes root in human service professions such as youth and community work, social work, teaching and health-based work, two key concepts feature in the discourse apparently promising to offer professionals certainty about how to be effective within the complexity and contradictions of post-modernity. The first concept – that of competence – has a variety of meanings and applications from the 'macro' societal level where it has been used by the National Council for Vocational Qualifications (NCVQ), now the Qualification and Curriculum Authority (QCA), as 'the basic building material for a whole assessment edifice' (Issitt, 1996), to the 'micro' level of individual task performance. The second concept – reflective practice – increasingly is identified as a key goal and process to be incorporated into professional training programmes. The reflective practitioner has a stance that is constantly refined in the work setting, enabling her/him to deal effectively with an uncertain world, otherwise characterized by Donald Schön as the 'swampy lowlands' of professional practice (Schön, 1992). If we consider the two concepts together it might be assumed that competence can be defined through occupational standards and reflective practice provides the means by which their delivery and maintenance is ensured.

However, there are a number of facets to these two concepts, which need to be examined in order to understand the implications of the paradigm shift for professional education and development. On the one hand, the valuing of work-based learning is to be welcomed, as the diversification of routes and access to professional qualification enables talented people from a variety of backgrounds to have their expertise accredited. As well as 'top-down' government initiatives there have also been grass roots struggles, which have occurred in youth and community work in particular, to get people's competence formally recognized (Bainbridge, 1988; Banks, 1990).

Yet there is confusion concerning the two concepts of competence and reflective practice both within the world of human service work and more generally. This stems in part from the mixed messages that come from the discourse concerning the terms raising a number of questions for exploration. Because the concepts are both concerned with work-placed learning is it useful or justifiable to make a connection, or, alternatively, do they have different ideological and methodological approaches? As a feminist I am interested in how an understanding of gender and other social divisions informs the discourse and application of the concepts, and whether an exploration of this would make a difference.

The need for a feminist understanding

In this chapter I show that both competence and reflective practice are contested concepts with diverse meanings and applications, and that it is important to understand how these affect women, who comprise more than half the population and almost half the workforce. Will work-based assessment of competence lead to more access to useful qualifications for women? Will it assist the breakdown of gender barriers in the workplace or exacerbate them? These issues gain increasing significance as the setting up of standards of occupational competence and NVQs is particularly well developed in occupations in which women predominate, such as health and social care (Issitt, 1996). The standards definition process has now progressed to the higher vocational levels and to minor professions such as social work, youth and community work and health promotion, qualification for which is usually assured through higher education. Alongside developments in competence-based education and training, which are taking place in these human service occupations, the notion of reflective practice now has particular currency (Yelloly and Henkel, 1995). Whilst feminism has been important in informing the value-base and methodology of this work (Langan and Day, 1992; Hanmer and Statham, 1988) feminist scholarship is at an early stage in considering the application of both these concepts (Issitt, 1996; Matthews, 1992).

What can a feminist critique offer?

I will show that a feminist critique[1] offers insights into the methodology and application of both concepts. As with other areas of scholarship, and social research is a good example here (Stanley and Wise, 1993), it has the potential to highlight contradictions as well as bringing the relationship of competence and reflective practice more sharply into focus. Importantly, for feminists, an objective will be to assess the usefulness of the concepts in transforming social relations and challenging inequalities due to gender and other forms of social exclusion.

I am conscious that in examining these concepts through a feminist lens I am using a methodology which itself is the subject to constant debate, whose discourse contains different perspectives and a number of 'unresolved problematics' (Dominelli, 1996, p 162). Although the feminist movement is diverse and does not speak with one voice, along with Dominelli I would argue that there are key principles within the various strands of feminism that seek to challenge the patriarchal power and structures. Aspects of feminist analysis that I will draw upon in this chapter to illuminate reflective practice and competence are the contribution of feminist critiques of social science methodology and feminist understanding of reflexivity and feminist transformation. I interpret this as being about making a difference in people's lives, building upon experience to create new knowledge and action that can bring about social change to challenge power inequalities due to gender. I will first consider reflective practice, and identify how this can be synthesized with feminism as a model against which the prevailing approach to the development of competence standards and assessment can be evaluated.

Reflective practice

Before presenting a feminist critique of the concept, I will outline some of its key features. Reflective practice has become very important in professional education, and has grown out of the need to develop an epistemology of practice that is more relevant than other theory that may be separate and not organic to the day-to-day work of professionals. Donald Schön (1987, 1992), has argued for many years that there has been a crisis in professional knowledge, which has left professionals ill equipped to meet the demands of practice. He sees the crisis as having a number of different causes and describes the inter- and intraprofessional conflicts regarding the nature of professional competence as a 'babble of voices' that can give no clear direction to help the practitioner. From outside the professions, various social movements have challenged the knowledge-base and elitism of the professional role with which its positivist knowledge base is ill equipped to deal.

For Schön a major problem that professionals have faced is the dominance of positivist epistemology in the education of professionals. He questions the assumed superiority of this to other forms of knowledge, as it inevitably leads to an overemphasis on a technically rational model of professionalism, which proposes inadequate 'blueprints' for problem-solving. This kind of knowledge separates the learning of theory from its application and sees research as an activity that is discrete from practice.

Unfortunately, Schön argues, professional work is not made up of problems for which there are formulaic answers dreamt up in institutions occupying the academic 'high ground' above the 'swampy lowlands' of practice. In reality, professional work is frequently engaged with the 'indeterminate zones of practice', which require a mixture of on-the-spot complex judgements, decision-making and action, in situations that are often unique. A purely technical solution would often mean excluding aspects of the problem and bringing about a partial solution. To be really effective the practitioner has to develop 'professional artistry' to allow her/him to be spontaneous and creative in problem-solving. She/he engages in 'reflection-in-action', using both tacit and explicit knowledge, experience and professional artistry in 'an action-present – a stretch of time within which it is still possible to make a difference to the outcomes of the action' (Schön, 1992, p 58).

We are now in a situation where a number of models of reflective practice have been developed and some writers have shown that the term is now used almost like a 'mantra' to be invoked to give training programmes credibility, without any real ideological consistency or depth in the way the concept is applied (Ecclestone, 1996). Zeichner (1995) provides a useful summary of the development of reflective practice in teacher education and shows that there are three key features to the way reflection is seen:

reflection as instrumental mediation of action – where knowledge is used to direct practice; reflection as deliberating among competing views of teaching – where knowledge is used to inform practice; and reflection as reconstructing experience – where knowledge is used to help teachers apprehend and transform practice' (Zeichner, 1995, p 18)

Reflective practice not only involves reflection-in-action in the action present, but reflection-on-action after the event and as a preparation for further action. This can take place at the individual level, in dialogue with a mentor, and collaboratively with peers. The synergy between knowledge and action has implications for research. This becomes an activity that is integrated with and not removed from practice, and theory is derived from as well as applied to the practice context. The practitioner becomes an action researcher (Hart and Bond, 1995), more effective both at immediate problem-solving, using research-mindedness to reflect upon and improve action.

Reflection is not an *ad hoc* activity, but it requires developing a way of working in which it becomes 'second nature' (Schön, 1992). Whilst there are other professional approaches – expert, managerial, and professional, it is

the reflective practitioner who recognises the limits of professional knowledge and action, builds up a cycle of critical reflection to maximise the capacity for critical thought, and produces a sense of professional freedom and a connection with rather than a distance from clients (Pietroni, 1995, p 43)

Feminism and reflective practice

There are many features common to reflective and feminist practice. In a number of spheres feminism has been important in precipitating the crisis in professional knowledge to which Schön refers. It has not only challenged existing knowledge bases from within and without the professions, but has been important in developing new ways of synthesizing theory and practice. Along with other radical practitioners in human service occupations (Bailey and Brake, 1977; Corrigan and Leonard, 1978; Dominelli and McLeod, 1989; Jeffs and Smith, 1990), feminists have challenged positivist assumptions about professionalism. This was borne out of ideology concerned to develop dialogical approaches that explored commonality with service users rather than professional distance. With the benefit of hindsight we can now see that aspects of this activity fit the reflective practice mode advocated above by

Pietroni (1995). Feminism not only operates at the level of ideology but is concerned to make a practical difference. It has therefore established and continues to pioneer new methodological approaches to human service work (Butler and Wintram, 1991; Krzowski and Land, 1988; Griffin, 1995). In social work and youth and community work, feminism has been part of a struggle to recognize that anti-discriminatory practice was central to the professional role and was fundamental to qualifications (Issitt, 1995). This value-base is now under attack as being 'politically correct nonsense' (Dominelli, 1996) but for many professionals it remains a cornerstone of their daily practice.

Thus feminism has not merely 'added' gender in or on to mainstream critiques but has transformed our ways of understanding knowledge and approaching social science (Fonow and Cook, 1991; Harding, 1987; Maynard and Purvis, 1994; Stanley and Wise, 1993). It has affected the methodology of social research, offering powerful critiques of the subjective/objective dichotomy through which the gathering of knowledge through positivist methods is seen as superior to that which is based around understanding subjective experience (Stanley and Wise, 1993). In relation to policy analysis in human service work, Pascall (1997) presents a comprehensive review of how feminism has 'changed the agenda of politics and social policy' (1997, p 2) showing the centrality of women's caring role in welfare. This has had a profound effect on knowledge and practice, and the contribution of feminist analysis is now recognized as a major force by mainstream writers (George and Wilding, 1994). It may be surprising, then, that feminism is not listed as one of the social movements that Schön (1992) has identified as challenging the elitism and expertise of professionals.

It seems therefore that the discourse arising from feminist critique and activity has been conducted in parallel with the discourse on reflective practice. Although Schön describes how the reflective practitioner deals with moral issues, and the competing demands of different interest groups, the impact of these groups on the knowledge and value-base of the reflective practitioner are not dealt with. Discussion of values is largely concerned with the micro level of action and does not provide a synthesis of the personal and political dimensions of reflective practice. So analysis that takes account of gender and other differences is missing from the discourse. Neither feminists nor writers promoting reflective practice seem to have taken account of each other's critique of positivism, in which both argue for the validity of different forms of knowledge and ways of seeing, and experiencing, the world.

Each discourse is therefore impoverished by lack of involvement with the other. So feminist social researchers who have written reflexively about their involvement as women researching other women – the differential power relationships involved, and the problems of getting feminist, qualitative approaches to research and social science taken seriously (Harding, 1987;

Oakley, 1981) – do not consciously define themselves as reflective practitioners, or relate their activity and methodology to that discourse. Is this because it goes without saying that feminist practice is reflective or that reflective practice is inherently feminist?

Towards a model of feminist reflective practice?

In order to begin to unravel this conundrum I will now consider how reflective practice matches with feminist reflexivity. There are two key aspects. First, as with reflective practice, feminist practice, through consciousnessraising and collective action, involves our engagement in ongoing critical evaluation and reflection. Through this we understand our motivation, actions, and involvements, recognizing the artificiality of separating ourselves from the work we are undertaking and producing; I have shown that this is particularly relevant to human service work. Second, feminism acknowledges that being reflective will be affected by one's experience of social difference and oppression in terms of race, class, gender, disability, etc, and this experience will affect the process and outcomes of any project. Thus feminist reflective practice will differ from the prevailing discourses on reflective practice, which are presented as gender-neutral. Even though both feminism and reflective practice are committed to notions of challenge and change, a feminist understanding of, and praxis in relation to, the 'personal and the political' enhances understanding of the dialectic between the individual and societal levels of activity, critique and experience. It enhances awareness of the frames that 'bound the phenomena to which they will pay attention' (Schön, 1995). When practitioners are not aware of their own way of framing roles and problems 'they do not attend to the ways in which they construct the reality in which they function; for them it is simply the given reality' (Schön, 1995, p 310).

It is axiomatic to the methodology of both feminism and reflective practice that knowledge and action is imperfect and unfinished and can always be improved and developed. However, without the incorporation of clear statements about the value-base and the social and political context, there is no guarantee that reflective practice will be concerned with social transformation to tackle unequal power relations. The term may be appropriated by those with different ideologies as Ecclestone shows, whose varying perspectives represent the different frames (Schön, 1995, p 309) through which a problem may be viewed. A feminist addition to Pietroni's summary of reflective practice presented earlier would aim to try and connect the personal with the professional and political, whilst incorporating the notion of reflection as a systematic activity as encapsulated in the list below. I present this not as a closed prescriptive model but as a basis for discussion and development. The feminist reflective practitioner:

- recognizes that professional knowledge is imperfect and can always be improved;
- realizes that technical expertise is necessary but there are not formulaic answers to complex questions – Schön's 'indeterminate zones of practice';
- operates within an integrated personal/professional/political value-base, which includes commitment to anti-oppressive practice, that seeks to understand and change the social and political context that affects practice;
- 'builds in a cycle of critical reflection to maximize the capacity for critical thought, and produces a sense of professional freedom and a connection with rather than a distance from clients'(Pietroni 1995).

This does not only involve looking back, ie 'reflection-on-action' but also 'reflection in action', using knowledge, skills and past experience to respond creatively to new situations in the here and now. Reflection is a collaborative as well as an individual process.

The incorporation of aspects of feminist reflexivity links reflective practice with social transformation. The feminist perspective I am suggesting pro-motes awareness of, and action in relation to, social divisions and difference. It ensures that reflective practice does not only operate at the individual prac-titioner level but incorporates feminist collectivity based upon dialogue and support for each other. Conversely, feminist practice is enhanced by an understanding of reflective practice whereby reflection is built in and sys-tematic, validated as a legitimate part of professional activity.

Where does this leave competence?

At the beginning of this chapter I suggested that identifying standards of occupational competence promised certainty, 'a port in the storm of post-modernity' (Hodkinson and Issitt, 1995). Ecclestone (1996) has shown that the shift towards work-based competence as the basis of assessment of quali-fication has often been equated with the promotion of reflective practice. Having established the considerable commonality between reflective and feminist practice and proposed the advantages of a feminist model, I will now use this as a way into 'deconstructing' the concept of competence, primarily in relation to its application to the definition of national occupational stan-dards and NVQs.

I have argued elsewhere that the definition of competence as 'the ability to perform work activities to the standard required in the workplace' (NCVQ, 1988) is a deceptively simple concept (Issitt, 1996; Hodkinson and Issitt, 1995; Issitt and Woodward, 1992). With the creation of NCVQ to oversee the development of national standards across all occupations, competence was equated with task-performance. This could be externally demonstrated in a way that was disconnected from the person who was undertaking the particular activity. Policy that aimed to restructure welfare and make the human service workforce operate more 'effectively', adopted the essentially thrusting language and metaphors of the marketplace in relation to education and training. The proponents of the paradigm shift were confident that qualification for an occupation would no longer be overreliant on knowledge-related educational 'inputs' but would be obtained through competence 'outputs' demonstrated 'on the job' (Jessup, 1990).

Thus the prevailing task-centred model, which equated competence with functional performance, is extremely powerful and operates at the political level of employment policy. Feminist understanding of the 'personal and the political' shows how 'macro' level employment policy in relation to competence also has particular resonance at the individualistic personal level when performance is assessed in the workplace. For the individual the term transcends task performance, and competence is experienced at the personal 'felt' level in terms of self-esteem (Matthews, 1992; Barnett and Baruch, 1979).

This is the level at which an individual will be judged as 'competent' or 'not yet competent', and previously internalized oppression due to gender, race, disability or class, so closely linked to self-esteem, may be reinforced by an expectation that competent behaviour involves behaving according to gender or other stereotypes (Kemshall, 1992). Alternatively, it may provide an opportunity to challenge this internalized oppression through gaining National Vocational Qualifications (NVQs)[2], enhancing women's personal self-esteem by accrediting their worth, and this previously may have gone unrecognized in their jobs (George, 1994; Callender *et al.*, 1993).

Using the model of feminist reflective practice we can see that people engage with the concept of competence through 'frame analysis', borne of their own particular understanding of reality, using the frame to translate the concept into something that makes sense for them, in a variety of ways, and gender will make a difference. Over and above the task-centred or person-centred approaches already identified, competence can be conceived of holistically and atomistically. Its holistic use is not only attached to a competent person but can also refer to the overall competence required in a particular occupation. It is used atomistically when overall occupational and individual performance is disaggregated into lists of separate actions that are hierarchically arranged. The assumption here is that all the competencies added together equal overall occupational competence (Ashworth and Saxton, 1990; Hyland, 1995; Issitt and Woodward, 1992). Different dimensions of competence can be expressed diagrammatically as shown in Figure 16.1.

Figure 16.1 allows for different models of competence, as well as movement between them or simultaneous incorporation of more than one approach. The dominant version originally promoted through NCVQ, which has provided the foundation for the work on standards development, would

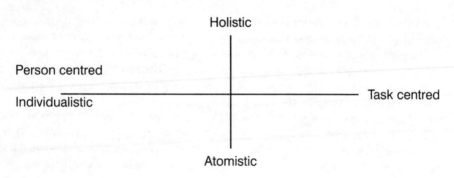

Figure 16.1 Dimensions of competence

be located primarily in the task-centred, individualistic and atomistic quadrants of the diagram.

There is now a considerable body of critical work that has highlighted methodological and political problems in relation to the dominant, task-centred model (Hyland, 1994; Field, 1995; Jones and Moore, 1995), raising questions about the objectivity and transparency of standards of competence. The functional analysis procedure used to define standards of competence and NVQs are rooted in positivist/behaviourist methodology and assume that the complex mix of knowledge, skills, attitudes and values can be broken down into measurable and observable performance. Human service work, which involves formal and informal interactions and varying relationships between people, is forced into a positivist/functionalist straitjacket of hierarchically arranged functions. Apparent scientific precision is assured through the detailed lists of performance indicators relating to each element of competence. This approach appears to fit with Schön's (1992) depiction of technical rationality, which falls short of the creativity required for reflective practice.

However, even when only operating at the level of technical rationality an objective means of assessing performance is illusory. Along with other critics, feminists would question the false dichotomy between 'objective' and 'subjective' knowledge that is set up by positivist methodology (Stanley and Wise, 1993; Coleman, 1991). They argue that there is not one version of reality, and women's experience of the world will be different from men's. Just as research grounded in positivist methodology is interpreted through the experience, feelings and beliefs of the researcher (Stanley and Wise, 1993), so it will be with the definition and assessment of competence. No matter how long the lists of criteria are, competence is still interpreted according to the subjective judgement of the assessor, who is an actor in the human interaction that assessment involves. Judgement will also be affected, consciously or unconsciously, by factors such as cultural background, gender and personal value-system. In trying to understand what goes on when assessing competence, feminist reflective practice would seek to incorporate awareness of the personal/political dimensions of the frames used by both the assessor and the candidate. The frames would include awareness of the socially constructed, yet subjective aspects of the 'selves' involved in relation to gender and other forms of social difference, culture, experience, personality, etc. Feminist reflective practitioners would be concerned to declare these openly and not hide behind a veneer of objectivity, pretending that these factors could be removed from the assessment process. Subjectivity is recognized and ways sought to use this in a positive, self-actualizing way (Hodkinson and Issitt, 1995) in order to operate fairly in relation to those wishing to have their competence assessed.

The feminist model of reflective practice is at odds with the methodology for competence definition and assessment, which is presented as 'empirically real and theory neutral' (Jones and Moore, 1995, p 85). This cannot only be challenged at the personal level when individual competence is assessed, but the 'transparency' of standards of occupational competence has also been questioned at the societal level. I have inferred earlier that the development of 'top-down', task-centred definitions of competence was part of a wider political agenda to give employers the key role in relation to vocational training (Hyland, 1995; Jones and Moore, 1995; Davies and Durkin, 1991). This is made clear by the White Paper 'Employment in the 1990s', which states that 'The system must be planned and led by employers as it is they who are best placed to judge skill needs' (Department of Employment, 1988), reinforced through later policy initiatives (eg DfEE, 1996). When describing the national standards programme the head of the former Employment Department's standards methodology unit highlights the importance of standards meeting the needs of employers, and that this relationship should have 'transparency' (Debling, 1989, p 81).

Jones and Moore (1995) argue that the emphasis on the primacy of employers emanates from a controlling ideology that extols the virtues of the market and offers a means of prescribing desirable behaviour of a compliant, unquestioning workforce. They state:

The competency model has been constructed not because it is good to think with but because it is good to use within the very particular policy context in which it has been active over recent years. (Jones and Moore, 1995, p 84)

But thinking as well as doing is central to feminist reflective practice, which extends the above critique to include a gender perspective. Because the controlling, pro-market ideology 'makes sex an inappropriate category of analysis in the marketplace' (Pascall, 1997, p 11), the definition of occupational standards of competence through functional analysis is not an objective, gender-neutral process but, in fact, a social product. Like 'skill', another term that is often used without reference to gender, it will reflect patriarchal power relations both in terms of the differential status of competence in 'male' and 'female' occupations and the language used to define it. As with skill, definitions of competence have to be understood in the context of a labour market in which the 'gender-stereotyping' of jobs has remained remarkably stable, even when the nature of work and the skills required to perform it have been radically transformed' (Wajcman, 1991, p 33). The implication here is that although women engaged in human service work may have both their personal and task competence validated through gaining NVQs (George, 1994; Callender *et al*, 1993) does this mean that since women remain in lower paid, lower status jobs their competence will be seen of less value, with a 'competence ceiling' that prevents their further progression (Issitt, 1996)? Dominelli's (1996) concern is that the translation into a competence framework of professional activity such as social work, in which women are numerically dominant, will provide a mechanism to downgrading its status.

Moreover, the functionalist underpinnings of task-centred, work-based competence may threaten the 'leading edge' approach of some radical professionals, including feminists, whose work is deeply challenging of patriarchal power at the personal and political levels and seeks to bring about change in human service work (Morley, 1993).

With the advent of NVQs what will now be the status of this kind of action for change, will it be deemed behaviour that is 'not yet competent' within a system of occupational standards that is retrospective and potentially serves to maintain the status quo? (Issitt, 1996, p 15)

Competence and feminist reflective practice – is reconciliation possible?

The analysis so far presented has been primarily concerned to 'deconstruct' competence through the feminist reflective practitioner's frame, in order to strip the concept to its ideological roots, showing how it impacts at the personal and political levels. I will now return to the question that I posed at the beginning of the chapter, ie whether it is useful to link the two concepts together in human service, and if so how a feminist model of reflective practice might fit.

Inevitably, the task-centred approach to competence presided over by the QCA has broken down as its inherent methodological problems render it unworkable in practice. This has resulted in a volte-face in relation to the initial principles that were vaunted as so fundamental in changing the nature of vocational education and training. Knowledge specification is now recommended for all NVQs (Beaumont, 1995), and in human service work other dimensions of competence, which include the person-centred, holistic aspects, and concerns about equal opportunities issues have now been incorporated. Is this therefore a vindication of the critique presented in this chapter? Does this represent a reconciliation between competence and reflective practice that includes feminist concerns?

The development of occupational standards and the NVQ assessment framework in human service work appears to have taken account of key features of the feminist model of reflective practice. From the early stages in health and social care the artificiality of the dichotomy between knowledge 'inputs' and practice 'outputs' was recognized by the specification of underpinning knowledge and skills. The foundational significance of the value-base was enshrined in Key Role '0' 'Promote and value the rights, responsibilities and diversity of people' (Care Sector Consortium, 1997). The connectedness between the 'self' of the individual practitioner, the quality of her/his and others' practice is perhaps covered by Key Role '1' 'Develop own and others' knowledge and practice to optimize the health and social well-being of people' (CSC, 1997).

Whilst concessions have been made to critics and practitioners who have been trying to work with the task-centred model, the problem that is continually encountered is that the methodological approach to defining and demonstrating competence rooted in functional analysis remains the same.

Thus the system based upon behaviourist/positivist assumptions can respond, but with a technically rational solution that reduces values to individual performance. It attempts to deal with complex interactions and decisions – what Schön (1987) has called 'indeterminate zones of practice' – by producing more detailed lists to prescribe behaviour. These may become ritualised and mechanistic in use. (Issitt, 1996, p 13).

The integration of values, reflexivity, knowledge and understanding and performance are proposed, according to Dominelli (1996), to give the appearance of 'political correctness', but at the personal level of experience this results in a process that is highly bureaucratic and difficult to manage. As Hyland (1994, p 62) argues:

In the last analysis, NVQs are primarily (and even obsessively) concerned with producing evidence to satisfy competence performance criteria, and this is quite different from the development of learning.

In trying to demonstrate their competence in human service, practitioners may become bogged down in detailed and repetitive evidence of performance, which has to be amassed and cross-referenced within and between elements and units of competence. Compiling the evidence becomes the focus, rather than reflection 'in' and 'on' action for human service, and the whole process, unless well resourced and supported, is potentially mystifying and oppressive.

Thus a number of issues remain unresolved in any attempt to reconcile a feminist conceptualization of reflective practice with an approach based on competence. Although occupational standards and work-based NVQs promise access to qualification, and a means of accrediting ability, it is by no means clear that advancement for women and other socially excluded groups in human service occupations can be assured without changes in the top-down methodology through which competence is defined and assessed. Whilst we need competent practitioners, we need to acknowledge the political dimension of what is presented as an 'objective' process. This means considering more 'grass-roots', person-centred inductive approaches that are less overwhelming and bureaucratic than current approaches.

Societal change has been at the heart of feminism for the last 30 years. The realization that the personal is political brought private, individual oppression out into the public domain. Feminist understanding offers the possibility for aspects of reflective practice that may still be outside the mainstream and oppositional to it, to develop and change the nature of professional activity in human service work (Issitt, 1996). If feminism, along with other movements to develop anti-oppressive practice, can prevent reflective practice from becoming individualized and narcissistic, what can it do for competence? Feminists, and other reflective practitioners, will need to continue to challenge and change 'top-down' processes to define and assess competence, as well as working to build alternatives to individualized competence models[3]. An important objective will be to support an integrated model of learning for the human service professions that enables practitioners to develop the criticality and creativity of feminist reflective practice that is more than competence alone.

Notes

1. I am using feminism as a way into understanding competence and anti-oppressive practice. I realize that feminism does not have the monopoly of this approach to analysis and anti-racist, anti-ablist, anti-heterosexist critiques would all have much to offer and have commonalities as well as differences with the feminist approach. I realize that womanism is a term that many women, particularly black women, feel is more accessible to them.
2. Although I am using the initials NVQ, the Scottish equivalent is SVQ (Scottish Vocational Qualification). The critique I develop can be applied to both.
3. At the time of writing I am engaged in research funded by the Nuffield Foundation into how women whose work has been informed by feminism use a variety of ways of conceptualizing competence and reflective practice.

References

Ashworth, P. D. and Saxton, J. (1990) 'On competence', *Journal of Further and Higher Education*, **14**(2) 3–25.
Bailey, R. and Brake, M. (eds) (1977) *Radical Social Work*, London, Edward Arnold.
Bainbridge, P. (1988) *Taking the Experience Route*, Leicester, CETYCW.
Banks, S. (1990) 'Accrediting prior learning: Implications for education and training in youth and community work', *Youth and Policy* **31**, 8–16.

Barnett, R. C. and Baruch, G. K. (1979) *The Competent Woman: Perspectives on Development*, New York, Irvington Publishers Inc.

Beaumont, G. (1996) *Review of 100 NVQs and SVQs*, London, NCVQ.

Butler, S. and Wintram, C. (1991) *Feminist Groupwork*, London, Sage.

Callender, C., Toye, J., Connor, H. and Spilsbury, M. (1993) *National Vocational Qualifications: Early indications of employers' take-up and use*, Brighton, Institute of Manpower Studies.

Care Sector Consortium (1997) *National Occupational Standards for Health Promotion and Care*, London, Local Government Management Board.

Coleman, G. (1991) *Investigating Organizations: A feminist approach*, University of Bristol, School for Advanced Urban Studies.

Corrigan, P. and Leonard, P. (1978) *Social Work Practice under Capitalism: A marxist approach*, Basingstoke, Macmillan.

Davies, B. and Durkin, M. (1991) 'Skill, competence and competencies in youth and community work', *Youth and Policy*, **34**, 1–11.

Debling, G. (1989) 'The Employment Department/Training Agency standards programme and NVQs: Implications for education', in J. Burke (ed.) *Competency-based Education and Training*, Lewes, Falmer.

DfEE (1996) *A Guide to achieving NTO Status*, Sheffield, DfEE.

Department of Employment (1988) *Employment in the 1990s*, London, HMSO.

Dominelli, L. (1996) 'Deprofessionalizing social work: Anti-oppressive practice, competencies and postmodernism', *British Journal of Social Work*, **26**, 153–75.

Dominelli, L. and McLeod, E. (1989) *Feminist Social Work*, Basingstoke, Macmillan.

Ecclestone, K. (1996) 'The reflective practitioner: Mantra or model for emancipation?', *Studies in the Education of Adults*, **28**(2), 146–61.

Field, J. (1995) 'Reality testing in the workplace: Are NVQs employment led?', in P. Hodkinson and M. Issitt (eds) *The Challenge of Competence: Professionalism through education and training*, London, Cassell.

Fonow, M. and Cook, J. A. (eds) (1991) *Beyond Methodology: Feminist scholarship as lived research*, Bloomington and Indianapolis, Indiana University Press.

George, M. (1994) 'The first rung', *Community Care*, 17 February.

George, V. and Wilding, P. (1994) *Welfare and Ideology*, Hemel Hempstead, Harvester Wheatsheaf.

Griffin, G. (ed.) (1995) *Feminist Activism in the 1990s*, London, Taylor & Francis.

Hanmer, J. and Statham, D. (1988) *Women and Social Work: Towards a woman-centred practice*, Basingstoke, Macmillan.

Harding, S. (ed.) (1987) *Feminism and Methodology*, Buckingham, Open University Press.

Hart, L. and Bond, M. (1995) *Action Research for Health and Social Care*, Buckingham, Open University Press.

Hodkinson, P. and Issitt, M. (eds) (1995) *The Challenge of Competence: Vocationalism through education and training*, London, Cassell.

Hyland, T. (1995) 'Behaviourism and the meaning of competence', in P. Hodkinson and M. Issitt (eds) *The Challenge of Competence: Vocationalism through education and training*, London, Cassell.

Hyland, T. (1994) *Competence, Education and NVQs: Dissenting perspectives*, London, Cassell.

Issitt, M. (1996) *Competence in the Quasi-market: Towards the development of a feminist critique*, Social Exclusion Research Monograph, Staffordshire University.

Issitt, M. (1995) 'Competence, professionalism and equal opportunities', in P. Hodkinson and M. Issitt (eds) *The Challenge of Competence: Vocationalism through education and training*, London, Cassell.

Issitt, M. and Woodward, M. (1992) 'Competence and contradiction', in P. Carter, T. Jeffs and M. K. Smith (eds) *Changing Social Work and Welfare*, Buckingham, Open University Press.

Jeffs, T. and Smith, M. (eds) (1988) *Welfare and Youth Work Practice*, Basingstoke, Macmillan.

Jessup, G. (1990) 'National Vocational Qualifications: Implications for further education', in M. Bees and M. Swords (eds) *National Vocational Qualifications and Further Education*, London, Kogan Page.

Jones, L. and Moore, R. (1995) 'Appropriating competence: The competency movement, the New Right and the culture change project', *British Journal of Education and Work*, 8(2) 78–92.

Kenshall, H. (1993) 'Assessing competence: Scientific process or subjective interference? Do we really see it?', *Social Work Education*, 12(1) 36–45.

Krzowski, S. and Land, P. (eds) (1988) *In Our Experience: Workshops at the Women's Therapy Centre*, London, The Women's Press.

Langan, M. and Day, L. (eds) (1992) *Women, Oppression and Social Work*, London, Routledge.

Matthews, A. (1992) *Does Gender Contribute to Perceptions of Job Competence?* London, NCVQ.

Maynard, M. and Purvis, J. (eds) (1994) *Researching Women's Lives from a Feminist Perspective*, London, Taylor & Francis.

Morley, B. (1993) 'Recent responses to "domestic violence" against women: A feminist critique', in R. Page and J. Baldock (eds) *Social Policy Review 5*, Canterbury, Social Policy Association.

NCVQ (1988) *The NCVQ Criteria and Related Guidance*, London: NCVQ.

Oakley, A. (1981) 'Interviewing women: A contradiction in terms', in H. Roberts (ed.) *Doing Feminist Research*, London, Routledge.

Pascall, G. (1997) *Social Policy: A new feminist analysis*, London, Routledge.

Pietroni, M. (1995) 'The nature and aims of professional education for social workers: A postmodern perspective', in M. Yelloly and M. Henkel (eds) *Learning and Teaching in Social Work: Towards reflective practice*, London, Jessica Kingsley.

Schön, D. (1995) *The Reflective Practitioner: How professionals think in action*, Aldershot, Arena.

Schön, D. (1992) 'The crisis of professional knowledge and the pursuit of an epistemology of practice', *Journal of Interprofessional Care*, 6(1), 49–63.

Schön, D. (1987) *Educating the Reflective Practitioner*, San Francisco, Jossey Bass.

Stanley, L. and Wise, S. (1993) *Breaking Out Again*, London, Routledge.

Wajcman, J. (1991) 'Patriarchy, technology, and conceptions of skill', *Work and Occupations*, 18(1), February, 29–45.

Yelloly, M and Henkel, M (eds) (1995) *Learning and Teaching in Social Work: Towards reflective practice*, London, Jessica Kingsley.

Zeichner, K. (1995) 'Conceptions of reflective practice in teaching and teacher education', in G. Harvard and P. Hodkinson (eds) *Action and Reflection in Teacher Education*, New Jersey, Ablex.

Chapter 17

Beyond competences: lessons from management learning

Ian Cunningham

Summary

This chapter goes beyond discussion of competence and competences. Ian Cunningham believes it is axiomatic that we want people who are competent at what they do. He argues that focusing on just the competence to do things is too limited as an aim of learning. As an alternative, the concept of capability succeeds in promoting a necessarily wider perspective.

Reference is made to a wide range of philosophical concepts and theories, and critical observation of current practice, to illustrate that more priority should be given to deciding what needs to be learned before addressing the processes and structures for learning.

Examples are drawn from the managerial world. However, it is suggested that there may be general lessons for education and training in the evidence and arguments quoted, within this broad case for a holistic approach to learning.

Introduction

In discussing capability there is a tendency for many people to see this concept as implying a largely mental/cognitive activity. I see it as involving also:

- feelings and emotions;
- physical aspects;
- issues of values, morals and spirituality;
- social factors, eg to do with relationships with others.

This perspective has been labelled 'holistic' and I will try to give my view of how this concept can be applied to good learning. As well as basing comments on practical experience and on authors quoted, I have also drawn on research conducted on chief executives and other top managers. This research was carried out in the USA and the UK with a view to developing fundamental, cross-culturally usable concepts and models. (Cunningham, 1988, 1994) (My colleague Graham Dawes also contributed to the research in the USA.)

The social domain

A major problem with the educational world in the UK is the individualistic orientation to learning. The focus on individuals must, of course, have a central place in planning learning, and I shall address this individual level. But before doing that I want to argue that in organizational life there is also an important focus on learning at the group or team level and on whole organization learning (as exemplified by the current concerns to develop learning organizations). Beyond the organization, there is a need to consider learning at the community level and in whole societies (as indicated in the learning society concept). And lastly there is the growing awareness of global learning needs, with the environmentalists being one group that has highlighted this issue.

I do not have space to do justice to these wider issues, but perhaps one example will help at least to record the dangers of self-centred individualism. In education if learners help each other and share their learning it is called cheating and people get punished for it. In the world outside educational establishments it is absolutely essential that people 'cheat'. Organizations, communities and whole societies cannot function effectively in the modern world unless people share their learning. Unless educational institutions address this issue they will continue to undermine attempts to create learning organizations, learning communities and learning societies.

Feelings and emotions

Let me next comment on 'emotional learning'. Mike Dixon, a columnist on the *Financial Times*, once commented to me that, in management, 'thinking is embedded in feeling'. This phrase struck a chord. Managers think out of an internal context of feelings and emotions; thoughts are not produced out of other thoughts. We think what it is possible for us to think as a result of the other dimensions of ourselves (as mentioned above – the emotional, the physical, the spiritual and the social).

Keutzer (1982), drawing on the work of Paul McLean and others, suggests that neurophysiological evidence supports the view that evolution of the neocortex has produced a split between the archaic (emotional) structures of the brain and the 'thinking cap' that governs rational thought. Emotion is the older partner – and, it is suggested, the more powerful. So that given the inevitable conflicts between reason and emotion, the reasoning part is 'compelled to provide spurious rationalisations for the senior partner's urges and whims' (Keutzer, 1982, p 79). Goleman (1995) makes a similar point when he says that 'the emotional faculty guides our moment to moment decisions'. Indeed the popularity of Goleman's book provides evidence that many people want to take seriously the research evidence he cites to support his argument for the centrality of 'emotional intelligence'.

Bramley (1977), from her experience as a student counsellor, argues that many students cover up emotional problems in unbalanced intellectual development. But, if we take Keutzer's hypothesis seriously, we can see that this strategy is misguided. And, as Bramley comments, 'When and if a student realises, on attainment of a good degree, that his intellectual ability cannot give him love and security for which he yearns, he may become very ill indeed, and certainly several suicidal young people whom I have known come into this category' (Bramley, 1977).

All this was well known in ancient wisdom, and in diverse cultures. To take one example from the Middle East:

Your reason and your passion are the rudder and the sails of your seafaring soul. If either your sails or your rudder be broken, you can but toss and drift, or else be held at a standstill in mid-seas. (Gibran, 1972)

Unfortunately, the lessons have not been learnt in the managerial world – or they have been forgotten or driven out in the learning environments of business schools. I will quote just one example. The *Boston Globe* of 13 October 1986 wrote up the 25-year class reunion of the Harvard Business School 1961 MBAs. Whilst it noted that there were positive comments about Harvard's role in making participants successful, there were significant concerns being raised. Edwin Stanley (Chairman of Stanley Investment and Management Inc.) said 'Business School did us a disservice with a compass locked on true north.' His criticism was of a narrowly focused driving ambition for success. Amos Hostetter (Chairman of Continental Cablevision) went further when he claimed that his personal life had been 'sublimated' to business success. 'I was being a coward and afraid of intimacy', he commented. One of the wives present criticized those who were raising these concerns. She said, 'I feel sorry for you guys. You shouldn't expect Harvard to teach you how to be human in your professional lives.'

I think that response was unfair. Business schools claim to equip people for managerial roles and if they pretend that personal feelings and values have no place, or they force the sublimation of these in a pseudo-rational, analytical atmosphere, then they do deserve to be criticized. La Bier's clinical research on young managers produced clear evidence of this problem. He found that there were managers who superficially were climbing the corporate ladder with apparent consummate skill and who behaved in ways that were totally 'normal'. However, from in-depth clinical study, he found that they were, to use his words, 'quite sick'. He described them as 'dominated by irrational passions of power lust, conquest, grandiosity and destructiveness or, conversely, by cravings for subjugation and humiliation' (La Bier, 1986, p 61).

On the other hand, he found another group who seemed to display some neurotic symptoms but were psychologically normal. These he saw as growing up through learning about and struggling with the difficulties of corporate life. This could be painful, and they sometimes showed it (for example through anxiety feelings or sleepless nights). The problem is that, as William Temple alluded to earlier this century, we are taught to think together and feel separately whereas we need to think separately and feel together. That is the mark of good collaborative practice, such as teamwork.

Evans and Bartolome (1980) discuss these issues drawing on writers such as Vaillant and Schein. They agree with the latter that 'the distinguishing characteristic of a top level executive is not his skill or ability but his emotional competence'. They show how, for instance, a successful manager may have to do an unpleasant task such as firing someone. They will feel bad about it, but face up to it and do it. In other words they experience negative feelings, but they deal with them appropriately. (Evans and Bartholome, 1980, p 155). Also see Schein (1978) and Vaillant (1977).

Metafeeling

The term I use to elucidate this emotional sophistication is metafeeling. This is, the emotionally mature person may feel bad but they feel OK about feeling bad. They know that life has its ups and downs, and they accept it. They experience crises, but work them through.

Metafeeling, then, is about how we feel about how we feel. People go to sad films, cry a lot and say how much they enjoyed it. They feel good about feeling sad. However, a person could experience some difficulty in life (for example, loss of a job), feel sad about it (reasonably), then feel bad about feeling sad. This can lead to a downward spiral of depression.

Some Buddhist monks have a routine of getting up in the morning, thinking of all the problems they and others have or could have, then laughing out loud about them. They recognize problems and the negative feelings around them. They are not covered up or pretended away. But then they are put in perspective.

Biorhythm evidence suggests that we go through cycles with ups and downs. It is suggested that we inevitably have emotional highs and lows, irrespective of what is going on in the world around us. Whilst I am not sure that the wilder claims about biorhythms are not too fanciful, it seems undeniable that people do experience patterns of internal change, eg hormonal, which have an effect on our emotional states. If we accept this then we can metafeel OK – we can know that we will not be on top form every day of our lives and that these variations are not to be blamed on anyone – least of all ourselves.

Connectedness

One of the important aspects of good learning seems to be about connecting. This includes internal connecting which integrates:

- thinking;
- feeling;
- physical (body);
- believing/valuing (including spiritual beliefs).

These internal processes need to come together. Holistic learning is not about developing each aspect sequentially. When we learn, in the best sense, we have feelings about what we think and we integrate these in our value/belief systems. A useful concept in explaining this connection is *centredness*.

We also engage in external connecting – that is we interact with the world around us. *Grounding* is the concept I will use to explore this. I will take the two concepts of centring and grounding in turn. They both came from Eastern thinking and are most visibly used in martial arts training, but are best seen as 'learning for life' in its broadest sense.

Centring

In some approaches to learning developed in China and Japan (such as Tai Chi and Aikido), the concept of the centre is important. It can be viewed as the centre of a single person, as their centre of gravity around which the body revolves (not literally!). It can also be seen that a person's centre is the centre of the universe from their point of view. It's the place from which to connect to others (people, things, animals, etc). So it has an ecological sense; the centre is the harmonizing focus of energy fields and patterns of relationships.

This can all sound pretty flaky, esoteric stuff if the language and way of thinking is new. But it is highly practical. There is a demonstrable difference between centred and uncentred people. Let me elaborate some features of centredness.

Harmony

'Harmony is an attunement of opposites, a unification of many, a reconciliation of dissentients' said Theon of Smyrna. Harmony is not, in music, unison. It is the aesthetic 'centring' of difference (different voices, different instruments). We each have these differences within us. Some psychologists and psychotherapists refer to our different parts as 'subpersonalities'. Berne (1964, 1974), in developing Transactional Analysis, used the idea of 'ego states', which he labelled 'parent', 'adult' and 'child'. Irrespective of their theoretical base, there is much agreement among psychotherapists that a key part of their work can be in helping a person integrate or harmonize or come to terms with these differences.

In terms of developing a holistic sense, the harmonizing required here is of head, heart and guts. Particularly as applied to centred managers, we are thinking of the person who:

- demonstrates harmonized energy;
- shows congruence and coherence in integrating theory and practice (in doing this, the person would bring together 'theory-in-use' and 'espoused theory', as Argyris and Schön (1974) suggest);
- is able to work with difference and ambiguity, and has the self-awareness to do this;
- 'listens to the inner voice' – this is a term Bennis (1989) uses about highly effective leaders. (The influence on Bennis is from Ralph Waldo Emerson's essay 'Self Reliance'.) The inner voice, if it is to be heard and believed, comes from the Centre;
- is able to be inside and outside at the same time – Postman and Weingartner (1969) call this 'the anthropological perspective', meaning someone who can understand the rituals, norms and culture of the group or organization (the insider perspective) and is able to stand outside, examine them and operate out of the inner voice;
- has personal theories and meanings that may not conform to the textbook (see McLean et al., 1982).

Balance

It is not that centred managers always feel 'in balance', but that they are aware of the value of balance. They recognize polarities and dualities and address them as such. However, we can get inappropriate balance as in the suggestion that the balanced middle manager has a chip on both shoulders! Without a centred way of operating, and attention to some of the factors above, balance on its own is insufficient.

I will mention some polarities that are relevant here, but they are not exhaustive of all the possibilities (see Cunningham, 1984).

Doing/being

Centred managers are aware of what they do and who they are. The verb 'to be' crops up in their language (eg 'I am...') (see Cunningham, 1992).

A related polarity is

Pro-activity/reactivity

Pro-activity is usually lauded as better than reactivity. But it is clear from my research that this criticism is of the wrong kind of reactivity. Wise reactivity is at the heart of the best customer care practices – flexible, thoughtful, caring responses to customer requests and demands. Pro-active organizations that push their technology on to the market, with little reactive wisdom in their responses to the market, tend to come unstuck eventually.

Taoists use the polarity yin/yang. This is often translated as yin (feminine) and yang (masculine) but the concepts are looser and more sophisticated (Cunningham, 1984). They can, for instance, be seen as subsuming pro-activity (in yang) and reactivity (in yin). Taoists emphasize the complementarity and interpenetration of these apparent opposites. The Taoist principle of mutuality suggests that it is not possible to have one pole without the other. The analogies are that there is no night without day, no light without dark and no valley without hills.

Theory/practice

This is a classic polarity that comes up a great deal in discussions about management. Business schools justify an overwhelming interest in theory by quoting aphorisms such as, 'There is nothing so practical as a good theory'. In their turn managers attack academics. Two 'question and answer' jokes indicate this:

1. *Question*: If you push the Professor of Marketing and the Professor of Finance off the roof of the University, which one hits the ground first?
Answer: Who cares?

2. *Question*: Why are academics buried 30 feet under the ground?
Answer: Because deep down they're OK.

A root cause of these divides is a dichotomy between what could be labelled two 'worlds'. First, there is a world of theory, which tends to be concerned with teaching generalizations about management in a classroom. As a shorthand I have called this the 'S' world as such teaching gives managers *solutions* to apply to their problems. They tend to be taught *specializations* (HR, marketing), *subjects* (economics, sociology) and *systems* (IT, OR). This 'S' world can also include precise *skills*, and often particular *structures*.

The other world is one of practice (the 'P' world). This is where managers learn most of what they need to learn. (Research suggests 80–90 per cent of the abilities successful managers use come from this world.) Managers learn by experience and from received wisdom (eg more experienced managers, mentors, etc). The learning is job based and is often a response to live *problems*. For example, if a new IT system is put in, managers have a problem if they do not know how to use it. So they learn. Such learning is very *people* orientated and is often about changing patterns of work and learning new *processes*. The 'P' world is readily recognizable to managers.

There are two difficulties with these two worlds. First, there is the 'S to P' issue. This is where managers are taught *solutions* and then have to find *problems* or *people* to use them on. Or, even worse, they distort problems to fit the solutions they have available.

To take my own career as an example, I was trained initially as a chemist. At one time I was offered a job as a research chemist in a pharmaceutical company. If I had taken it I might have been presented with the problem of alleviating or even curing a particular mental illness (say depression). The solution I was trained to provide was a chemical one. Presented with such a problem the only solution I would conceive would be a new drug. My training had convinced me to look for chemical solutions to such problems.

Some years after leaving the world of research chemistry I became involved in the field of psychotherapy. Here, presented with problems of mental illness, the therapist will commonly talk to the patient/client. He or she will look for solutions to the problem within the confines of the particular theoretical framework in which he or she has been trained. What the therapist will not usually do is search for a chemical solution to the problem, just as the average chemist would not think of refusing to search for a new drug and suggesting psychotherapy instead.

Mental illness presents major problems in Western countries. It is arguable that developing apt solutions to these problems is hampered by the inability of the various professions to talk to each other (and this problem seems to get worse as the subject boundaries are strengthened through increasing specialization).

This issue affects the managerial world quite broadly, and in training leads to difficulties such as 'the transfer of training' problem (a trainer euphemism for 'we taught them things that are no use in their work and therefore they don't apply them').

A different issue from the 'S to P' syndrome is 'P' only. This is where managers say 'I've learned all I need from experience. I don't need to explore new ideas being promoted by a bunch of ivory tower academics.' The difficulty with this approach is that experience is all about the past. If, as we assume, the future is not going to be like the past, this makes experience-only learning very limited.

As Fiedler (1992) has shown in his research, highly experienced managers/leaders function well in situations that require little or no learning.

These especially include high job stress situations such as firefighting. Someone leading a group of firefighters will draw on experience very heavily. They will not, in the middle of a fire, stop to think about learning issues. They work to well-rehearsed grooves, and stopping to think could be a dangerous activity. On the other hand, Fiedler's (and others') evidence suggests that in the low job stress world of the average organization, intellectual and creative ability is more likely to predict good leadership performance than experience. Note that I say that the average organization has low 'job stress', not necessarily low 'interpersonal stress', ie managers may not get on with each other (hence producing interpersonal stress) but their jobs are not inherently stressful (eg dangerous, as in firefighting).

The two dangers I have identified, namely 'S to P' and 'P only' need addressing. The answer seems to be 'P to S', that is going from problems to solutions, or from people to systems, etc. The point is that experience cannot be the only teacher. New ways of doing things are needed. There is a value in the expert, the professional, the academic. But they should be more in a role of responsiveness to the needs of people, problems, patterns and processes than they often are. This example shows the need for balance to be driven more from one direction. That is not to deny, though, the need for balance. And sometimes the backroom boffin will come up with a solution to a problem no one knew we had (or that we ignored).

Grounding

I have emphasized so far the idea of centring, and I have suggested the importance of internal balance and harmony. However, this is not enough. For instance, I quoted Bennis on 'listening to the inner voice'. But suppose the inner voice is coming from some disconnected, crazy place? At worst it could be a schizophrenic delusion.

Also, centred managers can be lively, creative entrepreneurs, but without connection into the wider society they may go off at tangents. The manager who is centred and grounded has a sense of these wider connections. They are the ones who take environmental and ecological issues really seriously. They do not just see their role as complying with the law or avoiding bad publicity if they pollute rivers. They see themselves as integrally involved in the planet and all life upon it.

Grounding can be grounding in:

- spiritual and religious beliefs that provide a well-worked-out faith;
- professional values – a sense of belonging to something bigger than the organization (as one civil engineer in a public organization said to me, 'If my employers were to ask me to build something I thought might be unsafe or unwise, I'd refuse because my professional values override my loyalty to my employer');

- family and community – a feeling of belonging and of intimate connection to others.

Grounding connects the inner to the outer worlds (and vice versa). It provides a solid base out of which the manager can operate. Grounded managers are not pushovers. This is literally true. I often demonstrate this in groups by using Ki Aikido techniques to show how if people physically ground themselves they literally cannot be pushed over. If, on the other hand, they are not physically grounded, they can be knocked sideways with a gentle push on the shoulders. People in organizations often intuitively recognize these differences. They recognize who is a lightweight and therefore easy to defeat in a conflict. And they recognize who not to take on in a fight.

Centring and grounding need to be brought together. Grounding without centring can lead to inertia and lack of change; centring without grounding can lead to burn out.

Morality and ethics

Rushworth Kidder (1992) has claimed to be the first Western journalist to visit the Chernobyl nuclear power plant after the accident there. He discovered that the accident had occurred because two engineers conducted an unauthorized experiment on reactor number four. In order to do this they had to override six separate computer-driven alarm systems. Now, these engineers were highly competent, highly able men. The accident did not occur because of human error, in the sense of someone making an unknown mistake. As Kidder commented, the accident was 'not a question of technology. It's a matter of ethics.' By this he meant that he saw the engineers' actions as requiring 'an ethical override'. The question I have from this is 'what was missing in their development and learning that left out ethics (or at least this kind of ethical issue)?'

Another incident points to this same problem. Richard Grabowski was, by all accounts, a brilliant aerospace engineering student. He was offered jobs with two prestigious companies, both of which would have involved designing weapons systems. On 16 October 1985, while considering these job offers, he committed suicide. His suicide note read:

If I were to live out my potential, I would only destroy life... I have such unbounded respect for the practical application of physical ideas that I would go so far as to murder humans... I am incapable of love. I am incapable of compassion. I can only respect rational, physical ideas. It is for this reason that I must die. If I were to continue living, I would only prolong my death. I cannot 'live' by any sense of my imagination producing weapons. (quoted in Skolimowski, 1986)

That is pretty terrifying stuff. What, again, was there in this person's learning and development that created this awful end for him? We can guess that examination of morality and ethics – and the struggles we need to make with moral and ethical choices – was missing. But in an era where old certainties no longer exist, where postmodern views of knowledge encourage a nihilistic relativism, new bases for action are necessary. This points to a moral basis for managerial activity – and therefore the need to learn to make moral choices.

I am not seeking to preach a particular moral position. That discussion, to do it full justice, belongs elsewhere. My point is about learning. It is possible to argue that rather than seeing ethics as an interesting option in the business school curriculum, we need to start managerial learning on a base of examining issues of morality, ethics, values and social responsibility. To decide what is right and good for a manager to learn must start from rightness and goodness being treated as moral questions.

There is much debate at present about what a good company is, or should be. Many, myself included, would say that the 'bottom line' is insufficient justification for the existence of a company or for measuring its success (goodness). Struggles with moral dilemmas, such as the interplay between the need for profit, the needs of employees, and the needs of the planet, are at the heart of the strategic learning that is needed in business. And moral development is both a learning issue and learnable.

Indeed, in Iris Murdoch's (1992) statement that 'learning is moral progress' we have a clue as to how to proceed. She points out that good learning develops wisdom and subtler visions, and it diminishes crass egoism. This kind of learning does not come from didactic preaching. It comes from individuals working openly with colleagues in exploration of moral dilemmas. Haste (1993) suggests that moral development comes from two factors. 'First, a caring community of which the individual feels a valued member, where mutual respect and justice are enacted, not just preached. Second, an environment which continually encourages reflection on the wider implications – including personal responsibility – of everyone's actions' (Haste, 1993).

The evidence of people coming out of higher education is that universities provide precisely the opposite environment. Indeed, in terms of all the criteria for holistic learning that I have identified, universities score badly. It is not that academic, cognitive development is unimportant – on the contrary it is of crucial importance. But my thesis is that an unbalanced education that assumes human beings are merely walking brains does not even work in its own terms. The denial of the emotions, of moral issues and of the social context of learning also produces poor cognitive activity.

Conclusion

This chapter has explored facets of 'good learning'. Whilst it has overlapped into the wider field of what makes a good manager, I have tried to keep the analysis within bounds. Hence there is much more that could be said about issues only alluded to here. The chapter is based on work more fully explored elsewhere (see Cunningham, 1994). The latter text also goes into detail on practical ways of solving some of the problems discussed here. However, as I indicated at the start of this chapter, we need to be clear on what is worth learning before we can address ways of meeting these needs – hence the focus of this piece.

References

Argyris, C. and Schön, D. (1974) *Theory in Practice,* San Francisco, Jossey-Bass.

Bennis, W. G. (1989) *On Becoming a Leader,* Reading, MA, Addison-Wesley.

Berne, E. (1964) *Games People Play,* London, Penguin.

Berne, E. (1974) *What do you say after you say Hello?,* London, André Deutsch.

Bramley, W. (1977) *Personal Tutoring in Higher Education,* Guildford, Surrey, Society for Research into Higher Education.

Cunningham, I. (1984) *Teaching Styles in Learner Centred Management Development,* Lancaster University, PhD thesis.

Cunningham, I. (1988) 'Patterns of managing for the future', *Industrial Management and Data Systems,* January/February, 18–22.

Cunningham, I. (1992) 'The impact of who leaders are and what they do', in K. E. Clark, M. B. Clark and D. P. Campbell (eds) *Impact of Leadership,* Greensboro, NC, CCL.

Cunningham, I. (1994) *The Wisdom of Strategic Learning,* Maidenhead, McGraw-Hill.

Evans, P. and Bartolome, F. (1980) *Must Success Cost So Much?,* London, Grant McIntyre.

Fiedler, F. E. (1992) 'The role and meaning of leadership experience', in K. E. Clark, M. B. Clark and D. P. Campbell (eds) *Impact of Leadership,* Greensboro, NC, CCL.

Gibran, K (1972) *The Prophet,* London, Heinemann.

Goleman, D. (1995) *Emotional Intelligence,* New York, Bantam.

Haste, H. (1993) 'Guilt and the struggle to teach right from wrong', *The Guardian Education,* March, 2–3.

Keutzer, C. S. (1982) 'Physics and consciousness', *Journal of Humanistic Psychology,* **22**(3), Spring, 74–90.

Kidder, R. (1992) 'Ethics: A matter of survival', *The Futurist,* March/April, 10–12.

La Bier, D. (1986) 'Madness stalks the ladder climbers', *Fortune,* 1 September, 61–4.

McLean, A. J., Sims, D. B. P., Mangham, I. L. and Tuffield, D. (1982) *Organization Development in Transition,* Chichester, John Wiley.

Murdoch, I. (1992) *Metaphysics as a Guide to Morals,* London, Chatto & Windus.

Postman, N. and Weingartner, C. (1969) *Teaching as a Subversive Activity,* Harmondsworth, Penguin.

Schein, E. M. (1978) *Career Dynamics,* Reading, MA, Addison-Wesley.

Skolimowski, H. (1986) 'Destruction through education', *The Scientific and Medical Network Newsletter,* **31**, p 1.

Vaillant, G. E. (1977) *Adaptation to Life,* Boston, Little, Brown.

Waldo Emerson, Ralph (1969) 'Self reliance', in Hendricks, S. (sel.) *Selections from Self Reliance Friendship, Compensation and Other Great Writings,* London, Hallmark.

Chapter 18

Professional competence: harmonizing reflective practitioner and competence-based approaches

Graham Cheetham and Geoff Chivers

Summary

This chapter describes a model of professional competence developed by the authors in connection with their current research into the way practitioners acquire and maintain the various aspects of their professional competence.

The model brings together a number of apparently disparate views of professional competence, including the 'functional outcomes' approach, a key feature of UK occupational standards and NVQs, and 'personal or behavioural competence' approaches, commonly used both within assessment centre settings and company-specific competency frameworks. It attempts to integrate these with the 'reflective practitioner' approach, suggested by Schön and now well recognized within many professional education programmes.

The model is currently being tested as part of a programme of empirical work across a range of different professions.

Note: a version of this paper has been published in the *Journal of European Industrial Training*, 1996, **20**(5), 20–30.

Introduction

The authors are currently researching into how professionals acquire the various aspects of their professional competence, and how this might be helped or hindered by formal development programmes. Their aim is to gather insights from professionals practising in a wide range of professions and to use these to help improve existing professional development programmes.

Before beginning our empirical work, we needed a suitable conceptual framework in the form of a comprehensive model covering all aspects of professional competence. We examined a variety of existing models, concepts and approaches relating to professional competence, or which might have a bearing upon it, but we concluded that although many had useful insights to offer, they each tended to concentrate on particular aspects of competence. None of them, in our view, offered the fully comprehensive model of professional competence we were seeking. We, therefore, set about trying to bring together a number of these different ideas and approaches into a single model.

Of course, we could not hope to reconcile every conflicting hypothesis. Instead, we looked for cohesive elements from the different approaches that could be made to complement each other, thereby producing a more holistic model than any of them, in our view, offered individually. Over a period of several months, and at least eight iterations, we arrived at our provisional model.

Key influences on the model

Some of the more important influences on the model are summarized below.

REFLECTIVE PRACTITIONER (SCHÖN, 1983; 1987)

Schön challenges the conventional (technical–rational) view of how practitioners operate. In his view, professionals do not solve problems simply by applying specialist or scientific knowledge. He believes they use a form of tacit knowledge – knowledge linked to specific activities, which he calls 'knowing-in-action'. Over time, they also develop repertoires of solutions and learn how to reframe difficult problems into ones they can deal with more easily. Their professional practice can be seen more as a form of artistry than applied theory.

For Schön, the crucial competence professionals need, both for developing their skills and for continuously improving them, is reflection (reflection-in-action and reflection-about-action).

UK OCCUPATIONAL STANDARDS/NVQS

For a number of years the UK government has been sponsoring the development of occupational standards for all types of occupation. The standards are used as a basis for National Vocational Qualifications (NVQs). The approach is firmly competence based, seeing competence as recognizable through job-specific outcomes.

Detailed lists of competences are derived through a procedure called 'functional analysis'. The competences are described in the form of performance criteria and range statements, the latter specifying the range of contexts in which competence should be demonstrated.

The approach accepts that knowledge and understanding, and to a lesser extent personal competence, underpin effective performance. Nonetheless, its primary focus is on functional competence (the ability to perform specific tasks, or functions, effectively within the workplace). The outcomes assessed are, therefore, primarily functional outcomes.

JOB COMPETENCE MODEL (MANSFIELD AND MATHEWS, 1985)

This model is closely linked to occupational standards and is meant to make their use more dynamic as well as assisting assessors in making judgements about the competence of candidates. The model sees competence as having three components:

1. the task component (ie the particular task to be performed);
2. task management (ie the skills needed when a number of tasks have to be performed together or in sequence);
3. the role (or job) environment (ie the skills needed to cope with the particular working environment or context).

BEHAVIOURAL COMPETENCE (BOYATZIS, 1982; KLEMP, 1980; SCHRODER, 1989)

In contrast to the occupational standards approach, which focuses on functional competence, a number of American researchers, especially in the field of management, focus heavily on behaviours or personal competence. This includes such things as self-confidence, stamina, interpersonal skills and presentation skills. Such characteristics may be more useful predictors of capability (ie future potential) than functional competences, which attest primarily to competence within an individual's current job role. Behavioural competencies are often used in assessment centre settings to assist in recruitment or for assessing an individual's promotion potential. They are also widely used as the basis of company-specific competency frameworks.

METACOMPETENCIES (HALL, 1986; HYLAND, 1992; NORDHAUG, 1990; REYNOLDS AND SNELL, 1988)

Some researchers have identified certain generic, high-level competencies, which appear to overarch other competencies or which may be important to their acquisition. They include such things as creativity, analysis, problem-solving and self-development.

CORE SKILLS (DFEE/NCVQ)

For a number of years, the UK government has been promoting the concept of core skills, now renamed key skills. These are generic, transferable skills, which are said to be important to most occupations (in all sectors and at all levels). They have been arrived at largely empirically from what employers persistently say they need from their employees. Core skills include such things as communication, IT and numerical skills and certain personal skills, such as working with others.

ETHICS (ERAUT *ET AL.*, 1994; OZAR, 1993)

Finally, we were influenced by recent works on ethics. Eraut *et al.*, for example, have carried out useful work in relation to the place of ethics and values within occupational standards. Ozar and others have written about the importance of ethics to effective professional performance and their place within professional development programmes. We, therefore, considered it important that there should be an explicit place for ethics and values within our model of professional competence.

The provisional model

The provisional model draws on each of the concepts mentioned above in addition to making use of a number of more general analytical tools such as Bloom's Taxonomy (Bloom, 1956). The model attempts to combine the strengths of the various approaches within a single, coherent framework. The resulting model is shown in Figure 18.1.

The model is of necessity quite elaborate and it will, therefore, be described in stages.

Core components

At the heart of the model are four 'core components' (not to be confused with the core skills mentioned earlier). These are:

- knowledge/cognitive competence (defined as 'the possession of appropriate work-related knowledge and the ability to put this to effective use');
- functional competence ('the ability to perform specific work-related tasks effectively');
- personal or behavioural competence ('the ability to adopt appropriate, observable behaviours in work-related situations)';
- values/ethical competence ('the possession of appropriate personal and professional values and the ability to make sound judgements based upon these in work-related situations').

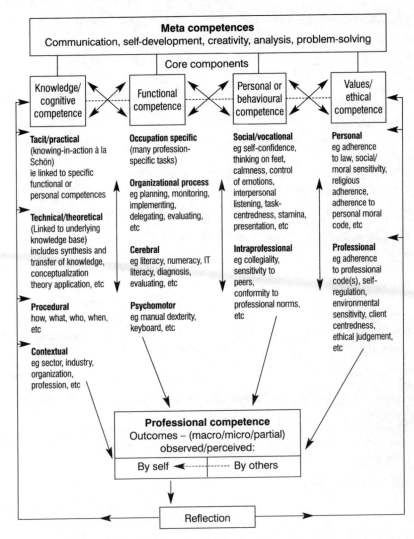

Figure 18.1 Provisional model of professional competence (compatible with 'outcomes' and 'reflective practitioner' approaches)

The linkage of cognitive competence with knowledge emphasizes the importance of the application of knowledge. Similarly, the linkage of values with ethical competence emphasizes that values, like knowledge, are of little use unless they are applied effectively.

Each of the core components is made up of a number of 'constituents'. Constituents are groups of individual competencies of a similar kind (constituent headings are shown in italic).

Knowledge/cognitive competence has been broken down into four constituents. These are:

- *tacit/practical* – this is knowledge linked closely to specific functional or personal competencies – similar to Schön's 'knowing-in-action';
- *technical/theoretical* – this relates to the underlying knowledge base of a particular profession, but also includes its application, transfer, synthesis, extrapolation, etc;
- *procedural* – this consists of the how, what, when, etc of the more routine tasks within professional activity;
- *contextual* – this is general background knowledge that is specific to an organization, industry, sector, etc.

The functional competence component has four constituents. These are:

- *occupation specific* – these are the numerous profession-specific tasks or functions;
- *organizational/process* – these are generic to all professions – eg planning, delegating, etc;
- *cerebral* – these are again generic competencies but which involve primarily mental activity – literacy, numeracy, etc;
- *psychomotor* – these are generic competencies of a more physical nature – manual dexterity, keyboard operation, etc.

The personal or behavioural competence component has two constituents:

- *social/vocational* – these are things like self-confidence, task-centredness, stamina etc;
- *intraprofessional* – these are behaviours that relate mainly to interaction with other professionals, such as collegiality, adherence to professional norms, etc.

Values/ethical competence also has two constituents:

- *personal* – these include such things as adherence to personal moral/religious codes, etc;
- *professional* – including adherence to professional codes, client-centredness, environmental sensitivity, etc.

Please note that the examples of competencies against each constituent heading are for illustrative purposes only and are not intended to be exhaustive. Note also that distinctions between different constituent groupings should not be viewed too rigidly. The main purpose of the constituent headings is to provide a checklist framework for the different types of competencies that might be involved. They may also have value in bringing together competencies of a similar nature that might be susceptible to similar development techniques.

Metacompetencies

Overarching the four core components are a number of metacompetencies. These can enhance or mediate competence in any of the core component areas (for example, creativity), or they may be essential for acquiring other competencies (for example, self-development). There may be other metacompetencies besides those shown in Figure 18.1.

Outcomes

The metacompetencies, the four core components, and their various constituents all interact together to produce a range of 'outcomes'. Outcomes may be of several kinds.

- 'macro-outcomes' – these are the broad, overall results of professional activity;
- 'micro-outcomes' – these are the outcomes of very specific activities under any of the core component headings;
- 'partial outcomes' – these are the result of a partially completed activity.

Outcomes, of whatever type, may be observed or otherwise perceived both by oneself and by others, though not perfectly by either party. Self-perception of outcomes is likely to be assisted by feedback from others, and this is indicated by the horizontal arrow between the 'self' and 'others' boxes in Figure 18.1.

Reflection

Self-perception of outcomes leads (or ought to lead) to 'reflection'. Professionals may reflect upon their performance against any of the core components (or more likely against any of their constituent competencies), or against any of the metacompetencies, or about their overall professional competence.

Schön (1983) suggests that reflection may also take place in the middle of an activity (what he calls 'reflection-in-action'). This is accommodated in the model through the concept of 'partial outcomes', referred to earlier (ie reflection against partial outcomes equates to Schön's reflection-in-action).

The main purpose of reflection is to improve professional competence. Therefore, the results of reflection are shown as feeding back into any of the core components and their various constituents or into any of the metacompetencies, thereby completing the cycle of continuous improvement.

Other features of the model

The sloping arrowed lines between each of the core component boxes illustrate that the core components may be heavily interrelated. For example, in order to execute a particular functional competence effectively, certain personal competencies may be needed. For example, 'delegation', which is seen in the model as a functional competence, may only be possible if a certain amount of 'assertiveness' is applied; the latter being clearly a behavioural or personal competence.

There are also interrelationships between different competencies within the same core component heading (these are illustrated in Figure 18.1 by the vertical arrowed lines).

Typical application of the provisional model

Figure 18.2 shows the model applied to a medical GP. This example is illustrative only and the details have not been confirmed by research. Nonetheless, this example may help to bring the provisional model to life.

Variations between professions

One fundamental difference between this model and certain other models is that it affords equal prominence to each of the core components. At the same time it allows for the possibility that different professions will require a different mix of the core components, as may different branches or job roles within the same profession. The mix required for a particular job role has been called the 'occupational competence mix' and is illustrated in Figure 18.3.

The relative importance of each of the core components to a particular occupation is indicated by the size of the segments. The metacompetencies, shown round the perimeter, can also vary in their relative size, illustrating that a different mix of metacompetencies may also be appropriate to different professions. Figure 18.4 compares two dissimilar professional roles – a barrister and a research chemist. It indicates that a barrister will require a strong cadre of personal competencies (such as self-confidence, presentation skills and ability to 'think on feet'), whereas a research chemist may not require such highly developed personal competencies (he or she may work mainly alone) but instead they will need a very strong knowledge base and a high order of cognitive competence.

These differences may seem obvious, yet they are often not fully reflected in initial professional development programmes, either in what is taught, or in the development methods used, or in the assessment processes applied.

A better understanding of the relative importance of each of the core components and metacompetencies to different occupations could help improve

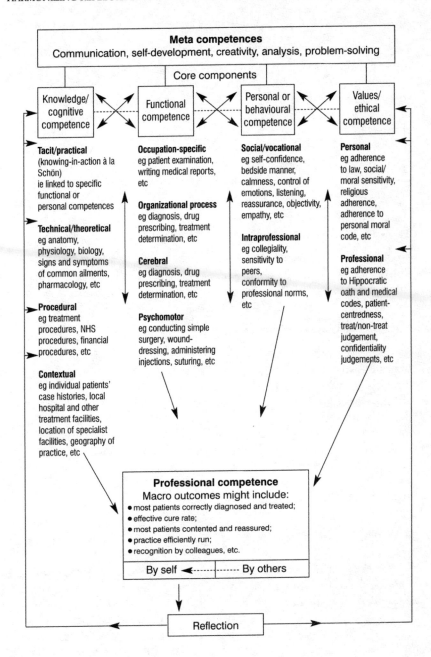

Figure 18.2 Example of the provisional model applied to a medical GP

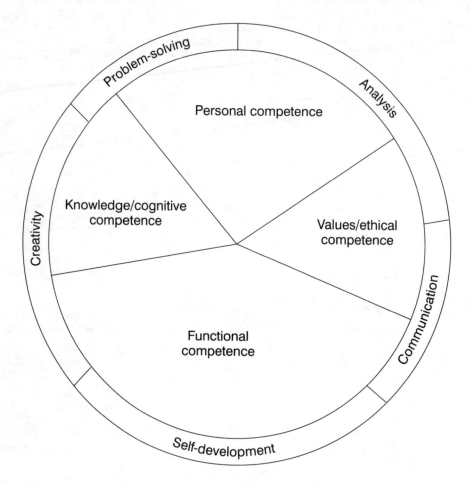

Figure 18.3 Occupational competence mix

the design of professional training by placing appropriate emphasis on the various components.

Figure 18.5 shows a three dimensional version of the model referred to as 'individual competence mix'. This illustrates the competence mix actually attained by a particular experienced individual. It indicates that even after the necessary occupational competence mix for the profession has been acquired, a practitioner may continue to develop each one of the components further, increasing the depth of competence within each towards the highest level of excellence in terms of professional performance. However, ongoing development is likely to proceed at different rates within different core component areas, as indicated by the variation in height between segments. For

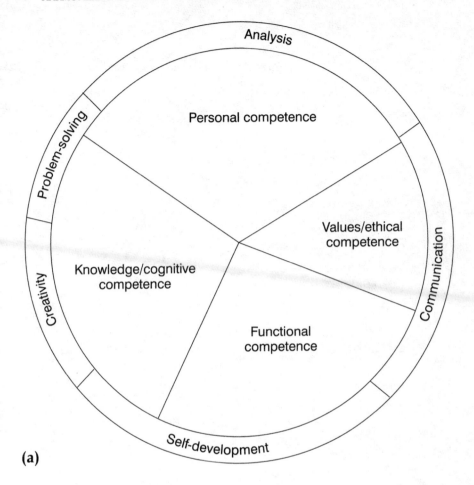

(a)

Figure 18.4 Occupational competence mix: comparison of contrasting professional roles for (a) a barrister and (b) a research chemist

simplicity, metacompetencies have not been included in the illustration, but these are also likely to be differentially developed.

Next steps in research

The empirical stage is investigating the validity of the provisional model within a number of different professions. An attempt is being made to draw up profession-specific versions of both the provisional model of competence and the occupational competence mix for each of the professions investigated.

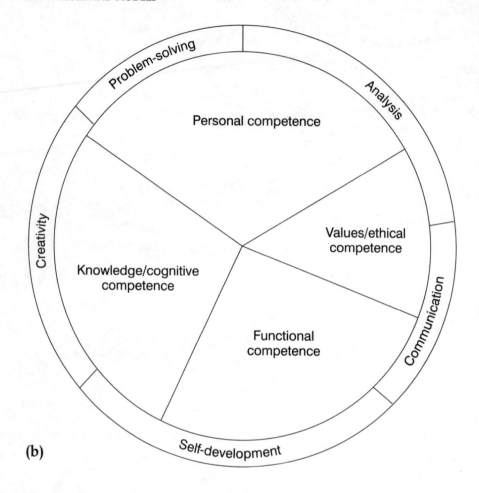

Figure 18.4 Occupational competence mix: comparison of contrasting professional roles for (a) a barrister and (b) a research chemist

The insights of experienced professionals are being sought as to how they acquired the different components of their professional competence and the extent to which this has been aided by formal development processes.

Other strands of empirical work are:

- the nature of professional practice;
- the nature of professional competence;
- competence accreditation;
- continuing professional development (CPD).

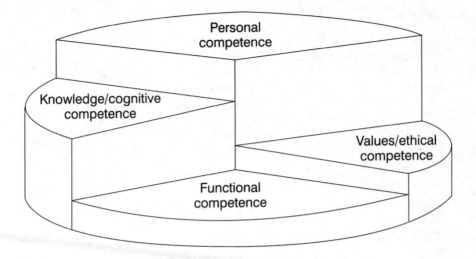

Figure 18.5 Individual competence mix for an experienced individual

It is hoped that through this work it may be possible to develop new paradigms for professional development that will help improve existing programmes.

Comments on any aspect of this chapter, and in particular on the professional model(s) described within it, would be welcomed by the authors (c/o Professor Geoff Chivers, Division of Adult Continuing Education, University of Sheffield, 196–198 West Street, Sheffield S1 4ET).

References

Bloom, B. S. (1956) *Taxonomy of Educational Objectives, Book 1: Cognitive Domain*, London, Longman.

Boyatzis, R. E. (1982) *The Competent Manager: A model for effective performance*, New York, Wiley.

Eraut, M., Steadman, S., Cole, G. and Marquand, D. (1994) *Ethics in Occupational Standards*, Sheffield, Employment Department.

Hall, D. T. (1986) *Career Development in Organizations*, San Francisco, Jossey-Bass.

Hyland, T. (1992) 'Metacompetence, metaphysics and vocational expertise', *Competence and Assessment*, **20**, 22–24, Sheffield, Employment Department.

Klemp, G. O. (1980) *The Assessment of Occupational Competence*, Washington DC, National Institute of Education.

Mansfield, B. and Mathews, D. (1985) *The Components of Job Competence*, Bristol, Further Education Staff College.

Nordhaug, O. (1990) *Individual Competences in Firms*, Philadelphia, Working Paper, Center for Human Resources, Wharton School, University of Pennsylvania.

Ozar, D. T. (1993) 'Building awareness of ethical standards', in L. Curry and J. F. Wergin (eds) *Educating Professionals*, San Francisco, Jossey-Bass.

Reynolds, M. and Snell, R. (1988) *Contribution to Development of Management Competence*, Sheffield, Manpower Services Commission.

Schön, D. A. (1983) *The Reflective Practitioner: How professionals think in action*, London, Maurice Temple Smith.

Schön, D. A. (1987) *Educating the Reflective Practitioner*, San Francisco, Jossey-Bass.

Schroder, H. M. (1989) *Managerial Competence: The key to excellence*, Iowa, Kendall/Hunt.

Part Six

Conclusion

Chapter 19

The challenge of developing the capable practitioner

Stan Lester

Between them the chapters in this book raise a wide range of issues about helping people to develop as capable practitioners, and about approaches to teaching and learning, to assessment, and (if more by inference) to organizing our educational institutions and systems to contribute to that goal. In attempting to pull together these issues in a conclusion of sorts, it seems to me that there are four key themes around which they revolve.

First, there is a need to work from more appropriate conceptual starting points than those which dominate professional development at present. Far from being just a matter of abstract philosophy, this is about the theories-in-use that run through our practice as educators; it is a central factor in ensuring that our systems for supporting learning and development are themselves capable. Second, there are issues about how the notion of the capable practitioner is translated into practice. This too has a structural influence on our ability to help people develop their capability, as anyone who has worked with UK competence statements will be aware. Third, there is the central area of practice itself: how can we as educators or 'learning practitioners' assist people to develop as self-managing, effective and eminently capable practitioners themselves? And finally, there is the issue of assessment and evaluation, which is pivotal in its ability to support or distort learning and development.

In this final chapter I will briefly enlarge on each of these themes, and point to some possible ways forward.

Building the foundations

Developing an agenda for capability requires different paradigms from the ones underlying the agendas of expertise and competence. The influence of positivism and the technical–rational model of professional development (cf Bines and Watson, 1992; Schön, 1983) has resulted in a one-way approach typified by presenting a body of knowledge to be learned and used, resistant to the notion of the practitioner as an active generator of knowledge and meaning. Competence-based approaches, with their functional and behavioural roots, may provide freedom to explore how to reach a level of competence, but the practitioner is not expected to decide or even challenge what 'competent' is; instead of being inducted into a body of knowledge, he or she is presented with an approved body of practice. In both traditions, what is effective knowledge and effective practice are treated as relatively unproblematic, and while the related development processes may be less or more flexible, the underlying structures are premised on stable-state assumptions and single-loop thinking (Argyris and Schön, 1974). Practitioners need 'maps' in the early stages of their development – they cannot be left to find their way in the dark or be subjected to the kind of reinventing of the wheel implied by the extremes of constructivism – but in terms of an underlying basis for professional development, technical–rational, behaviourist and functionalist perspectives do not provide adequate answers.

With reference to higher education, professional development is more than purely a matter of the pursuit of relevant knowledge and understanding, nor is it sufficient to focus on preparation for work or effectiveness in work roles. Discussions of reflective practice, self-managed learning, action learning, 'map-making' and the moral and emotional aspects of learning point to a rather different starting point, one which is potentially challenging to higher education because it is apt to reframe the notion of 'higher' learning itself. Developing capable practice is to say the least difficult when the development is based on foundations that lack capability – when there is a structural block which values conformity over creating what is of value. This tension is latent throughout the book, surfacing through both practical frustrations and conceptual discussions. It is only likely to be resolved when professional development is underpinned by ways of thinking that are neither narrowly instrumental nor intellectually detached, but include space for practitioners to exercise critique and creativity and engage in a dialogue between practice and practical theory.

From concept to practice

Operationalizing the capability agenda – making it tangible and practical – presents another challenge. As well as exploring the notion of the capable practitioner in its general sense, there is also the issue of what capability means in specific contexts – being a capable engineer, nurse, manager and so forth – as well as how it might be developed through, for instance, a law degree, a diploma in social work or a post graduate business programme. It is this issue of capability in context with which many of the preceding chapters engage. Through them, it is apparent that there is a tension between the broader notion of capability and some of the means used to describe it, just as the common sense notion of competence is proving extraordinarily difficult to capture in practice.

On the one hand, there is a pragmatic concern with being able to describe capability in terms that make it straightforward to communicate, develop and perhaps assess. This might involve asking questions such as what a capable practitioner does that is different from what a less capable one does; what kind of situations the practitioner needs to be able to act in (and on); and what kinds of things – understandings, abilities, skills and so on – contribute to capability. In theory, there should be little difficulty in building up a contextualized picture of the capable professional that communicates the information needed to assist development.

To borrow a metaphor from Brown and McCartney (Chapter 2), on the other hand there is a suspicion that capability, like the quality in Zen (Pirsig, 1974), can only be seen in its reflection; it is not amenable to being defined or dissected. There is a danger in attempting to disaggregate 'capability' that we miss the point, and instead of something dynamic and holistic produce at best a dry taxonomy of capabilities, and at worst a disconnected bullet-point list of competencies. I am reminded of an employer's comment in a recent study on key skills, which was to the effect that splitting them up and treating them as if they were unconnected would result in them being 'ground into dust' (Lester, 1997). Capability, in whatever context, is about more than a collection of parts.

A further danger in operationalizing capability lies in making the assumption that description, definition and disaggregation is somehow objective, of failing to see the perspective involved. It is unconsciously easy to create descriptions that embody current ways of doing things and current prejudices, building in interpretations that say less about being capable than about the describer's or definer's standpoint and context. If capability is about going beyond fitness for purpose, these kinds of assumptions need to be made explicit and open to challenge.

Overcoming this 'mystic–atomistic' tension perhaps revolves around realizing that capability is learned rather than taught, and that while the developing practitioner needs road maps and safety nets these are only for guidance; they are working descriptions that are open to enquiry and change by individual practitioners as they develop the insights to challenge and modify them. There is no inherent problem in attempting to describe and communicate capability in context and in practice, only in assuming that we can produce descriptions that are in some way objective or for that matter any more valid than the ones the capable practitioner will come to have in mind.

Teaching and learning

A theme that recurs constantly is that developing capability emphasizes learner-centred approaches, rather than ones based on transmitting knowledge and skills. From being a teacher or lecturer concerned with passing on content, the learning practitioner is asked to become a facilitator, questioner and perhaps mentor concerned foremost with the learning process. 'Content' knowledge and skills remain important, but it is no longer sufficient to see them as the only or even the main focus of professional development. Similarly, the 'expert' educator is not being asked to devalue their knowledge and expertise, but to make it available as a resource rather than putting it at the centre of the learning experience.

Contained within this approach is acknowledgement of and respect for the learner's experience and perspective, whether they are a seasoned practitioner or an 18-year-old school or college leaver. The experiences reflected in some of the chapters also point to the need for many learners to be assisted in moving from a passive approach, with its expectations of working to others' agendas, to a more active and self-managed style.

Without claiming that the language used here is more than transitional, it is interesting to observe how the metaphors used to describe teaching and learning reveal particular orientations or perspectives. The frequently used idiom of 'mechanisms' for 'delivering' learning has the unfortunate connotation that learning is a commodity that can be packaged and dropped off by a mechanical device, the learner having only to pick up and open the pack and install it. There is a need for less reliance on delivery systems (Schiff, 1970) where teachers give out and learners take in, and more use of realization systems in which the learning practitioner operates in something closer to a partnership with the learner. The individual teacher or lecturer is central to this, but the partnership will proceed on only a gradual scale unless there is the requisite support, development and (particularly in higher education) value placed on facilitating learning as much as on research and publication (cf Dearing, 1997; Booth, 1998). Therefore action is needed equally from those in faculties, institutions, professional bodies and public departments and agencies whose expectations and control of resources influence the parameters within which teachers work.

Assessment

Assessment traditionally performs a variety of functions, including indicating whether learners have learned what they are expected to learn, providing feedback on progress, operating entry gates to further educational opportunities and to jobs or careers, and enabling decisions to be made about awarding qualifications. It exerts a powerful influence on what and how people learn, and on how learning operates; to an extent the assessment tail frequently wags the learning dog, and there is much done in the name of education, training and development that would look faintly ridiculous if not for the excuse of assessment. In some respects educational systems are obsessed with assessment and accreditation, arguably to the detriment of their capability.

Assessment is a recurring issue throughout this book, sometimes in passing and sometimes as a more central concern, and several of the chapters indicate that, from a capability perspective, assessment is problematic. Assessment practice is lagging behind the leading edge of learning practice and there is a need for ways of generating feedback and making accreditation decisions that support rather than subvert or distract from the development of capability. Methods are being developed that seem to be supporting autonomous learning and self-evaluation, but they need to become more widespread and widely evaluated, and there is a need to question more often where assessment is needed at all and, where it is, how it can be made a more valid and constructive experience.

Conclusion

The questions posed in this book are important ones. Capable, intelligent practitioners – people who can work effectively in messy, indeterminate situations as well as in more neatly defined ones, manage conflicts of value, look beyond the solutions to problems and retain their humanity (and even humour) while they do so – are vital if we are to develop sustainable societies, economies and environments. That these practitioners need competence and knowledge for the contexts and situations they are working in almost goes without saying, but it is not in itself enough; they also need the capability to see and learn beyond the situation and beyond the present.

This capability agenda is therefore about more than the needs of employers and customers, and it cannot be limited to responding to government policy – although it needs to involve a dialogue with both, which enables the convergence needed for short-term essentials to exist in parallel with the divergence needed for longer-term changes and possibilities. Higher education, professional bodies and others responsible for professional development need to overcome the constraints of academic detachment on the one hand and of narrow instrumentalism on the other, and develop ways forward that have adequacy for the 21st century and beyond. The chapters in this book don't provide all the answers, nor could they, but they do start to ask some of the right kinds of questions.

References

Argyris, C. and Schön, D. A. (1974) *Theory in Practice: Increasing professional effectiveness*, London, Jossey-Bass.

Bines, H. and Watson, D. (1992) *Developing Professional Education*, Buckingham, SRHE/Open University Press.

Booth, C. (1998) *Accreditation and Teaching in Higher Education: Consultation paper*, London, Committee of Vice-chancellors and Principals.

Dearing, R. (1997) *Higher Education in the Learning Society*, Hayes, NCIHE Publications.

Lester, S. (1997) *The Wiltshire Key Skills Project: A summary of the research*, Chippenham, Chippenham College.

Pirsig, R. (1974) *Zen and the Art of Motorcycle Maintenance: An inquiry into values*, London, Random House.

Schiff, S. K. (1970) 'Training the professional', *University of Chicago Magazine*, Fall.

Schön, D. A. (1983) *The Reflective Practitioner*, New York, Basic Books.

Index